H. P. LOVECRAFT

H. P. LOVECRAFT: FOUR DECADES OF CRITICISM

Edited by
S. T. Joshi

Ohio University Press
Athens, Ohio

Library of Congress Cataloging in Publication Data
Main entry under title:

H. P. Lovecraft, four decades of criticism.

    Bibliography: p.
    Includes index.
    1. Lovecraft, Howard Phillips, 1890–1937—
Criticism and interpretation—Addresses, essays,
lectures. I. Joshi, S. T., 1958–
PS3523.0833Z66   813 ,.52   80-11535
ISBN 0-8214-0442-3 cloth
ISBN 0-8214-0577-2 paper

To
ANTHONY TOVATT
PETER GOODELL
and
ROBERT C. ROSE

Contents

ACKNOWLEDGEMENTS

"H. P. Lovecraft: An Appreciation," by Professor T. O. Mabbott, originally published in *Marginalia,* by H. P. Lovecraft; copyright 1944 by August Derleth and Donald Wandrei. Reprinted by permission of Arkham House Publishers, Inc., Sauk City, Wisconsin.

"Tales of the Marvellous and the Ridiculous," by Edmund Wilson, an alteration of an article of the same name from *The New Yorker,* 24 November 1945, appearing in *Classics and Commercials: A Literary Chronicle of the Forties,* by Edmund Wilson; copyright 1950 by Edmund Wilson. Reprinted by permission of Farrar, Straus and Giroux, Inc.

"A Literary Copernicus," by Fritz Leiber, Jr, a revision and expansion of an article entitled "The Works of H. P. Lovecraft: Suggestions for a Critical Appraisal" from *The Acolyte,* Fall 1944, appearing in *Something About Cats and Other Pieces,* by H. P. Lovecraft; copyright 1949 by August Derleth. Reprinted by permission of Arkham House Publishers, Inc., Sauk City, Wisconsin.

Excerpts from *The Supernatural in Fiction,* by Peter Penzoldt, Ph.D. Reprinted by permission of Humanities Press, Inc.

"The Cthulhu Mythos: A Study," by George T. Wetzel, a revision and expansion of an article of the same name appearing in *Howard Phillips Lovecraft: Memoirs, Critiques, and Bibliographies,* edited by George T. Wetzel; copyright 1955 by SSR Publications. Revised article published in *HPL,* edited by Meade and Penny Frierson; copyright by Meade and Penny Frierson. Reprinted by permission of the author.

"H. P. Lovecraft: Myth-Maker," by Professor Dirk W. Mosig, a revision and expansion of an article appearing in *I Miti di Cthulhu,* edited by August Derleth, Gianfranco de Turris, and Sebastiano Fusco, and in *Whispers,* December 1976; copyright 1976 by Stuart David Schiff. Revised article published in *The Miskatonic,* February 1976; copyright 1976 by Dirk W. Mosig. Reprinted by permission of the author.

"Through Hyperspace with Brown Jenkin: Lovecraft's Contribution to Speculative Fiction," by Fritz Leiber, Jr, a revision of an article appearing in *Shangri-L'Affaires,* September 1963. Revised article published in *The Dark Brotherhood and Other Pieces,* by H. P. Lovecraft and Divers Hands; copyright 1966 by August Derleth. Reprinted by permission of Arkham House Publishers, Inc., Sauk City, Wisconsin.

"Poe and Lovecraft," by Robert Bloch, a revision of an article appearing in *Ambrosia,* August 1973. Reprinted by permission of the author.

"Facts in the Case of H. P. Lovecraft," by Professor Barton L. St Armand, originally published in *Rhode Island History,* February 1972. Reprinted by permission of the author.

"Sade:
And when I vanish
I want all trace of my existence
to be wiped out"

> —Peter Weiss
> *The Persecution and Assassination of*
> *Marat as Performed by the Inmates of*
> *the Asylum of Charenton Under the*
> *Direction of the Marquis de Sade*

"Such is our condition that we are not permitted to arrive all at once at something reasonable no matter what it is. Before that it is necessary that we go astray for a long time, that we pass by all sorts of errors and degrees of impertinence."

> —Fontenelle
> *Digression sur les Anciens*
> *et les Modernes*

Preface

It is the belief of many that the time is "ripe" for objective, penetrating study of Howard Phillips Lovecraft to begin. Forty years have passed since his death; the majority of his work has, through the efforts of many fans and scholars, been saved from the probable oblivion of the pulp and amateur magazines where it originally appeared; his work is being disseminated and appreciated widely both here and abroad; Lovecraft is slowly gaining a position in American and world literature, although right now it is anyone's guess what that position ultimately will be.

In this book I have attempted to codify the astoundingly ambivalent interpretations imposed upon Lovecraft's work over the last thirty years. By including what are generally held by scholars to be some of the finer critical articles on Lovecraft, I have tried to indicate what ground has been covered in the field and what yet needs to be covered. In many ways the criticism of H. P. Lovecraft's work is at an amazingly backward stage; but this need not deny the fact that many keen minds have devoted their attention to the man and his work and have made lasting contributions—contributions that should form the basis for Lovecraftian critical study for the coming years and decades.

In the process of compilation I have been forced to be selective for a number of reasons, not the least of which is the fact that limited areas of Lovecraft's work have been covered again and again while other areas are still left untouched A crucial omission from this book is that body of articles on Lovecraft not written in English, so few of which have been translated. French critics in particular have significant and provocative views about Lovecraft—they consider him second only to Poe as America's greatest writer—but their work must here go unrepresented. German, Italian, and Spanish critics have been no less enthusiastic.

A word about procedures in this book. I have taken the liberty of annotating (sometimes heavily) the essays herein contained, not in an attempt to denigrate the undoubted talents of the authors, but either to offer corroboration or parallels where relevant or to present arguments as possible refutation. Dogma is the death of criticism, and contradicting views can oftentimes be enlightening and suggestive. Those footnotes that I have added are appended with my initials; those that are the authors' own have no initials following them. I have made no alteration of texts or footnotes save where noted and in the interests of bibliographic consistency. References in the footnotes have been quite abbreviated since my forthcoming bibliography of Lovecraft and Lovecraft criticism will provide full bibliographical details on virtually all items mentioned in this book.

xiii

It is astounding that, in so brief a time after his death, the facts of Lovecraft's biography and literary career have been so obscured. The reasons for this are perhaps two: firstly, the fact that Lovecraft never wrote any lengthy pieces of formal autobiography; secondly, the fact that Lovecraft's letters, the only true key to the man's life, never received wide distribution until only a decade ago. To obviate this situation I have felt it necessary to include, in the Introductory Notes, more strict biographical data than is perhaps usual. In this regard I am particularly grateful to Mr Kenneth W. Faig, Jr, who so arduously compiled much of the data therein.

The Appendices should be self-explanatory. The first gives the contents of what I, for bibliographic simplicity, have deemed *The Collected Works of H. P. Lovecraft,* published by Arkham House from 1963 to 1976. As these volumes are, save the paperbacks, the most easily available of Lovecraft's work, and as they include nearly comprehensive collections of the fiction and letters, I have used these volumes in the footnotes (where they are referred to as *Collected Works)* and elsewhere as the basic Lovecraft texts. The second appendix lists other worthy items of Lovecraft criticism which, due to spatial considerations, could not be included in this volume. Attention has particularly been given to biographical articles and memoirs, since aside from the Introductory Notes the essays in this book are entirely critical in nature. That this appendix lists but a small fraction of all that has been written on Lovecraft goes without saying; a full bibliography occupies several hundred pages.

A matter of some consequence in recent Lovecraftian studies is the use of the term "Cthulhu Mythos" to designate the vast myth-cycle which Lovecraft invented and which his associates (and, later, other macabre writers) elaborated upon. The debate as to whether the term is apt is not merely an argument over semantics, but touches upon the very core of Lovecraft's philosophical thought. As this debate has yet to be settled to anyone's satisfaction, I have chosen to refer, in my own comments in this book, to the myth-cycle simply as such, or as "the Lovecraft Mythos" (a title suggested to me by Mr Scott Connors). More on this matter will be found in Prof. Mosig's "H. P. Lovecraft: Myth-Maker."

In such a book as this it is inconceivable that many need not be thanked for their assistance in one way or another in its compilation. I must single out Mr Kenneth W. Faig, Jr and Prof. Dirk W. Mosig in particular for their constant help and guidance, but would like also to thank the following for their kind and indispensable aid: Robert Bloch, R. Boerem, Paul Buhle, Peter Cannon, Mrs Nancy Chudacoff of the Rhode Island Historical Society, Scott Connors, Douglas Edwards, R. Alain Everts, William Fulwiler, Donald M. Grant, Forrest D. Hartmann,

T. M. and P. T. Joshi, Prof. Edward S. Lauterbach, Robert Marten, Marc A. Michaud, Prof. Barton L. St Armand, J. Vernon Shea, Richard L. Tierney, James Turner of Arkham House, and George T. Wetzel. If the names of any other associates have been omitted, it has been through oversight and not intent.

I would also like to thank those authors who so kindly provided me with texts of their published work, those who supplied me with the texts of other writers, and in particular those who revised or wrote articles especially for inclusion in this book.

To the John Hay Library of Brown University, and in particular to Mr John H. Stanley, I express my hearty thanks for allowing me such liberal access to the Lovecraft Collection there; without which this book might never have reached completion in its present state. My thanks, too, to the Providence Public Library, the Library of the Rhode Island Historical Society, the Bracken Library of Ball State University, and the Muncie Public Libraries.

In fine, this volume does not intend to put forth a "standard" interpretation of H. P. Lovecraft, but does try to indicate and codify the trends in Lovecraft criticism during the last three decades. Criticism is itself an art, and like any must remain in flux.

Any errors in fact or interpretation that I have made in these pages reflects not on those many associates who have so unstintingly aided me but on my own incapacities.

—S. T. Joshi

INTRODUCTORY ESSAYS

H. P. Lovecraft: His Life And Work

By Kenneth W. Faig, Jr
and
S. T. Joshi

The criticism of the life and work of Howard Phillips Lovecraft (1890–1937) represents a singular chapter in the history of literature. Lovecraft the man has been labelled a "sexless misfit,"[1] an "eccentric recluse,"[2] a "horrifying figure,"[3] a "sick juvenile,"[4] or simply "strange;"[5] but others (most of whom knew and met Lovecraft) have said that he was "a great gentleman, in the truest sense of that much abused term,"[6] a "rational man before anything else,"[7] a "fascinating companion, teacher, and guide,"[8] and "not freakish, simply different."[9] Of his work still greater contradictions arise: he was a "ghastly writer,"[10] a "bad writer,"[11] "not a good writer,"[12] and an "atrocious writer;"[13] yet on the other hand he was "the supreme master of the tale of horror,"[14] "one of the most sensitive and powerful writers of [his] generation,"[15] and "the greatest American author of horror tales since Poe;"[16] his tales are "nearly always perfect in structure"[17] and are "superbly written;"[18] his style has been called both "distinguished"[19] and "undistinguished."[20] It is difficult to find an author in this century whose life, character, and mannerisms have been so minutely and voluminously documented; whose writings were so unrecognised in his lifetime, yet so widely known after his death. We must look to Poe and LeFanu to find writers whose lives have accumulated such bizarre legendry; to Conan Doyle to find one whose work has inspired such blatant imitation; and to Nathanael West to find one whose work has suffered such vicissitudes in critical acceptance. The reasons for all these occurrences are many, and to explain them requires an exploration not only of Lovecraft's life, work, and character, but many aspects of literature itself.

Lovecraft was born on 20 August 1890 in Providence, Rhode Island, and lived all but two years of his adult life there, in four different homes on or near historic College Hill, "a living museum of Colonial and Federalist architecture."[21] From these surroundings alone arose many of the predilections that would remain with Lovecraft for the rest of his life: his love of the past, of the Colonial and Georgian periods in history and literature, and of the beauty and mystery of nature. Lovecraft was possessed of a lifelong adoration of Old Providence and of New England; an adoration which was accentuated by his unfortunate "New York Exile" of the 1920's and which found sublime expression in such tales as *The Dream-Quest of Unknown Kadath* and *The Case of Charles Dexter Ward*. This feeling was not only an intellectual-aesthetic appreciation of the antiquities in New England, but had in addition a psychological aspect; for Providence and New England came to represent a haven of security, a familiar and comfortable milieu with which Lovecraft— whose "sense of place" was so acute—ever strived to harmonise himself. The importance of this setting, and of the city of Providence in particular, on Lovecraft's life, work, and thought cannot be overstressed.

The effect of Lovecraft's family—both ancestors and immediate relations—on his character has perhaps also been generally unemphasised. Much has been made of the death of Lovecraft's father, Winfield Scott Lovecraft, of paresis in 1898, after a term of five years passed in an insane asylum; yet Lovecraft, on the rare occasions that he spoke of his father at all, professed that he had hardly known him, and there seems ultimately little reason to doubt it. What may be as significant was the death in 1896 of Lovecraft's grandmother: the subsequent gloom into which the household was plunged impressed the young Lovecraft tremendously, and spurred hideous nightmares where faceless things that he labelled "night-gaunts" attacked him. Indeed, Lovecraft's maternal line, the Phillipses of old Rhode Island stock, is full of oddities: due to the colony's isolation, several of them married their first cousins, creating that vague element of incestuousness; a series of calamities struck the Phillips line in the middle of the nineteenth century, among which was the grisly death of one man who was accidentally caught in a water mill; and several of Lovecraft's relatives perished within the first two decades of his life.[22] Lovecraft was almost certainly aware of these developements, and they exerted a potent influence on his mind. They had much (though not all) to do with certain ideas that were central to his thought, among which were his fervent desire for racial purity and his literary theme of hereditary degeneration and unwholesome inbreeding (expressed in "The Rats in the Walls," "Facts concerning the Late Arthur Jermyn and His Family," "The Lurking Fear," "The Shadow over Innsmouth," and others).

With the death of Lovecraft's father, the upbringing of the child fell largely on his mother—who was even then showing signs of the neurosis which ultimately led to her confinement in a sanitarium—and his grandfather Whipple Phillips. Lovecraft had been reading as early as age four, feeding himself on the brothers Grimm and Jules Verne. He not long after discovered Greek mythology, and at age seven made first acquaintance with Edgar Allan Poe, the author who would by far have the largest influence on his work. Lovecraft had, indeed, begun to write fiction at about this time, and the bulk of this very early juvenilia is patently Poe-esque. Verse, too, emerged, largely of a classical or Georgian cast.

Lovecraft, as is commonly known, suffered from poor health for virtually all his life, and it was certainly no different in childhood. Ill health was the major factor in his failure to gain a diploma from high school and subsequently to enrol in college. Quiet, introspective, the young Lovecraft did not make a great many friendships, but those that he had were strong. His precocity would itself have precluded his being an "ordinary" boy; yet he was never—neither as a youth nor as a man—as "abnormal" as many would have us believe.

Before he was ten Lovecraft became captivated with a subject that, along with literature, would vie as his major intellectual interest—science. His study of astronomy led ultimately to the adopting of the major thesis in his philosophy, the cosmic outlook. When Lovecraft "discovered the myriad suns and worlds of infinite space,"[23] he could no longer take as much interest in human affairs *per se*: his interest eventually centred on the continuities of the historical time-stream, the appalling yet thrilling awesomeness (a basic dichotomy in Lovecraft's thought) of space and time, and the minute place of humanity in them. This was at once a rational and a quasi-mystic attitude, involving as it did certain triggers of his imagination, mainly visual—such as the witnessing of sunsets—and his dreams, which were certainly more vivid and coordinated than the ordinary man's.

Even as a boy, however, Lovecraft combined his scientific and literary interests by producing handwritten astronomy books and journals, such as *The Scientific Gazette* (1899, 1903-04, 1909), *The Rhode Island Journal of Astronomy* (1903-07, 1909), *Chemistry* (6 vols.), *The Science Library* (9 vols.), and many others. The image arises of the young Lovecraft dutifully sitting down every Sunday to pen these texts and to make either carbon or hectographed copies to distribute to his friends.

The death of Whipple Phillips in 1904 was doubly disastrous, for not only was Lovecraft "deprived of my closest companion," but "his death brought financial disaster"[24] to the family, and forced the Lovecrafts to move into a smaller home and share it with another family. For the rest of his life Lovecraft looked back with longing to his natal home—454

Angell Street—where he had passed such happy years.

The death of the grandfather more or less coincided with the emergence of Lovecraft's uncle, Dr Franklin Chase Clark, into the sphere of his existence. This "man of vast learning"[25] encouraged not only the youth's studies in science and literature but spurred his poetic efforts. The years from 1904 to 1908 are important not only for Lovecraft's prolific production of scientific works and of mystery and horror tales (the former inspired by Conan Doyle's Sherlock Holmes), but for the first appearance of Lovecraft's work in print. *The Providence Sunday Journal* of 3 June 1906 carried a brief letter by Lovecraft denouncing a local astrologer (a tactic which Lovecraft, a staunch defender of scientific truth against pseudoscientific or idealistic imagining, repeated in 1914 against the astrologer J. F. Hartmann), and the next two months saw him start regular astronomy columns for *The Pawtuxet Valley Gleaner* (Phenix, Rhode Island)[26] and *The [Providence] Tribune,* morning, evening, and Sunday editions. The former seems to have ceased at the end of 1906, but the latter continued more or less regularly until mid-1908.

Much of Lovecraft's fiction was destroyed in a "literary housecleaning"[27] that he effected in 1908; all that survived, aside from the early juvenilia which his mother saved,[28] were "The Beast in the Cave" (1905) and "The Alchemist" (1908). Both show Lovecraft's growing mastery of horrific effects and of the short story form, as well as his concern with human degeneration, reverse evolution, and other themes representative of his later work. The tales are manifestly Poe-esque, and the fact that Lovecraft often slavishly imitated various authors as they first caught his fancy might indicate his susceptibility to literary influences, an effect which caused one commentator to be quite baffled as to "what is really Lovecraft."[29] Later, of course, Lovecraft learned to assimilate these influences, and the basic originality of his work—in terms of philosophical intent—cannot be overlooked.

Lovecraft's life in the period from 1908 to 1913 seems curiously blank: as always he continued his omnivorous reading (thus gaining as much or more than a college education), and sporadically wrote poetry and scientific work. Such works as a sizeable astronomical notebook kept between 1909 and 1915[30] and the unpreserved *Inorganic Chemistry* (1910) may perhaps be the major literary products of the period.

As a result of the literary controversy conducted against John Russell and others in the pages of *The Argosy* (1913-14),[31] Lovecraft was recruited into the United Amateur Press Association (UAPA) by Edward F. Daas. Lovecraft rightly declares that "the benefit received from this affiliation can hardly be overstressed,"[32] and his involvement in amateur journalism was so crucial to his life and work that one writer has said:

"His connexion with Amateur Journalism was directly responsible for making him the man he was during the last ten or eleven years of his life."[33] Even before his death Lovecraft was a legend in amateur journalism, being one of the strongest and most influential forces ever to come within its scope. It was not only that he published vast amounts of his work—essays, fiction, poetry—in many different amateur journals, or that he held many offices, including those of President, Vice-President, and Official Editor; but he became intimately enmeshed with its political and literary set-up. Yet Lovecraft gained as much from amateur journalism as he gave to it: his encountering of opinions that differed radically from his helped to widen his own horizons, to reduce the dogmatism of his views, and to make him more tolerant of others. His own magazine, *The Conservative* (of which thirteen issues were produced from 1915 to 1923), was filled with heated arguments on amateur journalism controversies and on the current national and international political scene, and also contained discussions of modern art and literature. Lovecraft's work in amateur journalism divides into two roughly distinct periods: from 1914 to 1925 (for the UAPA and at the same time, from as early as 1917 to 1925, for the rival National Amateur Press Association), and in the early 1930's, for the NAPA. He never lost touch with amateur journalism, and was submitting work to amateur journals long after it was appearing professionally.

In terms of literary output, nonfiction and poetry predominated during the period from 1912 to 1919. Lovecraft at this time was phenomenally prolific as a poet, such that, as was his wont, he used many pseudonyms when he published his work. Relatively little of this verse is horrific, being largely satiric, pastoral, philosophical, and, in small part, propagandist (note "Temperance Song," "Germania—1918," and others). Intensely derivative, this early poetry is not as central to his work as even his early fiction and certain of his essays; though a few works—"The Poe-et's Nightmare," "Nemesis," *et al.*—do hold much significance. It may be somewhat incorrect to say that Lovecraft was "imitating" the Georgian poetic masters; for he had been reading them since his very early youth, and as a matter of course considered them (as well as Poe) models of style whom it was logical to follow. If many of these poems are somewhat dry and mechanical,[34] some of them are indeed profound, *all* are finely and properly crafted, and all contain redeeming elements of humour, pathos, wit, and horror. For a period of roughly a decade Lovecraft radically reduced his serious poetic output, but upon its brief recommencement in late 1929 (when such notable works as "The Ancient Track," "The East India Brick Row," and the *Fungi from Yuggoth* were penned), it showed signs of a stylistic originality and unaffectedness which indicates that Lovecraft had the capability to be a poet of the first water.

In 1917, of course, Lovecraft commenced, after a nine-year hiatus, the writing of horror fiction. The year before, he had allowed his "The Alchemist" to be published in *The United Amateur,* and W. Paul Cook, noting the promise it showed, strongly urged Lovecraft to take up his fictional pen again. This Lovecraft did, producing "The Tomb" and "Dagon," the first of his tales that are considered part of his mature fiction, in quick succession in the summer of 1917. Lovecraft's output of fiction was never large, and in terms of volume and time expended, both his occupation as literary revisionist and his correspondence (which became heavy at about the time of his entrance into amateur journalism) dwarfed his fiction. Lovecraft, moreover, was rather slow in beginning again to write fiction: only two major stories were written in 1917 and one in 1918; late 1919, and especially 1920, saw an increase in quantity, though his tales were still short and did not in general contain the tightness of plot and style that typified his later work.

R. Alain Everts believes that Lovecraft may have been revising the manuscripts of others as early as 1912,[35] but his revisory work obviously increased as he entered amateur journalism. For the rest of his life it provided his major source of income, since his selling of what little fiction he wrote was somewhat erratic. It is futile to argue that Lovecraft "wasted" his time in this revising: without the money it brought in Lovecraft might not have been able to write any stories at all. Moreover he attracted, because of his own work in horror-fiction, the patronage of would-be macabre writers, and in the course of revising or ghost-writing tales incorporated various elements of his philosophy or his myth-cycle into them; many of them were, indeed, tantamount to original fiction. Of course, this revision of horror tales was a very small part of his revisory work, which ran the gamut from verse to textbooks to novels.

During Lovecraft's early involvement in amateur journalism, he did not by any means abandon his scientific writing: astronomical articles of his appeared in both *The [Providence] Evening News* (1914–18) and in *The Asheville [N.C.] Gazette-News* (1915). These were the last such articles that he wrote, and Lovecraft allowed himself much freedom in them: many included snatches of poetry and others discussed astronomical *curiosa* and history.

"About 1919," records Lovecraft, "the discovery of Lord Dunsany . . . gave a vast impetus to my writing."[36] In the ensuing two or three years Lovecraft strove in many of his tales stylistically to imitate the Irish fantaisiste. What is interesting, however, about Lovecraft's involvement with Dunsany is that he had written "Polaris," a tale which could be said to have "Dunsanian" touches, well before he encountered Dunsany's work. Actually there is no great mystery for this similarity, for it seems evident that both writers were using the style of the King James Bible[37] (note especially Dunsany's *The Gods of Pegāna).* Since the atmosphere of dreams and dream-like images can best be achieved by the use of such a solemn, formal, and archaic style—involving the use of unfamiliar and exotic words (some mythical) to create the sense of magical unreality—it may not be surprising that such independent affinity was had. Nonetheless, we can readily see why Lovecraft received "an electric shock"[38] upon reading Dunsany, since he here encountered a writer whose themes, style, and outlook seemed so to parallel his own.

In 1921 Lovecraft's mother died after a two-year confinement in a sanitarium; Lovecraft was overwhelmed by her death, and for weeks did little. It has been stated that Lovecraft was a "mother's boy," dominated by the female members of his family. It is true that after 1915, with the death of Dr F. C. Clark, there were no major male figures in his family who had any great influence on him, and that for the rest of his life he lived either with his mother, his wife, or his two aunts; yet we have seen that Whipple Phillips was an able, if not complete, replacement for the father that Lovecraft never knew, and that Dr Clark also had a large hand in shaping his intellectual growth. The effects of Lovecraft's being an only child, of his lack of a "real" father, of his being constantly in the company of adults, can not now be fully answered; but the over-protectiveness of his mother might—at least toward the end—have been offset by his increasing epistolary ties and his personal acquaintance with friends and associates.

The death of his mother fortuitously coincided with Lovecraft's meeting of his future wife, Sonia H. Greene (Davis), an immigrant Russian Jew several years older than he. After a three-year romance, the two married and set up housekeeping in Brooklyn. But the marriage was not a success, and after two years a separation was obtained.

Lovecraft's marriage is rightly one of the most controversial aspects of his life, for it raises questions about his character heretofore never encountered. The reasons for the failure of the marriage cannot be explained away by such laughably feeble and simplistic motives as Lovecraft's "need for loneliness"[39] or his "reclusiveness" or his "xenophobia," all which misrepresent Lovecraft significantly: the reasons were many and complex. The marriage brought together two strong-willed individuals, each of whom refused to make concessions to the other. On Lovecraft's side, the ingrained habits of thirty-four years of bachelorhood had much to do with the separation, as did his psychological-aesthetic need for Providence and New England. Lovecraft, unused as he was at earning a steady income, could find no work, and his lack of previous employment made it impossible for him even to locate a job in literary circles, for which he was without doubt thoroughly competent.⁴⁰ In spite of this, Lovecraft was able to enjoy himself: visits to museums and libraries, night-long literary discussions, and pedestrian explorations of the city spiced the weeks and months of his "New York Exile." Here we see the heyday of the Kalem Club, Lovecraft's informal circle of friends in New York, so named because last names beginning in K, L, and M predominated. But it was to be expected that the Dunsanian glamour of New York, with its dizzying spires and skyline, would soon fade and give way to a recognition of the decadence and insalubriousness of the city, of its oppressive vastness and its teeming crowds; and this gradually but surely began to wear him down. Lovecraft's distrust of foreigners (which shall be discussed at length later) increased as a natural result of the trying circumstances, and it might be said that toward the last few months of his New York stay he was reaching a level of acute psychological disturbance. That Sonia Davis was more of a hindrance than a help can be inferred from the testimony of Lovecraft's friends, who have remarked that she was an unusually domineering woman; and at this stage Lovecraft had come to expect self-sufficiency in his thoughts and actions.

Some years before the marriage Lovecraft had discovered the world of professional publication of his fiction. Having in 1921 been asked by G. J. Houtain, an amateur journalism acquaintance, to write a series of six short tales with a recurring central character for the cheap professional magazine *Home Brew,* Lovecraft complied by producing "Herbert West—Reanimator;" this was published, as "Grewsome Tales," in 1922;⁴¹ the following year Lovecraft wrote another serial for *Home Brew,* "The Lurking Fear." When the legendary *Weird Tales* was founded in 1923, Lovecraft was urged to contribute to it, and his first submissions were readily accepted. *Weird Tales* became the major market for his stories, and it eventually published all but four of his important tales,⁴² many of his revisions of other writers' horror tales, and some of his horrific poetry as well.

In the mid-1920's emerged the final major influence on Lovecraft's work—Arthur Machen. The Machen influence can be detected in such tales as "Cool Air" (1926),⁴³ "The Dunwich Horror" (1928), "The Whisperer in Darkness" (1930), and others. Also around this time came another developement in Lovecraft's work—the growing length of his tales as he found more and more that his concepts required the spaciousness of the novelette or short novel to be justified. With "The Rats in the Walls" (1923) the developement begins, continuing through such tales as

"The Shunned House" (1924), "Imprisoned with the Pharaohs" (1924), "The Horror at Red Hook" (1925), and "The Call of Cthulhu" (1926). Lovecraft's last short story was "The Strange High House in the Mist" (1926); in the ten years that followed he wrote no original fiction under 10,000 words in length.

Lovecraft's ecstatic return to Providence from the hated New York in 1926 launched a burst of literary productivity such as he never experienced before or afterward. Aside from continuing his major essay, "Supernatural Horror in Literature," which has been begun in late 1925, he produced in the next year several lengthy tales, including "The Call of Cthulhu," *The Dream-Quest of Unknown Kadath, The Case of Charles Dexter Ward,* and "The Colour out of Space." With the first tale we detect the first important contribution to Lovecraft's celebrated mythcycle. The beginnings of the cycle can be traced as far back as "Dagon" (1917), but more properly it begins with such preliminary tales as "The Nameless City" (1921) and "The Festival" (1923), and gains coherence with "The Call of Cthulhu." It would, however, be somewhat improper to distinguish too strongly between tales that are part of the cycle and those that are not, for in truth all his works express the central theme in Lovecraft's philosophy—"that common human laws and interests and emotions have no validity or significance in the vast cosmos-at-large"[44] —and the sole difference lies in which tales do or do not use the artificial pantheon of gods, places, and other such effects as central plot elements. While it is convenient at times to divide Lovecraft's work into certain loose and inexclusive categories—based perhaps on use of pseudomythological beings, common plot themes and settings, and the like—it is wise always to keep its fundamental philosophical unity in mind.

With "The Colour out of Space" we may also trace the tendency of Lovecraft's later work toward the *genre* of science-fiction; a tendency which may conceivably be stretched to earlier works such as "Beyond the Wall of Sleep" (1919). It is quite debatable that Lovecraft actually wrote "science-fiction"—the more so since none can agree as to what "science-fiction" is—but his importance in the developement of the field is now established. Such tales as "The Whisperer in Darkness," *At the Mountains of Madness,* and "The Shadow out of Time" use many techniques and mechanics of plot that can be classified as those of "science-fiction."

Almost without question the final decade of Lovecraft's life were his crowning years. His tales were selling with tolerable frequency, though he had some major setbacks;[45] his antiquarian travels became more extensive, as he several times visited Quebec, Charleston, New Orleans, and other sites; he met several associates whom he had previously known only by correspondence—Henry S. Whitehead, E. Hoffmann Price,

R. H. Barlow, to name only a few; his income from revisory work and professional magazine appearances was enough to allow him a moderately comfortable though necessarily a financially cautious existence; and he could leisurely appreciate hitherto unknown sites in Providence and New England, sites which saw exquisite description in such tales as "The Dunwich Horror," "The Whisperer in Darkness," and "The Haunter of the Dark" (1935).

During this period his work was, albeit slowly and on a very modest level, finding a wider recognition. Although Lovecraft always remained tremendously popular with the readerships of both the amateur journals and of *Weird Tales,* his tales now began appearing on the honour rolls of the O'Brien *Best Short Stories* annuals, and were being anthologised both in this country and in England; his work came to the attention of Vincent Starrett, Bertrand K. Hart, William Bolitho, and other important literary figures. In spite of all these circumstances, Lovecraft had only one true book published in his lifetime—*The Shadow over Innsmouth,* published by his friend William Crawford under the imprint of The Visionary Publishing Co. in 1936. Earlier, in 1928, W. Paul Cook had printed up sheets of *The Shunned House,* but never bound them; and Lovecraft also had eight small pamphlets issued from 1915 to 1936.[46] Lovecraft's failure to have a book published—either a novel or a collection of tales—by a major commercial firm has often been commented upon, but the fact is not difficult to explain: at the time, major publishers were extremely reluctant to publish collections of weird tales by obscure authors; specialty firms such as Arkham House, DAW Books, and Gnome Press did not come into existence until well after Lovecraft's death, only flourishing from the 1950's on. The only way, therefore, that Lovecraft could have a book brought out was to resort to the amateur presses of his friends and colleagues. Several publishers—Vanguard, Alfred A. Knopf, Loring & Mussey, Putnam's, and others—did indeed query Lovecraft about his work, but nothing came of these efforts. The publishers frequently asked for novel-length tales by Lovecraft; and he had the 50,000-word *The Case of Charles Dexter Ward* lying in manuscript since 1927, but appeared so discouraged as to its quality that he never made an effort to prepare it for publication.

It was ultimately Lovecraft's nonprofessional attitude toward his work that resulted in the lack of greater material success in his life. He was first and foremost an amateur, and considered writing for money both morally repugnant and aesthetically suicidal. Lovecraft wrote often that he was not and could not be a hack writer: he refused to *produce* work designed to meet the expectations of anyone aside from himself. It is true that he did do much work of this kind, for he was a literary revisionist by trade;

but he differentiated clearly between this work and his own original fiction. For the same reason he intensely disliked any editorial alterations of a tale once it was completed: not only did it reduce the unity and individuality of the story, but even the slightest change disturbed the subtle psychological effect of his pattern of words, phrases, and sentences. Despite the remarks of several commentators, Lovecraft was exceedingly careful about the smallest nuances of spelling, punctuation, and grammatical structure, for he knew well the hypnotic power of certain effects of syntax and phonology.

As the years passed, Lovecraft grew more and more uncertain about the quality of his fiction. Statements like ''I simply lack whatever it is that enables a real artist to convey his mood'' and ''I'm farther from doing what I want to do than I was 20 years ago''[47] expressed his own feelings toward his work for the last several years of his life. He wrote less and less in his later years. We have already noted that several of his tales languished in manuscript and were published only after his death;[48] others were sold only with the help of his friends and agents.[49] Lovecraft was quite disinclined to submit a work for publication after it had been once rejected, for this constant peddling would create that aura of commercialism that was so abhorrent to him.

Yet Lovecraft was writing till the very end of his life. Although his last fictional effort seems to have been the collaboration with Robert H. Barlow, ''The Night Ocean'' (Autumn 1936), he was continuing his bewilderingly vast correspondence up to the day before he was taken to Jane Brown Memorial Hospital on 10 March 1937, where he would die painfully five days later of cancer of the intestine, a disease whose symptoms had appeared well over a year earlier but which Lovecraft never had treated. Three days later a handful of friends and relatives saw him interred at Swan Point Cemetery in the family plot, where, though only after forty years, a small marker now heads his grave. It bears the inscription: ''I Am Providence.''[50]

Immediately upon Lovecraft's death, plans were made to organise a collection of his tales. August Derleth and Donald Wandrei, after receiving the Lovecraft papers from Lovecraft's distant cousin and literary executor, R. H. Barlow, set out to interest publishers in an omnibus of his fiction; but they were turned down by both Scribner's and Simon and Schuster. The latter firm, however, suggested that the two publish the book themselves, and this they set out to do. Arkham House released its first book in 1939, bearing the title *The Outsider and Others* by H. P. Lovecraft. Containing thirty-six stories plus the essay, ''Supernatural Horror in Literature,'' the book was an immense 553 pages long. The editors, Derleth and Wandrei, at the time envisioned a trilogy of volumes by Lovecraft, the first being a fiction omnibus, the second a collection of "the remaining prose, fiction and nonfiction, selected poems, and various miscellaneous pieces,"[51] and the third a volume of *Selected Letters*. Yet their goal proved to be too conservative. The second of the projected volumes—*Beyond the Wall of Sleep*—did emerge in 1943; but, when the editors found that the letters by Lovecraft that they received from correspondents were too vast for immediate publication, they issued a further "stop-gap"[52] volume of miscellany, *Marginalia* (1944). From then on, Arkham House has been issuing such stop-gap volumes periodically—*Something about Cats and Other Pieces* (1949), *The Shuttered Room and Other Pieces* (1959), *The Dark Brotherhood and Other Pieces* (1966)—while reissuing the fiction, collecting a volume of horror tales revised by Lovecraft, *The Horror in the Museum and Other Revisions* (1970), and publishing the "posthumous collaborations" of Lovecraft and Derleth. The editing and publishing of the *Selected Letters*—which expanded from a projected single volume to three volumes to five volumes—has taken nearly forty years.

Not long, however, after the initial Lovecraft omnibuses started appearing from Arkham House, other publishers began issuing Lovecraft themselves. Bartholomew House, Ben Abramson, the World Publishing Company, Avon Books, Victor Gollancz, Panther Books, Belmont Books, Lancer Books, and, more recently, Ballantine Books gave the Lovecraft fiction a wide distribution in the United States and England. Translations of Lovecraft into other languages were in existence as early as 1946, but did not become extensive until the mid-1950's, when several volumes of Lovecraft in French began appearing. German, Dutch, Spanish, Italian, Polish, Japanese, and many other foreign editions have followed.

The renewed scholarly interest in Lovecraft during this decade has resulted in the unearthing and publishing of much of Lovecraft's more obscure work, such as essays in amateur journals, unreprinted poems, and other marginalia.[53] This reprinting is helping critics and scholars to assess Lovecraft the writer more completely and to illuminate hitherto unclear aspects of his life. More work in this direction yet needs to be done, especially in connexion with Lovecraft's unpublished works and letters.

Lovecraft has become an established and important writer of this century whose work has already had a vast influence on horror and science-fiction literature; and we can expect this influence to grow in the coming decades. But we cannot yet leave Lovecraft the man and writer without first examining some of the key aspects which we have still left untouched.

As for his fiction, we find several complementary patterns relating to his basic one of the cosmic quality. One that has already been mentioned is the use of dreams. As noted, Lovecraft had, from the age of six on, extremely vivid dreams, many of which he transcribed directly into stories.[54] Yet virtually all his works were either based (at least in part) on dreams or incorporate dreams or dream-images. Indeed, it would not be going too far to say that the peculiar passivity of most of Lovecraft's narrators —a technique which has often been castigated—may have been used to strengthen the dream-like quality of his work; this, and the constant use of the first person, transfers the dream-images into our own minds. Other stray factors perhaps come together if we take this approach, such as the fact that many of Lovecraft's climactic scenes occur in darkness or semi-darkness. Lovecraft was not necessarily implying that the incidents he outlines are imaginary—the contrary is probably the case, since Lovecraft was manifestly wanting to show that his incidents actually occurred, that the vast entities peopling his tales actually exist, thus showing the inconsequentiality of mankind in relation to them. However, aside from wanting to transform his own dreams into words, Lovecraft wished to obscure our grasp of reality so as to make the incident or incidents which reveal an apparent suspension of natural law—a fact that Lovecraft considered the greatest source of terror—more credible.

Central to Lovecraft's entire work and thought was the concept of time. Lovecraft often felt that he had suffered a dislocation in time and that he was most at home in the eighteenth century, "or, at any rate, his conception of the eighteenth century."[55] Defeat of time, and the horrors that can result when time is confounded or disordered, play a role in many of his tales. We have an obvious example in "The Shadow out of Time," but we see in such tales as *The Case of Charles Dexter Ward* that the past itself—being manifested in this instance as ancestral legacy—can irrupt into the present and create circumstances which could affect "all civilisation, all natural law, perhaps even the fate of the solar system and the universe."[56] All his tales of hereditary degeneration (notably "The Rats in the Walls") include the idea that the past (in this case each human's past, stretching back to a time when we were not fully human) cannot die, and can still have a potent influence on the present and future. Yet in Lovecraft there is, as in his appreciation of nature, both a horror and an adoration of time and the past: in some tales he postulates that "time could not exist in certain belts of space;" this he depicts not as a horrifying but as a "picturesque"[57] situation, for the potentialities of knowledge gained in such a state—an understanding of the continuities of time, space, and history—was fascinating to Lovecraft. The concept of time is in Lovecraft a manifold one, and is not linked only to his love of bygone eras.

We need say little more about Lovecraft's work save again to indicate that fiction was not the only important body of his work, nor yet his poetry and essays: although he seemed never to consider them literary works as such, Lovecraft's letters dwarf, in sheer volume, the rest of his output combined. He wrote an estimated 100,000 letters, totalling several million words, and among his correspondents were Rheinhart Kleiner, Alfred Galpin, Maurice W. Moe, James F. Morton, Edward H. Cole, his aunts Mrs F. C. Clark and Mrs Annie E. P. Gamwell, Samuel Loveman, Frank Belknap Long, Clark Ashton Smith, August Derleth, Donald Wandrei, Wilfred Blanch Talman, Bernard Austin Dwyer, Woodburn Harris, Vincent Starrett, B. K. Hart, Elizabeth Toldridge, E. Hoffmann Price, Robert E. Howard, J. Vernon Shea, Robert Bloch, R. H. Barlow, Duane Rimel, Virgil Finlay, Willis Conover, and many others. An indication of the size of this body of his work can be gained by realising that less than 1000 of these letters, many of them highly excerpted, fill the five volumes of *Selected Letters,* a cumulative total of over 2000 pages.

Lovecraft the man has been called many things, and among the major charges against his character is his "racism." It is clear, however, that Lovecraft's ethnocentric views were typical of his time, his social position, and his milieu; it is not that his views were more pronounced than other "old Americans" of the early twentieth century, but that they were repeatedly, coordinately, and strongly expressed on paper. It is not to the point that we should call Lovecraft "wrong" about his attitudes, for by extension we would be obliged to call virtually every man and every civilisation up to and somewhat after his time, from the Greeks and before, "wrong;" and we must also bear in mind that all aspects of "racism" have taken on more sinister hues to those generations that know of the horrors of World War II. Lovecraft's attitudes remained only vocal, and there is no recorded instance of any action on his part against minorities. Many of his closest friends, including his wife, were not of the pure Nordic stock that he so concerned himself with. Moreover, his views did not remain, as they may have been towards youth, uncoordinated or impulsive: basing his theories on Darwin, Huxley, and others, he sincerely considered it detrimental for "incompatible" peoples and races to intermingle too heavily, lest culture-patterns become congealed into an amorphous homogeneity. His beliefs were for a time accentuated by his witnessing of the beautiful old homes in his own Providence destroyed or renovated by the foreigners who were flooding into the city and the country during his early years. It was not the destruction of the homes *per se* that he resented: it was, symbolically, the reduction of that aura of the past which he felt should be preserved in the name of culture, and which he seemed psychologically to need. From the 1920's on, his views became gradually less extreme, and in his later years he was probably less concerned with "racial purity" than many members of his social station. Let us not, however, explain the matter away entirely: Lovecraft's stance led him to adopt many illogicalities and misconceptions, and it is not to his credit that he infiltrated not only his letters but his poems ("New-England Fallen," "The Teuton's Battle Song," etc.) and even stories ("The Horror at Red Hook," "He," etc.) with his sentiments.

Lovecraft's political thought underwent as profound a change during his life as did his racial views. At first an ostentatiously staunch Anglophile with a severely conservative outlook, he changed in "a mere fifteen years . . . [into] a confirmed liberal who envisioned a form of fascistic socialism entailing governmental ownership of industry, artificially allotted employment, regulated salaries and old age pensions, and similar measures."[58] This is only a further indication of the flexibility of Lovecraft's mind: a tireless searcher for truth, he was able to discard or modify his beliefs in the face of new evidence or experience.

The claim that Lovecraft was an "eccentric recluse" falls to the ground when we observe the wide travels that he made during the last fifteen to twenty years of his life. That Lovecraft was reclusive in his youth can perhaps not be denied, particularly during the period from 1908 to 1914; but though he never met many of his major colleagues (Clark Ashton Smith, August Derleth, Robert E. Howard, Robert Bloch, *et al.*), there were on the other hand many whom he did meet. His home was always open to guests, though his predilection for sleeping during the day and working at night sometimes created problems. It is certainly not correct that Lovecraft was a snob: he "mingled with all kinds of people, and was not a snob at all—as every single one of his living friends (teachers, professors, manual labourers, printers, the high and the low) can attest."[59] It may be true to an extent that Lovecraft preferred indirect contact with others, i.e. through correspondence; but it was rare that Lovecraft turned down the company of a friend.

Was Lovecraft's fondness for the eighteenth century—its manners, its literature, the philosophical currents running through it, its art—a vast pose and affectation, as some have suggested? The statement is somewhat untenable, for Lovecraft grew up with the eighteenth century, and his continuous and voluminous reading of its literature made him feel perfectly at home with it. He wrote on one occasion: "The eighteenth century is my illusion. . . . What [it] really was, was the *final* phase of that perfectly unmechanised aera which as a whole gave us our most satisfying life. It was not so aesthetically great as the Elizabethan age, and in no way comparable to Periclean Greece and Augustan Rome. Its hold upon [me] is due mostly to its *proximity*. . . ."[60] Lovecraft loathed the nineteenth century, thinking much of its literature hollow (especially the Victorian, though he found many kind words for Poe, Baudelaire, and the Decadents) and its art and architecture grotesque, a "desert of illusions, pomposities, and hypocrisies."[61] The twentieth century, on the other hand, repelled him with its *avant-garde* literary and artistic trends, its defiance of tradition for the sake of defiance. Lovecraft merely considered eighteenth-century England a more pleasant, rational, and unaffected age in which to immerse himself. His use of archaisms in his early writings (e.g. "traffick") was only a natural result of his reading of old texts; later he abandoned many of them, though retaining some (as well as his English spellings) out of personal preference. His letters have now disproven the belief that Lovecraft was, because of his fascination with the past, not aware of the contemporary scene: to his correspondents he often wrote intelligently and perceptively about the modern world political situation, modern literature and philosophical thought, and modern scientific breakthroughs.

If Lovecraft's pose as an old man—typified by the signing of his letters as "Grandpa Theobald"—indicated a wistful longing to maintain the sedate and classical calm of an elderly gentleman-philosopher and teacher, it reflected no less his manifold wit. He could be as pungently satiric as a Bierce ("Ad Criticos," the pseudonymous replies to the astrologer Hartmann, etc.), as outrightly hilarious as a Wodehouse ("Ibid," "Sweet Ermengarde," "To Mistress Sophia Simple, Queen of the Cinema"), and as genially amusing as an Austen ("To Charlie of the Comics," "To Phillis," etc.). Other works reveal hilarious self-parody, while in others ("Alfredo," "A Reminiscence of Dr. Samuel Johnson") we see Lovecraft penning some beautiful works of parody and sarcasm with tongue firmly in cheek.

The feature of Lovecraft's character that has attracted the most praise, even from adverse critics, is his brilliant erudition. Lovecraft not only read vastly, but remembered all that he read: his memory was often a source of wonderment to his friends. It was only in his early years that this learning was "bookish": when he emerged from the over-protection of his mother and tempered his knowledge with experience, the result was the phenomenal intellect exhibited in his later letters. We can only catalogue the areas of knowledge with which Lovecraft was more than adequately familiar: astronomy, literature, aesthetics, philosophy, chemistry, psychology, history (especially ancient Greek and Roman, English, and Colonial American), architecture, politics, art, linguistics, and others.

Lovecraft's health and his relative poverty have been gone into often enough in the past. Whether his inability to stand cold temperatures was congenital or resulted from some combination of later effects—sequestration, malnutrition, etc.—may now be impossible to determine; indeed, it is questionable whether Lovecraft suffered so severely from starvation as has commonly been believed. August Derleth has tried to destroy this myth, and he is probably correct in saying that Lovecraft's "eating habits were often dictated by necessity, but just as often by choice."[62] However parsimonious Lovecraft's diet may seem to us, it seemed quite to suffice for him. His diet was, of course, far from ideal: sugar, chocolate, coffee, and other such edibles formed a disconcertingly large part of it. It could then be said that Lovecraft was, if not in a state of semi-starvation, probably in a state of chronic malnutrition; and we know that his reluctance to visit doctors—stemming as much from disinclination as from shortage of money—indirectly caused his premature death.

This has not been an attempt to explain away the many peculiarities and paradoxes that make up Lovecraft's life and character: we can ask ourselves why he continued to hold, in light of his supreme rationality, racial views which seem to us illogical; why he made so few efforts at gaining material success when, with not a great deal of effort nor a great compromising of his views, he could have obtained it in good measure; why he sometimes could be shockingly unthinking—his astounding impromptitude in keeping appointments is well known—and other times be most generous and considerate; why he was so puerilely dogmatic up to and beyond the age of thirty; why his unusually reserved sexual attitudes were what they were; and many other aspects not properly understood. Our goal has been to map out, in a general way, the life, work, character, and thought of "one of the most interesting men of his generation,"[63] and to reduce the distortions about him that have spread over the past decades, and so render the interpretation of his work the more facile. Lovecraft remains one of the most controversial writers of this century, and his work has been subject to bewilderingly manifold interpretations. Lovecraft the man has been pictured both as a saint and as a fiend; but is it not clear that his true character lies somewhere between the extremes? The paradoxes in Lovecraft's life are representative of the basic paradox of the human condition. That he so escapes facile categorisation and simplistic generalisation is only a tribute to the rich complexity of his mind and character.

Notes

1. J. W. Thomas, "H. P. Lovecraft: A Self-Portrait" (M.A. thesis: Brown University, 1950), p. 96.

2. Lin Carter, *Lovecraft: A Look Behind the "Cthulhu Mythos,"* p. xi; even L. Sprague de Camp realises the inaccuracy of this statement, saying that "during the last decade of his life, he was hardly more eccentric or more reclusive than most professional authors" (*Lovecraft: A Biography,* p. 59).
3. Colin Wilson, *The Strength to Dream,* p. 1.
4. Isaac Asimov; quoted in de Camp, *op. cit.,* p. 440.
5. S. Eisner, "H.P.L.—Imagination's Envoy to Literature (Some Introductory Remarks)", *Fresco,* VIII, 3 (Spring 1958), 2.
6. E. A. Edkins, "Idiosyncrasies of HPL," p. 7.
7. A. Derleth, "Lovecraft as Mentor," p. 169.
8. Helen V. Sully, "Memories of Lovecraft: II," *The Arkham Collector,* 4 (Winter 1969), 119.
9. J. Chapman Miske, "H. P. Lovecraft: Strange Weaver," *Scienti-Snaps,* III, 3 (Summer 1940), 9.
10. Brian W. Aldiss, *Billion Year Spree,* p. 177.
11. C. Wilson, *op. cit.,* p. 8.
12. Edmund Wilson, "Tales of the Marvellous and the Ridiculous."
13. C. Wilson, "Prefatory Note" to *The Philosopher's Stone* (New York: Crown, 1971), p. [6].
14. Drake Douglas, *Horror!,* p. 264.
15. J. O. Bailey, *Pilgrims Through Space and Time,* p. 179.
16. Prof. John A. Taylor; quoted in de Camp, *op. cit.,* p. 440.
17. P. Penzoldt, *The Supernatural in Fiction,* p. 171.
18. Douglas, *op. cit.,* p. 266.
19. Dust jacket to *The Outsider and Others.*
20. E. Wilson, *op. cit.*
21. De Camp, *op. cit.,* p. 8.
22. Thanks are due to Prof. Henry L. P. Beckwith for pointing out some of these factors.
23. Lovecraft to Edwin Baird, 3 February 1924; in *Collected Works,* V, p. 302.
24. Lovecraft to Rheinhart Kleiner, 16 November 1916; in *Collected Works,* V, p. 40.
25. *Ibid.,* p. 38.
26. Reprinted, as *First Writings . . . ,* by Necronomicon Press (1976).
27. De Camp, *op. cit.,* p. 45.
28. Lovecraft writes to J. Vernon Shea (19–30 July 1931), "I do . . . have copies of some 8-year-old junk which my mother saved—'The Mysterious Ship' & 'The Secret of the Grave.' " (Ms. letter in the Lovecraft Collection, John Hay Library, Brown University.) Actually, the story "The Secret of the Grave" was not preserved, but "The Secret Cave" was.
29. Penzoldt, *op. cit.,* p. 166.
30. Cf. David H. Keller, "Lovecraft's Astronomical Notebook," *The Lovecraft Collector,* 3 (October 1949), 1–4.
31. Cf. Sam Moskowitz, "H. P. Lovecraft and the Munsey Magazines," in *Under the Moons of Mars,* pp. 373–79.
32. "Autobiography—Some Notes on a Nonentity," in *Beyond the Wall of Sleep,* p. xiii.
33. W. Paul Cook, *In Memoriam: Howard Phillips Lovecraft,* p. 55.
34. Lovecraft himself realised this fact, signing one poem ("A Mississippi Autumn," *Ole Miss,* Dec. 1915) as "Howard Phillips Lovecraft, Metrical Mechanic."
35. R. Alain Everts (pers. comm.), January 1977.
36. "Autobiography . . .", p. xiii.
37. We owe this observation to Mr J. Vernon Shea.
38. Lovecraft to Clark Ashton Smith, 14 April 1929; in *Collected Works,* VII, p. 328.
39. C. Wilson, *The Strength to Dream,* p. 2.
40. Revisory work was undoubtedly continued, but even when Lovecraft was single this failed to provide enough of an income on which to live; the situation was clearly worse when Lovecraft had a wife to support. As it turned out, of course, his wife began to support him.

41. Lovecraft was to have received $5 per instalment for the series; but researches by R. Alain Everts have indicated that this money, at least in full, was never paid him.
42. The exceptions were *The Dream-Quest of Unknown Kadath* (1926-27), "The Colour out of Space" (1927), *At the Mountains of Madness* (1931), and "The Shadow out of Time" (1934-35).
43. It has been suggested that the plot of "Cool Air" could have been taken either from Poe's "Facts in the Case of M. Valdemar" (cf. Penzoldt) or from Machen's "Novel of the White Powder" (cf. J. Vernon Shea, "H. P. Lovecraft: The House and the Shadows").
44. Lovecraft to Farnsworth Wright, 5 July 1927; in *Collected Works,* VI, p. 150.
45. The rejection of *At the Mountains of Madness* by *Weird Tales* in 1931 "probably did more than anything to end my effective fictional career." Lovecraft to E. Hoffmann Price, 12 February 1936; in *Collected Works,* IX, p. 224.
46. *The Crime of Crimes* (1915); *United Amateur Press Association: Exponent of Amateur Journalism* (1916); *Looking Backward* (1920?); *The Materialist Today* (1926); *Further Criticism of Poetry* (1932); *The Cats of Ulthar* (1935); *Some Current Motives and Practices* (1936); *Charleston* (1936).
47. Lovecraft, *loc. cit.*
48. Aside from *The Case of Charles Dexter Ward,* the other major one is *The Dream-Quest of Unknown Kadath,* published in 1943.
49. "In the Vault" (1925) and "The Dreams in the Witch House" (1932), sold by August Derleth; *At the Mountains of Madness,* sold by Julius Schwartz; "The Shadow out of Time," sold by Donald Wandrei.
50. This venture, to which many Lovecraftians contributed, was led by Prof. Dirk W. Mosig.
51. August Derleth and Donald Wandrei, "By Way of Introduction," in *Beyond the Wall of Sleep,* p. ix.
52. Derleth and Wandrei, "Foreword" to *Marginalia,* p. vii.
53. Cf. such specialty firms as Necronomicon Press (West Warwick, R.I.); Donald M. Grant (West Kingston, R.I.); Silver Scarab Press (Albuquerque, N.M.); The Strange Company (Madison, Wis.); Gerry de la Ree (Saddle River, N.J.); Roy A. Squires (Glendale, Cal.); Whispers Press, and others.
54. Notable examples are "The Statement of Randolph Carter," "Celephais," and "The Shadow out of Time." Indeed, an entire book containing dream-inspired tales and letter excerpts in which Lovecraft describes his dreams has been published—*Dreams and Fancies* (1962).
55. W. T. Scott, "The Haunter of the Dark: Some Notes on Howard Phillips Lovecraft," *Books at Brown,* VI, 3 (March 1944), 2.
56. *The Case of Charles Dexter Ward,* in *Collected Works,* II, p. 171.
57. "The Dreams in the Witch House," in *ibid.,* p. 270.
58. James Turner, "Preface" to *Collected Works,* IX, pp. xxxiv-xxxv. Insofar as Lovecraft, even in his later years, could be both socialistic and unduly nationalistic, it may be improper to label him a "liberal" in the classical sense; yet we may note that many of the governmental policies he advocated were indeed adopted by several countries in the renaissance of modified "liberalism" following World War II.
59. R. Alain Everts to S. T. Joshi, 17 September 1975.
60. Lovecraft to James F. Morton, 30 October 1929; in *Collected Works,* VII, p. 50.
61. *Ibid.* Many historians and thinkers—notably Lewis Mumford, Arnold Toynbee, and Lord Clark—share his views.
62. Derleth, "Myths About Lovecraft," *The Lovecraft Collector,* 2 (May 1949), 1.
63. C. Wilson, *The Strength to Dream,* p. 10.

Lovecraft Criticism: A Study

By S. T. Joshi

Why has criticism of H. P. Lovecraft been so mixed? The question divides into the matters of why he has been so condemned and why so vastly praised. Aside from the incidental vagaries and prejudices of individual critics, the essential reasons for his unpopularity are perhaps these: firstly, Lovecraft, despite his frequent borrowings of concepts and styles from other writers, was fundamentally a highly original writer; secondly, his style was not at all like that of his contemporaries, tending to reflect both the classically correct Georgian and the sober and precise style such as that found in scientific journals; thirdly, the weird tale has, until very modern times, not generally been regarded as a legitimate form of writing; and fourthly, Lovecraft's publishing in the pulp magazines of his day and, later, the championing of his work by the fans of the pulps caused him to appear a most dubious sort of literary figure. Perhaps each of these reasons needs to be dealt with more carefully.

Lovecraft's outlook, as expressed through his fiction and stated bluntly in his letters and essays, was that of what he himself called "cosmic indifferentism." Being a mechanist materialist philosophically, he felt that the existence of man on this planet represented nothing more than an infinitesimally small and incidental (and, as he wryly suggested in *At the Mountains of Madness,* perhaps accidental) occurrence in the universe; the lifespan of humanity would be a mere second in infinity. In his fiction this was reflected by the hinting of the awesome gulfs of space and the awesome vistas of time. Lovecraft's myth-cycle, with its titanic entities—Yog-Sothoth, Azathoth, Cthulhu, Nyarlathotep, *et al.*—, is not an indication that Lovecraft was some odd mystic who created mythical "gods" and beings in an attempt to escape "reality," but a crystal clear reflexion of his cosmic outlook: the very indifference of these incalculably powerful entities to the inconsequential creatures called human beings is the source of terror in Lovecraft's tales. These beings—labelled "gods" by men because they seemed to reflect "godlike" powers—are not interested either in the preservation or the destruction of men, but exist merely to further their own ends; and if men by chance stumble upon them or get in their way, then they are simply exterminated. This reflexion of man's ludicrously minute position in the cosmos is perpetually conveyed in his fiction, and may perhaps be Lovecraft's major contribution to literature. The majority of critics, however, have not understood this, being distracted by what they consider a puerile exhibition of mystical "gods" and creatures whose outlandish names (devised to further the sense of their "outsideness") seem to have attracted more attention than their philosophical significance. Then, too, Lovecraft's oftentimes gruesome physical horror has been depreciated, when in fact it is often more symbolic and psychological than physical: note the hideous monster who narrates "The Outsider," and who symbolises both the grotesqueness in man (for his is a "leering, abhorrent travesty on the human shape")[1] and, by his very grotesqueness, an utter alienage from normality.

Lovecraft's style of writing is very clearly not modern; as Robert Bloch meant in another sense, "It is difficult to believe that Howard Phillips Lovecraft was a literary contemporary of Ernest Hemingway."[2] We have not the brisk, terse, casual, and often simple style that typifies modern American and, to a lesser extent, modern English fiction; what we encounter instead is a soberly erudite and precise style, a modernisation of a style in vogue two centuries ago. Lovecraft searched for the *mot juste* as assiduously as did Flaubert; he revised and polished his fiction to an extent now considered absurd and superfluous. The style has been called "artificial,"[3] pretentious, and false; yet since Lovecraft's literary diet in his childhood consisted primarily of eighteenth-century literature, this style came to him so naturally—as is evidenced by his letters, which were written spontaneously and instinctively—that we can hardly call it affected. The major reason for its unpopularity is simply that this style is no longer used nor is in vogue; such depreciations of it reflect little more than the literary tastes of our time. The same can be said of the objections to Lovecraft's use of such words as "hideous," "horrible," "ghastly," and other such bluntly horrific adjectives, voiced by such critics as Edmund Wilson, Colin Wilson, L. Sprague de Camp, and others: such a use of adjectives was popular in the weird fiction up to the time of Poe, and from then on it was looked down upon; the use of this technique cannot be intrinsically incorrect, since a single generation or two might suffice to restore it to public favour.

As for the prejudice held against the horror tale as a sort of "poor relation" to mainstream literature, this has been evident ever since the decline of the popular Gothic novels of the eighteenth and early nineteenth centuries; only the rise in popularity and acceptance of the related *genre* of science-fiction (and also of the fantasy tales of such writers as Charles Williams, C. S. Lewis, and J. R. R. Tolkien) in the last decade or two has allowed the purely weird tale itself to become "respectable" in the eyes of critics. Edmund Wilson seemed to have an especial loathing of weird fiction which went beyond mere prejudice against the *genre* as a whole, but, as late as 1944, Winfield Townley Scott was epitomising the sentiment held by most critics at that time and following: "The purpose of shocking—of frightening or horrifying—is in literature a meretricious one." Scott continued to say that he refused "to regard weird tales, no matter who writes them, as great literature" because "there is 'enough horror in real life without dragging it in from outside,' as [Elliott] Paul once put."[4] The subjectivity and irrelevance of such a view is immediately manifest, for the very fact that there is "horror in real life" vindicates the existence of the weird tale as an art form, if by art we mean (as Lovecraft noted) a "treatment of life."[5] Moreover, Scott and other critics ignore the fact that the greatest macabre writers have almost invariably used the weird as a vehicle to express personal, profound, and complex philosophies of life and literature. The time is past when mature critics can brush aside the work of Poe, Bierce, and Lovecraft from its place in American and world literature.

August Derleth has written that "it was to be expected that the place of original publication [of Lovecraft's fiction] would be held against it."[6] Pulp magazines have never attracted the praise of critics, and perhaps rightly so, since the overwhelming majority of the material contained in them is cheap, puerile, formula-ridden hack-work; yet to the credit of *Weird Tales* and other pulps it can be said that they provided markets for many authors now considered great—Tennessee Williams and Ray Bradbury are only two—, that they were now and then far superior in format and content (both literary and artistic) to general-fiction magazines, and, of course, that they were the precursors of the reputed science-fiction magazines of today. Yet, scattered as Lovecraft's fiction was in the cheap pulps, amidst the frequently frightful trash that cluttered most issues (though at times ennobled by the literate work of Lovecraft's colleagues, Clark Ashton Smith, Donald Wandrei, Frank Belknap Long, Henry S. Whitehead, C. L. Moore, and others), it became very easy to pass off Lovecraft's tales as hack-work. If Lovecraft's work was indeed so fine, it might have been argued, why did he not publish in more prestigious journals? But here the prejudice against the horror tale came into play: reputed magazines included very little imaginative fiction because, firstly, it was not considered proper or valuable, and secondly, it was not popular with the readerships of the magazines. Meanwhile, Lovecraft and other sincere weird writers, having few markets, had to publish where they could. Then, too, the championing of Lovecraft by the legions of horror and science-fiction fans, whose articles were not impressive criticism, tended to create the image that Lovecraft was some anomalous writer who was enjoying a brief popularity with uncritical readers.

For all these reasons, Lovecraft was either ignored by major critics or judged harshly, subjectively, or jokingly. Material about Lovecraft had been appearing as early as the 1910's, in the amateur presses; and when Lovecraft began publishing in *Weird Tales,* readers flooded the "Eyrie," the letter column of the magazine, with praises of his tales. After his death, minor critical and biographical articles began appearing in fanzines such as *Golden Atom, Fantasy Commentator, Fantasy Advertiser,* and elsewhere. Whole magazines (of which the first were *The Acolyte* and *The Lovecraft Collector*) were devoted exclusively to Lovecraft, and his talents were loudly—and perhaps excessively—praised. Lovecraft was quickly becoming the centre of a sort of cult. Edmund Wilson's article, therefore, was intended to "prove" how ridiculous was such a cult, and how puerile were Lovecraft's writings. But by around 1950, it was clear that Lovecraft would not "fade away."' Recognising this fact, Dr Peter Penzoldt devoted space to him in his study, *The Supernatural in Fiction* (1952).

But the main critical/biographical/bibliographical work was still being done by fans and by the associates and correspondents of Lovecraft; within a decade and a half of his death, such colleagues as Frank Belknap Long, August Derleth, Donald Wandrei, E. Hoffmann Price, Rheinhart Kleiner, W. Paul Cook, Samuel Loveman, Mrs Muriel Eddy, his wife Sonia Davis, R. H. Barlow, and others had produced memoirs of Lovecraft, while other members of the "Lovecraft Circle," or those associated with it—Fritz Leiber, Joseph Payne Brennan, Derleth, Matthew H. Onderdonk, George T. Wetzel, and others—were attempting brief critical appraisals. What hampered these studies—and what has hampered the effectiveness of much Lovecraft criticism until recent times —was the unavailability of much of the important body of Lovecraft's work. While letters by Lovecraft had found print as early as the 1920's, the letters never received anything approaching wide distribution until the publication of the *Selected Letters* volumes, beginning in 1965; and the difficulty of assessing Lovecraft completely and objectively without examining his letters is amply testified by the uninformed criticisms of Edmund Wilson, Colin Wilson, Brian W. Aldiss, Damon Knight, and others. Criticism before the late 1960's concentrated only on Lovecraft the fiction-writer and, on rare instances, the poet; what was not considered was the breadth of his philosophy and erudition (though this was indicated by many of his correspondents, who had first-hand knowledge of it) and the scope of his "cosmic indifferentism," the key to the understanding of the Lovecraft *oeuvre.*

At this point there can be touched upon another reason for the many misconceptions that have arisen concerning Lovecraft's life and work: August Derleth. As Prof. Dirk W. Mosig points out in "H. P. Lovecraft: Myth-Maker," Derleth's unwillingness or inability to understand the Lovecraft works caused him to conceive and disseminate a highly distorted impression of Lovecraft; and, due to the fact that Derleth, being Lovecraft's publisher and champion, was considered the "authority" on his subject, his views, oftentimes fallacious, were adopted by the majority of critics and scholars. Perhaps Derleth's most serious fault was in writing his "posthumous collaborations" with Lovecraft, which are not only intrinsically poor but which present a perversion of Lovecraft's cosmic myth-cycle. It can be said that Derleth, though perhaps unintentionally and certainly with no malicious intent, has delayed the advancement of objective Lovecraft criticism for nearly thirty years. It is a tribute to such early scholars as Fritz Leiber, Jr, George T. Wetzel, and Matthew H. Onderdonk that they saw through Derleth's misconceptions and interpreted Lovecraft's work on its own terms; as a result, their articles to this day remain some of the finest critical studies on Lovecraft ever written.

The first master's thesis on Lovecraft was written as early as 1950, with James Warren Thomas' "H. P. Lovecraft: A Self-Portrait;" but the attention of the academic world on Lovecraft did not become extensive until the 1960's. That decade saw the writing of five papers on Lovecraft, including the valuable Koki and St Armand theses and the first doctoral dissertation, by Maria Tranzocchi of Rome University. In the first six years of this decade, eight papers have already been written.

Articles about Lovecraft in other languages have been trickling in ever since the late 1950's, but did not become voluminous until the 1960's and 1970's. French critics have been leading champions of Lovecraft, and Italian, Spanish, and German critics have not been far behind.

While memoirs of Lovecraft have always been with us, formal biographies have been curiously scarce. The sad state of Lovecraft biographies can be indicated by the fact that August Derleth's inadequate *H.P.L.: A Memoir* (1945) was long considered the "standard" biography. The first full-length biography was written forty years after Lovecraft's death, this being L. Sprague de Camp's dubious *Lovecraft: A Biography* (1975). While de Camp has included a vast amount of research (some of it incorrect) in his book, he has allowed himself to pass subjective value judgements on Lovecraft's life and character, and to attempt much posthumous psychoanalysis, with debatable results. De Camp's biography should ultimately serve, insofar as it does attempt to offer a unified and full chronological view of Lovecraft's life, as a guideline of research for future, more objective biographies.

But de Camp is far from being the first to attempt armchair psycho-analysis on Lovecraft: this began as early as 1945, with Marjorie Farber, and has continued through Colin Wilson and others. Yet only recently (though Penzoldt had suggested it two decades before), with scholars such as Prof. St Armand and Prof. Mosig, has the Lovecraft *oeuvre* been logically explored in a psychoanalytical-literary framework, thus adding a fascinating dimension to the appreciation and understanding of Love-craft.

Peripheral both to Lovecraft's own work and to Lovecraft criticism are those works by other authors which imitate Lovecraft's style or em-body or elaborate upon the themes expressed in his fiction, generically called tales of the Yog-Sothoth Cycle of Myth, or Cthulhu Mythos. Authors of such tales include not only some of Lovecraft's major corre-spondents, whom he himself urged to add to his myth-cycle (August Derleth, Frank Belknap Long, Robert E. Howard, Robert Bloch, Clark Ashton Smith), but writers on the fringe of the Lovecraft circle (Carl Jacobi, Joseph Payne Brennan, Hugh B. Cave, Henry Kuttner, Manly Wade Wellman), and writers completely dissociated from Lovecraft, writing their fictions long after his death (J. Ramsey Campbell, Brian Lumley, Richard L. Tierney, Lin Carter, Colin Wilson, James Wade). But while the influence of Lovecraft is patent in these obvious cases, it can also be felt in the work of Kurt Vonnegut, Jr, Ray Bradbury, Jorge Luis Borges, and other writers not normally associated with Lovecraft. Lovecraft's fiction is of too narrow a literary scope to influence future writers in the manner of Poe's detective or horror tales, but it is very like-ly that the concepts embodied in his work could have an effect on litera-ture. More work in the tradition of Colin Wilson's ''Lovecraftian'' novels or Fred Chappell's novel *Dagon*—which strive not to imitate slavishly Lovecraft's style or to rehash Lovecraft's own plots, but to elaborate upon his ideas—might be looked for in the future.

While brief articles on Lovecraft have recently appeared in such periodicals as *Time, Yankee,* and the *New York Times Book Review,*[8] The major critical work on Lovecraft is still being done in the amateur presses and fanzines. The establishment some years ago of the Esoteric Order of Dagon, an amateur press association devoted to Lovecraft, has resulted in the publishing of thousands of pages of Lovecraft-related material, some of it valuable. Another, more scholarly amateur press association, the Necronomicon, headed by R. Alain Everts, is also pro-viding much important biographical, bibliographical, and critical re-search on Lovecraft, as are such semi-professional periodicals as *Whispers* and *Nyctalops*. Major recently-published memoirs—*Lovecraft at Last* by H. P. Lovecraft and Willis Conover; Frank Belknap Long's *Howard Phillips Lovecraft: Dreamer on the Nightside*—and the recent or forthcoming critical/biographical studies by Prof. Mosig, Prof. St Armand, Prof. James Merritt, Prof. John Taylor Gatto, and Prof. Philip A. Shreffler[9] might indicate that the major critical work on Lovecraft—particularly in the realms of his philosophical and literary thought and his place in intellectual history—has yet to be done.

Modern scholarship seems to be on the brink of a new assessment of H. P. Lovecraft—an assessment shorn of the inaccuracies and misconceptions of the past, amalgamating the finest critical thought of prior scholarship, and augmenting it with new discoveries. If the present compilation in any way helps in that new assessment—which should reveal the strengths and weaknesses of Lovecraft's entire literary output, his key position in weird fiction, science-fiction, and American and world literature, and the extent of his cosmic thought, the like of which literature has rarely if ever seen—then its purpose will have been admirably fulfilled.

Notes

1. *Collected Works,* I, p. 58.
2. See Bloch's "Poe and Lovecraft."
3. See Penzoldt's *The Supernatural in Fiction,* p. 165.
4. W. T. Scott, "His Own Most Fantastic Creation: Howard Phillips Lovecraft," in *Exiles and Fabrications,* p. 52.
5. Lovecraft to Zealia Brown (Reed) Bishop, 12 June 1927; in *Collected Works,* VI, p. 144.
6. See "H. P. Lovecraft and His Work."
7. *Ibid.*
8. Philip Herrera, "The Dream Lurker," *Time* (11 June 1973); Bartlett Gould, "Rhode Island's Genius of Grue," *Yankee* (October 1969); Marc Slonim, "European Notebook," *New York Times Book Review* (17 May 1970).
9. Prof. Mosig, *H. P. Lovecraft* (Twayne); Prof. St Armand, *The Roots of Horror in the Fiction of H. P. Lovecraft* (Dragon Press); Prof. Merritt, an untitled biography; Prof. Gatto, *The Major Works of H. P. Lovecraft,* a Monarch Study Note; Prof. Shreffler, *The H. P. Lovecraft Companion* (Greenwood Press).

A Chronology of Selected Works by H. P. Lovecraft

This list claims to exclude no known work of fiction by Lovecraft, but certain items of poetry and nonfiction (most of the latter consisting of essays on amateur journalism) have been omitted for the sake of space. The dating of the items should not be considered certain save for the fiction: some have been dated purely in terms of publication. These latter dates are printed in italic type. Manuscripts, chronologies, and letters have been examined, however, and the dating of the fiction is probably quite accurate. Abbreviations used: (np): not published; (x): destroyed or lost. Some titles have been abbreviated.

1897–1902

Fiction

The Noble Eavesdropper (1897?)
The Secret Cave or John Lees Adventure (1898)
The Mystery of the Grave-Yard (1898)
The Haunted House (x)
The Secret of the Grave (x)
John, the Detective (x)
The Mysterious Ship (1902)

Poetry

The Poem of Ulysses, or The Odyssey (8 Nov. 1897) (np)
The Iliad (1898?) (x)
The Aeneid (1898?) (x)
Ovid's Metamorphoses (1900) (np)
Poemata Minora, Vol. I (1902) (x)
Poemata Minora, Vol. II (inc. "Ode to Selene or Diana;" "To the Old Pagan Religion;" "On the Ruin of Rome" [np]; "To Pan;" "On the Vanity of Human Ambition" [np] (1902)

Non-Fiction

Mythology for the Young (1897?) (x)
Egyptian Myths (1897?) (x)
The Art of Fusion Melting Pudling & Casting (1898?) (np)

Chemistry (6 vols.; 4 extant)
(np)
Early Rhode Island (x)
An Historical Account of Last
Year's War with SPAIN

(1899?) (x)
Antarctic Atlas (x)
Voyages of Capt. Ross, R.N.
(x)
Wilkes's Explorations (x)

1903

Non-Fiction

The Rhode Island Journal of
Astronomy (2 Aug.-Apr.
1907; 69 issues) (np)
The Scientific Gazette (16
Aug.-31 Jan. 1904; 32

issues) (np)
Astronomy/The Monthly
Almanack (Aug.-Feb. 1904;
9 issues) (np)

1904

Non-Fiction

The Science Library (?) (9
vols.; 3 extant; inc. "1.
Naked Eye Selenography"
[np]; "2. The Telescope"
[np]; "3. Life of Galileo"
[x]; "4. Life of Herschel
(revised)" [x]; "5. "Saturn

and His Rings" [np]; "6.
Selections from Author's
'Astronomy' " [x]; "7. The
Moon, Part I" [x]; "8. The
Moon, Part II" [x]; "9. On
Optics" [x])

1905

Fiction

The Beast in the Cave (21 Apr.)

Poetry

De Triumpho Naturae (July)

1906

Nonfiction

Letter to *Providence Sunday Journal* (27 May)
Letter to *Scientific American* (16 July)
Astronomy articles for *Paw-* *tuxet Valley Gleaner* (*July– Dec.;* 17 articles) and *Providence Tribune* (*Aug.–June 1908;* 20 articles)

1907

Fiction

The Picture (x)

1908

Fiction

The Alchemist

1909

Nonfiction

Astronomical notebook (to 1915) (np)

1910

Nonfiction

A Brief Course in Inorganic Chemistry (x)

1912

Poetry

On the Creation of Niggers *(4 Mar.)*
Providence in 2000 A.D. New-England Fallen (Apr.)

1913

Poetry

On a New-England Village Quinsnicket Park
  Seen by Moonlight (7 Sept.)

Nonfiction

Letters in *Argosy (Sept.–Oct.
  1914)*

1914

Poetry

1914 *(Mar.)* To Members of the Pin-Feath-
On a Modern Lothario *(July)* ers *(Nov.)*
To General Villa *(Nov.)*

Nonfiction

Astronomy articles for *Provi-* *(Sept. –Dec.;* 6 articles)
  dence Evening News (Jan.– Department of Public
  May 1918; 53 articles) Criticism *(Nov.–May 1919;*
"Bickerstaffe" pieces in 16 articles)
  Providence Evening News

1915

Poetry

The Power of Wine *(Jan.)* March *(Mar.)*

The Simple Speller's Tale
(*Apr.*)
Elegy on Franklin Chase Clark
(*Apr.*)
The Bay-Stater's Policy (*June*)
The Crime of Crimes (*July*)
Fragment on Whitman (*July*)
On Receiving a Picture of
Swans (Sept.)
Unda, or The Bride of the Sea

(Sept.)
Gems from "In a Minor Key"
(*Oct.*)
The State of Poetry (*Oct.*)
The Magazine Poet (*Oct.*)
A Mississippi Autumn (Nov.?)
On the Cowboys of the West
(*Dec.*)
To Samuel Loveman (*Dec.*)

Nonfiction

Astronomy articles in *Asheville Gazette-News* (*Feb.–May?*; 19? articles)
The Crime of the Century
(*Mar.*)
The Morris Faction (*Mar.*)
The Question of the Day
(*Mar.*)
Metrical Regularity (*July*)
In a Major Key (*July*)
The Dignity of Journalism

(*July*)
The Conservative and His
Critics (*July; Oct.*)
The Youth of Today (*Oct.*)
The Renaissance of Manhood
(*Oct.*)
Liquor and Its Friends (*Oct.*)
More "Chain Lightning"
(*Dec.*)
Systematic Instruction in the
United (*Dec.*)

1916

Poetry

A Rural Summer Eve (*Jan.*)
The Teuton's Battle Song
(*Feb.*)
R. Kleiner, Laureatus (*Apr.*)
Ye Ballade of Patrick von
Flynn (*Apr.*)

Temperence Song (*Spring*)
The Beauties of Peace (*June*)
The Rose of England (*Oct.*)
An American to Mother
England
The Poe-et's Nightmare

Nonfiction

Revolutionary Mythology
(*Oct.*)
Old England and the

"Hyphen" (*Oct.*)
In the Editor's Study (*Oct.–July 1923;* 7 articles)

1917

Fiction

The Tomb (June)

Dagon (July)

A Reminiscence of Dr. Samuel Johnson (*Sept.*)

Poetry

Futurist Art (*Jan.*)

Elegy on Phillips Gamwell (*Jan.*)

Lines on Gen. R. E. Lee (*Jan.*)

The Rutted Road (*Jan.*)

The Nymph's Reply to the Modern Business Man (*Feb.*)

Fact and Fancy (*Feb.*)

Pacifist War Song—1917 (*Mar.*)

Britannia Victura (*Apr.*)

The Poet of Passion (*June*)

Ode for July Fourth, 1917 (*July*)

On the Death of a Rhyming Critic (*July*)

To Mistress Sophia Simple, Queen of the Cinema (Aug.)

Autumn (*Nov.*)

To Greece, 1917 (*Nov.*)

Sunset (*Dec.*)

An American to the British Flag (*Dec.*)

Old Christmas (Dec.?)

Nonfiction

Concerning "Persia—in Europe" (*Jan.*)

The United's Problem (*July*)

The Truth About Mars (*Autumn*)

President's Message (for *United Amateur*) (*Sept.– July 1918;* 6 articles)

1918

Fiction

Polaris

The Mystery of Murdon Grange (np; x)

The Green Meadow (with W. V. Jackson) (1918? 1919?)

Poetry

Astrophobos (*Jan.*)

A Winter Wish (*Jan.*)

To Jonathan Hoag (Feb.)

Laeta; a Lament (*Feb.*)

The Volunteer (*Feb.*)

Ad Britannos, 1918 (*Apr.*)

Psychopompos (May?)
Nemesis (June)
On a Battlefield in Picardy
  (*July*)
The House (*July*)
To the American Flag (July?)

Phaeton (*Aug.*)
August (*Aug.*)
Hellas (*Sept.*)
To Arthur Goodenough (*Sept.*)
The Eidolon (*Oct.*)
Germania—1918 (*Nov.*)

Nonfiction

At the Root (*July*)
The Despised Pastoral (*July*)
Anglo-Saxondom (*July*)
Merlinus Redivivus (*July*)

Time and Space (*July*)
The Literature of Rome (*Nov.*)
The Simple Spelling Mania
  (*Dec.*)

1919

Fiction

Beyond the Wall of Sleep
Memory
Old Bugs
The Transition of Juan
  Romero (16 Sept.)

The White Ship (Nov.)
The Doom that Came to
  Sarnath (3 Dec.)
The Statement of Randolph
  Carter (late Dec.)

Poetry

Theodore Roosevelt (*Jan.*)
Spring (*Apr.*)
Damon—A Monody (*May*)
Hylas and Myrrha (*May*)
A Cycle of Verse (inc.
  "Clouds;" Mother Earth;"
  Oceanus") (*July*)
Monody on the Late King

Alcohol (*Aug.*)
The Dead Bookworm (*Sept.*)
The City (*Oct.*)
To Edward John Moreton
  Drax Plunkett (*Nov.*)
Wisdom (*Nov.*)
Bells (*Dec.*)
The Nightmare Lake (*Dec.*)

Nonfiction

The Brief Autobiography of
  an Inconsequential Scribbler
  (*Apr.*)
Helene Hoffman Cole—Lit-
  terateur (*May*)
The Case for Classicism (*June*)

Americanism (*July*)
Idealism and Materialism—A
  Reflection (*July*)
Bolshevism (*July*)
The Commonplace Book (to
  1937)

1920

Fiction

The Terrible Old Man (28 Jan.)
The Tree
The Cats of Ulthar (15 June)
The Temple
Facts concerning the Late
    Arthur Jermyn & His Family
The Street (?)
Life and Death (?) (x)
Poetry and the Gods (with
    Anna Helen Crofts)
Celephais (early Nov.)
From Beyond (16 Nov.)
Nyarlathotep (early Dec.?)
The Picture in the House (12
    Dec.)
The Crawling Chaos (with
    W. V. Jackson) (1920?
    1921?)
Ex Oblivione (1920? 1921?)

Poetry

To Phillis (*Jan.*)
Tryout's Lament for the
    Vanished Spider (*Jan.*)
On Reading Lord Dunsany's
    Book of Wonder (*Mar.*)
To a Dreamer (25 Apr.)
Cindy: Scrub Lady in a State
    Street Skyscraper (*June*)
On a Grecian Colonnade in a
    Park (*Aug.*)
On Religion (*Aug.*)
The Dream (*Sept.*)
October (*Oct.*)
November (*Oct.*)
Christmas (*Nov.*)
Regnar Lodbrug's Epicedium

Nonfiction

Literary Composition (*Jan.*)
Looking Backward (Feb.)
For What Does the United
Stand? (*May*)
Life for Humanity's Sake
    (*Sept.*)

1921

Fiction

The Nameless City (Jan.)
The Quest of Iranon (28 Feb.)
The Moon-Bog (Feb.? Mar.?)
The Outsider
The Other Gods (14 Aug.)
The Music of Erich Zann
    (Dec.)
Herbert West—Reanimator
    (Sept.–mid-1922)

Poetry

To Mr. Hoag (*Feb.*)
To a Youth (*Feb.*)
Sir Thomas Tryout (*Nov.*)

To Mr. Galpin (*Nov.*)
Medusa: A Portrait (Dec.)

Nonfiction

The Defence Reopens! (Jan.)
(np)
What Amateur Journalism
and I Have Done for Each
Other (21 Feb.)
Winifred V. Jackson: A
"Different" Poetess (*Mar.*)

The Defence Remains Open!
(Apr.) (np)
The Haverhill Convention
(*July*)
Final Words (Sept.) (np)
Nietzscheism and Realism

1922

Fiction

Hypnos (May)
What the Moon Brings (5 June)
Azathoth (June)
The Horror at Martin's Beach
(with Sonia Davis)

Four O'Clock (with Sonia
Davis)
The Hound (Sept.)
The Lurking Fear (Nov.)

Poetry

On a Poet's 91st Birthday
(*Feb.*)

To Zara (Aug.)

Nonfiction

The Poetry of Lilian Middle-
ton (14 Jan.) (np)
A Confession of Unfaith (*Feb.*)

Lord Dunsany and His Work
(14 Dec.)

1923

Fiction

The Rats in the Walls (Aug.?
Sept.?)

The Unnamable
Ashes (with C. M. Eddy, Jr)

The Ghost-Eater (with C. M. Eddy, Jr)
The Loved Dead (with C. M. Eddy, Jr)
The Festival

Poetry

To Damon (*Aug.*)

To Endymion (*Sept.*)

Nonfiction

Review of *Ebony and Crystal*
by Clark Ashton Smith

1924

Fiction

Deaf, Dumb and Blind (with C. M. Eddy, Jr)
Imprisoned with the Pharaohs (Feb.–Mar.)
The Shunned House (Oct.)

Poetry

To Mr. Hoag (*Feb.*)

Providence (*Nov.*)

Nonfiction

The Omnipresent Philistine
(*May*)

1925

Fiction

The Horror at Red Hook (1–2 Aug.)
He (11 Aug.)
In the Vault (18 Sept.)

Poetry

My Favourite Character (31 Jan.)
Primavera (*Apr.*)
A Year Off (24 July)
To an Infant (26 Aug.)
October (Oct.?)

Nonfiction

The Poetry of John Ravenor Bullen (*Sept.*)

Supernatural Horror in Literature (late 1925–June 1927)

1926

Fiction

The Descendant (?)
Cool Air (Mar.)
The Call of Cthulhu (Summer)
Two Black Bottles (with W. B. Talman) (June–Oct.)
Pickman's Model

The Silver Key
The Strange High House in the Mist (9 Nov.)
The Dream-Quest of Unknown Kadath (Autumn–22 Jan. 1927)

Poetry

Hallowe'en in a Suburb (*Mar.*)
The Return (*Dec.*)

Yule Horror (Dec.)

Nonfiction

The Materialist Today
The Cancer of Superstition

(with C. M. Eddy, Jr) (Oct.)
Cats and Dogs (23 Nov.)

1927

Fiction

The Case of Charles Dexter Ward (Jan.–1 Mar.)
The Colour out of Space (Mar.)

The Very Old Folk (2 Nov.)
The Last Test (with de Castro)
History of the *Necronomicon*

Poetry

Ave Atque Vale (Oct.)

Nonfiction

Introduction to Bullen's *White Fire* (Aug.)

Vermont: A First Impression (29 Sept.)

1928

Fiction

The Curse of Yig (with Zealia
Bishop) (Spring)
Ibid (?)

The Dunwich Horror (Summer)

Nonfiction

Observations of Several Parts
of America

1929

Fiction

The Electric Executioner
(with Adolphe de Castro)

The Mound (with Zealia
Bishop) (Dec.–early 1930)

Poetry

Recapture (*Fungi from Yuggoth*, XXXIV) (Nov.)
The Outpost (26 Nov.)
The Messenger (30 Nov.)

East India Brick Row (Dec.)
The Ancient Track (Dec.)
Fungi from Yuggoth (35 sonnets; 27 Dec.–4 Jan. 1930)

Nonfiction

Travels in the Provinces of
North America (np)

A Descent to Avernus
(*Summer*)

1930

Fiction

Medusa's Coil (with Zealia
Bishop) (May)

The Whisperer in Darkness (24
Feb.–26 Sept.)

Nonfiction

An Account of Charleston (17 July)
A Description of the Town of

Quebeck (Sept.?–14 Jan. 1931)

1931

Fiction

At the Mountains of Madness (Feb.–22 Mar.)

The Shadow over Innsmouth (Nov.?–3 Dec.)

Nonfiction

Some Causes of Self-Immolation (13 Dec.)

1932

Fiction

The Dreams in the Witch House (Jan.–28 Feb.)
The Man of Stone (with Hazel Heald)

Through the Gates of the Silver Key (with E. H. Price) (Oct.–Apr. 1933)

Nonfiction

Further Criticism of Poetry (18 Apr.)

In Memoriam: Henry St. Clair Whitehead (Dec.)

1933

Fiction

The Horror in the Museum (with Hazel Heald)

Winged Death (with Hazel Heald)

Out of the Eons (with Hazel
    Heald)
The Thing on the Doorstep

(21–24 Aug.)
The Horror in the Burying
    Ground (with Hazel Heald)

Nonfiction

Some Repetitions on the
    Times (22 Feb.) (np)
Some Dutch Footprints in
    New England
Supernatural Horror in Litera-

ture (revised) (*Oct.–Feb.
    1935*)
Some Notes on a Nonentity
    (23 Nov.)

1934

Fiction

The Battle that Ended the
    Century (with R. H.
    Barlow) (June)
Collapsing Cosmoses (with R.
    H. Barlow) (June?)

The Book (?)
The Thing in the Moonlight (?)
The Shadow out of Time
    (Nov.–Mar. 1935)

Nonfiction

The Weird Work of William
    Hope Hodgson (Summer)
Notes on Writing Weird Fic-
    tion (June?)
Some Notes on Interplanetary
    Fiction (July)

Mrs. Miniter—Estimates and
    Recollections (16 Oct.)
Homes and Shrines of Poe
    (late)
The Unknown City in the
    Ocean

1935

Fiction

"Till A' the Seas" (with R. H.
    Barlow) (Jan.)
The Challenge from Beyond
    (with C. L. Moore, A. Mer-
    ritt, F. B. Long, R. E.
    Howard) (Aug.)
Satan's Servants (with Robert

Bloch)
The Diary of Alonzo Typer
    (with William Lumley)
    (Oct.)
The Haunter of the Dark
    (Nov.)

Nonfiction

What Belongs in Verse
(*Spring*)
Heritage or Modernism:
   Common Sense in Art

Forms (*Summer*)
Some Current Amateur Verse
   (Dec.)
[On Roman Architecture] (x)

1936

Fiction

In the Walls of Eryx (with
   Kenneth Sterling) (Jan.)

The Night Ocean (with R. H.
   Barlow) (Autumn?)

Poetry

The Odes of Horace, III, ix
   (22 Jan.)
In a Sequester'd Providence
   Churchyard Where Once

Poe Walk'd (Aug.)
To Mr. Finlay (20 Nov.)
To Clark Ashton Smith
   (Nov.?)

Nonfiction

Charleston (Jan.)
Some Current Motives and
   Practices (4 June)
In Memoriam: Robert Ervin
   Howard (5 July)

Suggestions for a Reading
   Guide (Fall)
Literary Review
Supernatural Horror in Litera-
   ture (revised/abridged)

n.d.

Fiction

Sweet Ermengarde

Poetry

Alfredo (play)

Nonfiction

Some Backgrounds of Fairy-
land (1926-1936?)

I
GENERAL STUDIES

H. P. Lovecraft: An Appreciation

By T. O. Mabbott

The recognised authority on Edgar Allan Poe, Professor Thomas Ollive Mabbott (1897–1968) of Hunter College devoted several articles to Lovecraft. Aside from "H. P. Lovecraft: An Appreciation," he wrote a review of The Outsider and Others *and an essay on "Lovecraft as a Student of Poe." Mabbott's knowledge of Lovecraft was not profound, but, as he himself states, he did become by the following article (published in 1944) "the first academic person to review Lovecraft."*

Lovecraft is one of the few authors of whom I can honestly say that I have enjoyed every word of his stories. He wrote every word of his stories. He wrote every kind of prose—earning money as a ghost-writer, to compose what he really wanted to write. His essays that I have seen are occasionally amusing. His study, "Supernatural Horror in Literature," makes one feel he could have been a remarkable interpreter of Literature. And while his poetry seems to me mostly written "with his left hand," it includes that marvellous bacchanalian song (in "The Tomb") with the magnificent line,

Better under the table than under the ground[1]

which makes one think he might under some circumstances have been a fine poet. But it was a writer of weird fiction that he chose to be primarily, and that choice seems to me justified by what he wrote.

His gifts were unusual. He was a scientist at heart, and that gave him a love of clarity. But he was also a dreamer, and could command the record of his own dreams, so as to make his readers yield "to shadows and delusions here." But mere style and clarity and careful planning cannot make a writer outstanding. There must be a narrative power for the writer of stories to excel, and that narrative power was the greatest of Lovecraft's gifts. It could outbalance his one greatest weakness—as recognised by himself, a tendency to melodrama, to kill off a dozen victims where one would have served better. It could have outbalanced a dozen weaknesses he did not have.

From time to time he is compared to Poe. There is little basis and no necessity for comparison. He was a great appreciator, admirer, and even interpreter of Poe (his recognition of the central theme of the "House of Usher" as the possession of but one soul by brother, sister, and the house itself seems to have been as novel as it is obviously correct)[2] and he shared to a large extent Poe's views of the purpose of literature and the attitude the artist should have toward the weird. Lovecraft says in "The Unnameable":

> It is the province of the artist . . . to rouse strong emotion by action, ecstasy, and astonishment.[3]

Poe thought the creation of a mood the end—and by mood something rather like ecstasy is meant. Lovecraft said to Mr E. Hoffmann Price, "But don't you shudder and ask, Can these things really be?" and Poe said to a friend he feared "demons take advantage of the darkness to carry people away—though I do not believe there are any demons." I do not think any better attitude or theory can be held by the writer of weird tales—one reads dozens of them in which the writer betrays his own incredulity, and it is always fatal to the artistic effect. The two writers had a similar attitude, and one that would work for them. The chief difference is hard to explain although it is easy to feel; Poe was more interested in method of thought, Lovecraft more in a record of ideas; yet Lovecraft tried to make his tales consistent with each other, while Poe could allow the devil to read human minds in one tale and not in another with insouciance. It is also notable that Poe, like most writers, was only occasionally interested in the weird, while Lovecraft confined himself to a single *genre*.

But Lovecraft is not to be thought of an as imitator of Poe. Almost every writer of weird stories since 1850 has either admired and borrowed some things from Poe or attempted to avoid being like him. Lovecraft was among the admirers. Since 1935, say, Lovecraft himself has exerted an influence, and he has good followers.[4] But Lovecraft can stand on his own feet, and does this without reference to his influence or the influences upon him. Few writers have ever won their way with less ballyhoo. Yet, meeting with Lovecraft's works, men of letters like Stephen Vincent Benét have commended them,[5] and a prominent professor of English recently remarked to me on the enthusiastic delight with which he read Lovecraft's stories—for pleasure. A good wine needs no bush, and while

I think it too soon to say what place Lovecraft will have in American Literature, I have no doubt that it is an honourable place that should be accorded this truest amateur of letters.

As a sort of postscript, I should like to add that I feel it appropriate, that, as the first academic person to review Lovecraft, I have this opportunity to make a certain apology for the present book from an academic standpoint.[6] It seems to be generally felt that Lovecraft's great gift was for fiction. His writings were voluminous enough so that a selection of them is necessary. But it is certainly a good principle that in such a selection, we should be given all of the man's best work, and all of the work in his best field of endeavour. The stories here collected are for the most part early, or fragmentary, and there is a presumption that none represents him at his best. But while no fair critic should base an estimate of Lovecraft on this material, it will satisfy certain quite justifiable desires. One is that we can here see what the earliest work was like. The other is that, if we belong to the class that does enjoy all the stories, we can feel that we are not deprived of even a single one that survives.

Many men corresponded with H.P.L., and it is a matter of great regret to me that I was not of their number. Yet perhaps he would like it that a tribute should be written by one who did not know him, but who recognised through his publications alone a great lover of beauty and clear thinking, and of all that is characteristic of civilisation—and best of all, one truly devoted to what so many only pretend devotion, the pure cause of literature as a "friend to ease the cares and lift the soul of man." And in the language of his favourite period, I remain, his humble servant.

Notes

1. *Collected Works,* III, p. 15.—S.T.J.
2. See "Supernatural Horror in Literature," in *Collected Works,* III, p. 378.—S.T.J.
3. From *Collected Works,* III, pp. 196–97. Lovecraft spelled the title of the tale "The Unnamable," which is peculiar considering his predilection for English spelling variations.—S.T.J.
4. Technically, the first "Lovecraft-influenced" tale may have been Frank Belknap Long's "The Space-Eaters" (1927), which was the first tale to elaborate upon Lovecraft's myth-cycle. August Derleth, Clark Ashton Smith, Robert Bloch, and others also used elements of the myth-cycle before Lovecraft's death.—S.T.J.
5. William Rose Benét has written that his brother "was entirely familiar with the work of H. P. Lovecraft long before that little-known master of horror was brought to the attention of the critics." See W. R. Benét's "My Brother Steve," *The Saturday Review of Literature,* 15 Nov. 1941.—S.T.J.
6. The reference is to *Marginalia* (1944), in which this essay appeared, and which contained some of Lovecraft's revisions and collaborations, early tales, essays, and other appreciations by friends and critics.—S.T.J.

Tales of the Marvellous
and the Ridiculous

By Edmund Wilson

Edmund Wilson's celebrated "Tales of the Marvellous and the Ridiculous" originally appeared in The New Yorker *for 24 November 1945. The article was little more than a review, but because of Wilson's high status in criticism (he has been called the dean of American critics), his low opinion of Lovecraft took root in American literary circles, and harmonised all too well with that American prejudice toward imaginative fiction which Wilson (1895–1972) possessed to an unusual degree. This article, then, gains its importance not intrinsically (for its errors of fact and interpretation are self-evident) but historically. As much as any, it may have caused the neglect of Lovecraft's work and thought by American literary scholarship. The article was included in Wilson's oft-reprinted* Classics and Commercials: A Literary Chronicle of the Forties, *for which it was slightly revised.*

When a year and a half ago, I wrote a general article about horror stories,[1] I was reproached by several correspondents for not having mentioned the work of H. P. Lovecraft. I had read some of Lovecraft's stories and had not much cared for them; but the books by and about him have been multiplying so and the enthusiasm of his admirers has been becoming so insistent that I have felt I ought to look into the subject more seriously. There have appeared, mostly in 1945, a collection of his *Best Supernatural Stories;* an unfinished novel, *The Lurker at the Threshold,* completed by August Derleth; a volume of his miscellaneous writings, with appreciations by various writers: *Marginalia;* an essay by him on *Supernatural Horror in Literature;* and *H.P.L.: A Memoir,* by August Derleth. Lovecraft, since his death in 1937, has rapidly been becoming a cult. He had already his circle of disciples who collaborated with him and imitated him, and the Arkham House (in Sauk Center [sic], Wisconsin), which has published *Marginalia* and *The Lurker at the Threshold,* is named from the imaginary New England town that makes the scene of many of his stories. It seems to be exclusively devoted to the productions of Lovecraft and the Lovecraftians. A volume of his letters has been announced.

I regret that, after examining these books, I am no more enthusiastic than before. The principal feature of Lovecraft's work is an elaborate concocted myth which provides the supernatural element for his most admired stories. This myth assumes a race of outlandish gods and grotesque prehistoric peoples who are always playing tricks with time and space and breaking through into the contemporary world, usually somewhere in Massachusetts. One of these astonishing peoples, which flourished in the Triassic age, a hundred and fifty million years ago, consisted of beings ten feet tall and shaped like giant cones.[2] They were scaly and irridescent, and their blood was a deep green in colour. The base of the cone was a viscous foot on which the creatures slid along like snails (they had no stairs in their cities and houses but only inclined planes), and at the apex grew four flexible members, one provided with a head that had three eyes and eight greenish antennae, one with four trumpet-like proboscises, through which they sucked up liquid nourishment, and two with enormous snippers. They were prodigiously inventive and learned, the most accomplished race that the earth has bred. They propagated, like mushrooms, by spores, which they developed in large shallow tanks. Their life-span was four or five hundred years.[3] Now, when the horror to the shuddering revelation of which a long and prolix story has been building up turns out to be something like this, you may laugh or you may be disgusted, but you are not likely to be terrified—though I confess, as a tribute to such power as H. P. Lovecraft possesses, that he at least, at this point in his series, in regard to the omniscient conical snails, induced me to suspend disbelief. It was the race from another planet which finally took their place, and which Lovecraft evidently relied on as creations of irresistible frightfulness, that I found myself unable to swallow: semi-invisible polypous monsters that uttered a shrill whistling sound and blasted their enemies with terrific winds. Such creatures would look very well on the covers of the pulp magazines, but they do not make good adult reading. And the truth is that these stories were hack-work contributed to such publications as *Weird Tales* and *Amazing Stories,* where, in my opinion, they ought to have been left.

The only real horror in most of these fictions is the horror of bad taste and bad art. Lovecraft was not a good writer. The fact that his verbose and undistinguished style has been compared to Poe's is only one of the many sad signs that almost nobody any more pays real attention to writing. I have never yet found in Lovecraft a single sentence that Poe could have written, though there are some—not at all the same thing—that have evidently been influenced by Poe. (It is to me more terrifying than anything in Lovecraft that Professor T. O. Mabbott of Hunter College, who has been promising a definitive edition of Poe, should contribute to the Lovecraft *Marginalia* a tribute in which he asserts that "Lovecraft is one of the few authors of whom I can honestly say that I have enjoyed every word of his stories," and goes on to make a solemn comparison of Lovecraft's work with Poe's.) One of Lovecraft's worst faults is his incessant effort to work up the expectations of the reader by sprinkling his stories with such adjectives as "horrible," "terrible," "frightful," "awesome," "eerie," "weird," "forbidden," "unhallowed," "unholy," "blasphemous," "hellish" and "infernal." Surely one of the primary rules for writing an effective tale of horror is never to use any of these words—especially if you are going, at the end, to produce an invisible whistling octopus.[4] I happened to read a horror story by Mérimée, "La Vénus d'Ille," just after I had been investigating Lovecraft, and was relieved to find it narrated—though it was almost as fantastic as Lovecraft—with the prosaic objectivity of an anecdote of travel.[5]

Lovecraft himself, however, is a little more interesting than his stories. He was a Rhode Islander, who hardly left Providence and who led the life of a recluse. He knew a lot about the natural sciences, anthropology, the history of New England, American architecture, eighteenth-century literature and a number of other things. He was a literary man *manqué,* and the impression he made on his friends must partly have been due to abilities that hardly appear in his fiction. He wrote also a certain amount of poetry that echoes Edwin Arlington Robinson—like his fiction, quite second-rate; but his long essay on the literature of the supernatural horror is a really able piece of work. He shows his lack of sound literary taste in his enthusiasms for Machen and Dunsany, whom he more or less acknowledged as models, but he had read comprehensively in this special field—he was strong on the Gothic novelists—and writes about it with much intelligence.

As a practitioner in this line of fiction, he regarded himself rightly as an amateur, and did not, therefore, collect his stories in book-form.[6] This was done after his death by his friends. The "Cthulhu Mythos" and its fabricated authorities seem to have been for him a sort of boy's game which he diverted his solitary life by playing with other horror story fanciers, who added details to the myth and figured in it under distorted names. It is all more amusing in his letters than it is in the stories themselves. His illustrator, Virgil Finlay, he would address as "Dear Monstro Ligriv," and he was in the habit of dating his letters not "66 College Street, Providence" but "Kadath in the Cold Waste: Hour of the Night-Gaunts," "Brink of the Bottomless Gulf: Hour That the Stars Appear Below," "Burrow of the Dholes: Hour of the Charnel Feasting," "Bottomless Well of Yoguggon: Hour That the Snout Appears," etc.[7] He cultivated a spectral pallor. "He never liked to tan," writes a friend, "and a trace of colour in his cheeks seemed somehow to be a source of annoyance."⁸ The photograph which appears as a frontispiece in *H.P.L.: A Memoir* has been printed—with design, one supposes—in a pinkish transparent red that makes him look both insubstantial and sulphurous.

But Lovecraft's stories do show at times some traces of his more serious emotions and interests. He had a scientific imagination rather similar, though much inferior, to that of the early Wells. The story called "The Colour out of Space" more or less predicts the effects of the atomic bomb, and "The Shadow out of Time" deals not altogether ineffectively with the perspectives of geological aeons and the idea of controlling time-sequence. The notion of escaping from time seems the motif most valid in his fiction, stimulated as it was by an impulse toward evasion which had pressed upon him all his life: "Time, space, and natural law," he wrote, "hold for me suggestions of intolerable bondage, and I can form no picture of emotional satisfaction which does not involve their defeat—especially the defeat of time, so that one may merge oneself with the whole historic stream and be wholly emancipated from the transient and ephemeral."⁹

But the Lovecraft cult, I fear, is on even a more infantile level than the Baker Street Irregulars and the cult of Sherlock Holmes.

Notes

1. "A Treatise on Tales of Horror," *The New Yorker*, XX, 15 (27 May 1944), 72, 75–78, 81–82; in *Classics and Commercials*, pp. 172–81.—S.T.J.
2. These are the beings, of course, described in "The Shadow out of Time."—S.T.J.
3. Lovecraft states that their life-span was "four or five thousand years;" cf. *Collected Works*, I, p. 398.—S.T.J.
4. See the Introductory Notes, p. 21.—S.T.J.
5. Lovecraft himself praises the "terse and convincing prose" of "La Vénus d'Ille;" cf. "Supernatural Horror in Literature," in *Collected Works*, III, p. 372.—S.T.J.
6. As noted in the Introductory Notes, Lovecraft did try hesitantly to land collections of his work, but these efforts came to naught. That this circumstance was fundamentally caused, at least in part, by Lovecraft's amateur spirit is more than likely.—S.T.J.
7. Cf. Derleth's *H.P.L.: A Memoir*, pp. 61–62.—S.T.J.
8. Cf. W. Paul Cook's *In Memoriam: Howard Phillips Lovecraft*, p. 9; in *Beyond the Wall of Sleep*, p. 428.—S.T.J.
9. Lovecraft to August Derleth, 21 November 1930; in *Collected Works*, VII, p. 220.—S.T.J.

A Literary Copernicus

By Fritz Leiber, Jr

The following article by Fritz Leiber, Jr (1910–   ) is believed by many to be the finest general critical essay on Lovecraft. It represents a revision and expansion of an article called, "The Works of H. P. Lovecraft: Suggestions for a Critical Appraisal." Leiber and Lovecraft corresponded in the last few months of the latter's life, and Leiber has continued to write articles and reviews about Lovecraft, as well as Lovecraftian parodies ("To Arkham and the Stars"); but unlike many of the "Lovecraft circle," his voluminous fiction (horror and science-fiction tales) is not greatly influenced by Lovecraft, nor does it imitate his style.

I

Howard Phillips Lovecraft was the Copernicus of the horror story. He shifted the focus of supernatural dread from man and his little world and his gods, to the stars and the black and unplumbed gulfs of intergalactic space. To do this effectively, he created a new kind of horror story and new methods for telling it.

During the Middle Ages and long afterwards, the object of man's supernatural fear was the Devil, together with the legions of the damned and the hosts of the dead, earthbound and anthropomorphic creatures all. Writers as diverse as Dante and Charles Maturin, author of *Melmoth the Wanderer,* were able to rouse terror in their readers by exploiting this fear.

With the rise of scientific materialism and the decline of at least naive belief in Christian theology, the Devil's dreadfulness quickly paled. Man's supernatural fear was left without a definite object. Writers seeking to awaken supernatural fear restlessly turned to other objects, some old, some new.

Horror of the dead proved to be a somewhat hardier feeling than dread of the Devil and the damned. This provided the necessary ground for the genre of the ghost story, ably exploited by Montague Rhodes James and others.

Arthur Machen briefly directed man's supernatural dread toward Pan, the satyrs, and other strange races and divinities who symbolised for him the Darwinian-Freudian "beast" in man.

Earlier, Edgar Allan Poe had focused supernatural dread on the monstrous in man and in nature. Abnormal mental and physiological states fascinated him, as did the awesome might of the elements, natural catastrophes, and the geographic unknown.

Algernon Blackwood sought an object for horror especially in the new cults of occultism and spiritualism, with their assertion of the preternatural power of thoughts and feelings.

Meanwhile, however, a new source of literary material had come into being: the terrifyingly vast and mysterious universe revealed by the swiftly developing sciences, in particular astronomy. A universe consisting of light-years and light-millennia of black emptiness. A universe containing billions of suns, many of them presumably attended by planets housing forms of life shockingly alien to man and, likely enough in some instances, infinitely more powerful. A universe shot through with invisible forces, hitherto unsuspected by man, such as the ultraviolet ray, the X-ray—and who can say how many more? In short, a universe in which the unknown had vastly greater scope than in the little crystal-sphered globe of Aristotle and Ptolemy. And yet a real universe, attested by scientifically weighted facts, no mere nightmare of mystics.

Writers such as H. G. Wells and Jules Verne found a potent source of literary inspiration in the simple presentation of man against the background of this new universe. From their efforts arose the genre of science-fiction.

Howard Phillips Lovecraft was not the first author to see in this new universe a highly suitable object for man's supernatural fear. W. H. Hodgson, Poe, Fitz–James O'Brien, and Wells too had glimpses of that possibility and made use of it in a few of their tales. But the main and systematic achievement was Lovecraft's. When he completed the body of his writings, he had firmly attached the emotion of spectral dread to such concepts as outer space, the rim of the cosmos, alien beings, unsuspected dimensions, and the conceivable universes lying outside our own space-time continuum.

Lovecraft's achievement did not come overnight. The new concept of the horror story did not spring full-grown from his mind. In his earlier tales he experimented with the Dunsanian strain and also wrote a number of effective stories in the vein of Poe, such as "The Statement of Randolph Carter," "The Outsider," "Cool Air," and "The Hound."[1] He shared Machen's horror of the human beast and expressed it in "The Lurking Fear," "The Rats in the Walls," "The Horror at Red Hook," and "Arthur Jermyn."[2] Though even in these briefer tales we find broad hints of the new concept: vast life forms from earth's past in "Dagon" and a linkage of a human being's insanity with the appearance of a new star in "Beyond the Wall of Sleep." But with "The Call of Cthulhu" the line of developement becomes clearly marked, as shown by the opening sentences: "The most merciful thing in the world, I think, is the inability of the human mind to correlate all its contents. We live on a placid island of ignorance in the midst of black seas of infinity, and it was not meant that we should voyage far. The sciences, each straining in its own direction, have hitherto harmed us little; but some day the piecing together of dissociated knowledge will open up such terrifying vistas of reality, and of our frightful position therein, that we shall either go mad from the revelation or flee from the deadly light into the peace and safety of a new dark age."[3]

For a while Lovecraft tended to mix black magic and other traditional sources of dread with the horrors stemming purely from science's new universe. In "The Dunwich Horror" the other-dimensional creatures are thwarted by the proper incantations, while witchcraft and the new Einsteinian universe appear cheek-by-jowl in "The Dreams in the Witch House." But when we arrive at "The Whisperer in Darkness," *At the Mountains of Madness,* and "The Shadow out of Time," we find that the extraterrestrial entities are quite enough in themselves to awaken all our supernatural dread, without any mediaeval trappings whatsoever. White magic and the sign of the cross are powerless against them and only the accidents of space and time—in short, sheer chance—save humanity.

In passing, it is to be noted that Lovecraft, like Poe, was fascinated by great natural catastrophes and new scientific discoveries and explorations, as is understandable from one who chose cosmic horror for his theme. "The Whisperer in Darkness" begins with the Vermont floods of 1927 and one notes other possible linkages: reports of oceanic earthquakes and upheavals and "Dagon" and "The Call of Cthulhu;" the inundation of acres of woodland by a man-made reservoir and "The Colour out of Space;" threat of demolition of some old warehouses on South Water Street, Providence, and the poem "Brick Row," which is dated 7 December 1929, and may have been the germ of Lovecraft's great sonnet cycle *Fungi from Yuggoth,* written between 7 December 1929, and 4 January 1930;[4] regional decay and degeneration and "The Lurking Fear" and "The Shadow over Innsmouth;" ravages of German submarine warfare and "The Temple;" polar exploration and *At the Mountains of Madness;* discovery of the planet Pluto by C. W. Tombaugh in 1930 and "The Whisperer in Darkness," featuring that discovery and written in the same year.

It is a great pity that Lovecraft did not live to experience the unparalleled New England hurricanes of 1938, when the downtown heart of his own Providence was invaded by the sea, to the accompaniment of terrific wind and downpour. What a story that would eventually have got out of him!

II

The universe of modern science engendered a profounder horror in Lovecraft's writings than that stemming solely from its tremendous distances and its highly probable alien and powerful nonhuman inhabitants. For the chief reason that man fears the universe revealed by materialistic science is that it is a purposeless, soulless place. To quote Lovecraft's "The Silver Key," man can hardly bear the realisation that "the blind cosmos grinds aimlessly on from nothing to something and from something back to nothing again, neither heeding nor knowing the wishes or existence of the minds that flicker for a second now and then in the darkness."⁵

In his personal life Lovecraft met the challenge of this hideous realisation by taking refuge in traditionalism, in the cultivation of mankind's time-honoured manners and myths, not because they are true, but because man's mind is habituated to them and therefore finds in them some comfort and support. Recognising that the only meaning in the cosmos is that which man dreams into it, Lovecraft treasured beautiful human dreams, all age-worn things, and the untainted memories of childhood. This is set forth clearly in "The Silver Key," the story in which Lovecraft presents his personal philosophy of life.

In the main current of Lovecraft's supernatural tales, horror of the mechanistic universe gave shape to that impressive hierarchy of alien creatures and gods generally referred to as "the Cthulhu mythos," an assemblage of beings whose weird attributes reflect the universe's multitudinous environments and whose fantastic names are suggestive renderings of nonhuman words and sounds. They include the Elder Gods or Gods of Earth, the Other Gods or Ultimate Gods, and a variety of entities from distant times, planets, and dimensions.

Although they stem from that period in which Lovecraft mixed black magic in his tales and was attracted to Dunsanian pantheons, I believe it is a mistake to regard the beings of the Cthulhu mythos as sophisticated equivalents of the entities of Christian daemonology, or to attempt to divide them into balancing Zoroastrian hierarchies of good and evil.

Most of the entities in the Cthulhu mythos are malevolent or, at best, cruelly indifferent to mankind. The perhaps benevolent Gods of Earth are never mentioned directly, except for Nodens, and gradually fade from the tales. In *The Dream-Quest of Unknown Kadath* they are pictured as relatively weak and feeble, symbols of the ultimate weakness of even mankind's traditions and dreams. It is likely that Lovecraft employed them only to explain why the more numerous malevolent entities had not long ago overrun mankind, and to provide a source of incantations whereby earthlings could to some degree defend themselves, as in "The Dunwich Horror" and *The Case of Charles Dexter Ward.* In later tales, as we have mentioned, Lovecraft permitted mankind no defence, except luck, against the unknown.[6]

In contrast to the Elder Gods, the Other Gods are presented as powerful and terrible, yet also—strange paradox!—". . . blind, voiceless, tenebrous, mindless . . ." (*The Dream-Quest*).

Of the Other Gods, Azathoth is the supreme deity, occupying the topmost throne in the Cthulhu hierarchy. There is never any question of his being merely an alien entity from some distant planet or dimension, like Cthulhu or Yog-Sothoth. He is unquestionably "god," and also the greatest god. Yet when we ask what sort of god, we discover that he is the blind, idiot god, ". . . the mindless daemon-sultan . . .," ". . . the monstrous nuclear chaos. . . ."

Such a pantheon and such a chief deity can symbolise only one thing: the purposeless, mindless, yet all-powerful universe of materialistic belief.

And Nyarlathotep, the crawling chaos, is his messenger—not mindless like his master, but evilly intelligent, pictured in *The Dream-Quest* in the form of a suave pharaoh. The Nyarlathotep legend is one of Lovecraft's most interesting creations. It appears both in the prose poem and the sonnet of that name. In a time of widespread social upheaval and nervous tension, one looking like a pharaoh appears out of Egypt. He is worshipped by the fellahin, "wild beasts followed him and licked his hands." He visits many lands and gives lectures with queer pseudoscientific demonstrations, obtaining a great following—rather like Cagliostro or some similar charlatan. A progressive disintegration of man's mind and world follows. There are purposeless panics and wanderings. Nature breaks loose. There are earthquakes, weedy cities are revealed by receding seas, an ultimate putrescence and disintegration sets in. Earth ends.

Just what does Nyarlathotep "mean"? That is, what meanings can most suitably be read into him, granting that, by him, Lovecraft may not consciously have "meant" anything. One possibility is that the pharaoh-charlatan expresses the mockery of a universe man can never understand or master. Another is that he symbolises the blatantly commercial, self-advertising, acquisitive world that Lovecraft loathed (Nyarlathotep always has that aura of the salesman, that brash contemptuousness). Yet a third possibility is that Nyarlathotep stands for man's self-destructive intellectuality, his awful ability to see the universe for what it is and thereby kill in himself all naive and beautiful dreams.

In this connexion it is to be noted that Lovecraft, to his last month a tireless scholar and questioner, was the embodiment of the one noble feeling scientific materialism grants man: intellectual curiosity. He also expressed this passion in his supernatural tales. His protagonists are often drawn into the unknown as much as they dread it. Quaking at the horrors that may lurk there, they yet cannot resist the urge to peer beyond the rim of space.[7] "The Whisperer in Darkness," perhaps his greatest story, is remarkable for the way in which the horror and fascination of the alien are equally maintained until almost the very end.

This alchemist-like yearning for "hidden knowledge" was one of the forces which led Lovecraft to create that remarkable series of imaginary but deceptively realistic "secret books," chief among them the *Necronomicon,* which are featured prominently in his later stories.

III

Lovecraft's matured method of telling a horror story was a natural consequence of the importance of the new universe of science in his writings, for it was the method of scientific realism, approaching in some of his last tales (*At the Mountains of Madness* and "The Shadow out of Time") the precision, objectivity, and attention to detail of a report in a scientific journal. Most of his stories are purported documents and necessarily written in the first person. This device is common in weird literature, as witness Poe's "MS. Found in a Bottle," Haggard's *She,* Stoker's *Dracula,* and many others, but few writers have taken it as seriously as did Lovecraft.

He set great store by the narrator having some vitally pressing motive for recounting his experiences, and was ingenious at devising such motives: justificatory confession in "The Thing on the Doorstep" and "The Statement of Randolph Carter;" warning, in "The Whisperer in Darkness" and *At the Mountains of Madness;* attempt by the narrator to clarify his own ideas and come to a decision, in "The Shadow over Innsmouth;" scholarly summing up a series of events, in *The Case of Charles Dexter Ward* and "The Haunter of the Dark."[8]

The scientifically realistic element in Lovecraft's style was a thing of slow growth in a writer early inclined to a sonorous and poetic prose with an almost Byzantine use of adjectives. The transition was never wholly completed, and like all advances, it was attended by losses and limitations. Disappointingly to some readers, who may also experience impatience at the growing length of the stories (inevitable in scientific reports), there is notably less witchery of words in, say, "The Shadow out of Time" than "The Dunwich Horror," though the former story has greater unity and technical perfection. And Lovecraft's own restricted and scholarly life hardly fitted him to be an all-over realist. He always observed a gentlemanly reserve in his writings and depicted best those types of characters which he understood and respected, such as scholars, New England farmers and townsmen, and sincere and lonely artists; while showing less sympathy (consider "He") and penetration in the presentation of business men, intellectuals, factory workers, "toughs," and other admittedly brash, uninhibited, and often crude denizens of our modern cities.

There were three important elements in Lovecraft's style which he was able to use effectively in both his earlier poetic period and later, more objective style.

The first is the device of *confirmation* rather than revelation. (I am indebted to Henry Kuttner for this neat phrase.) In other words, the story-ending does not come as a surprise, but as a final, long-anticipated "convincer." The reader knows, and is supposed to know, what is coming, but this only prepares and adds to his shivers when the narrator supplies the last and incontrovertible piece of evidence. In *The Case of Charles Dexter Ward* the reader knows almost from the first page that Ward has been supplanted by Joseph Curwen, yet the narrator does not state this unequivocally until the last sentence of the book. This does not mean that Lovecraft never wrote the revelatory type of story, with its surprise ending. On the contrary, he used it in "The Lurking Fear" and handled it most effectively in "The Outsider." But he did come more and more to favour the less startling but sometimes more impressive confirmatory type.

So closely related to his use of confirmation as to be only another aspect of it, is Lovecraft's employment of the terminal climax—that is, the story in which the high point and the final sentence coincide. Who can forget the supreme chill of: "But by God, Eliot, *it was a photograph from life,*" or "*It was his twin brother, but it looked more like the father than he did,*" or "They were, instead, the letters of our familiar alphabet, spelling out the words of the English language in my own handwriting," or ". . . the face and hands of Henry Wentworth Akeley."[9] Use of the terminal climax made it necessary for Lovecraft to develop a special type of story-telling, in which the explanatory and return-to-equilibrium material is all deftly inserted before the finish and while the tension is still mounting. It also necessitated a very careful structure, with everything building up from the first word to the last.

Lovecraft reinforced this structure by what may be called *orchestrated prose*—sentences that are repeated with a constant addition of more potent adjectives, adverbs, and phrases, just as in a symphony a melody introduced by a single woodwind is at last thundered by the whole orchestra. "The Statement of Randolph Carter" provides one of the simplest examples. In it, in order, the following phrases occur concerning the moon: ". . . waning crescent moon . . . wan, waning crescent moon . . . pallid, peering crescent moon . . . accursed waning moon. . . ." Subtler and more complex examples can be found in the longer stories.

Not only sentences, but whole sections, are sometimes repeated, with a growing cloud of atmosphere and detail. The story may first be briefly sketched, then told in part with some reservations, then related more fully as the narrator finally conquers his disinclination or repugnance toward stating the exact details of the horror he experienced.[10]

All these stylistic elements naturally worked to make Lovecraft's stories longer and longer, with a growing complexity in the sources of horror. In "The Dreams in the Witch House" the sources of horror are multiple: ". . . Fever—wild dreams—somnambulism—illusions of sounds—a pull toward a point in the sky—and now a suspicion of insane sleepwalking. . . ."[11] While in *At the Mountains of Madness* there is a transition whereby the feared entities become the fearing; the author shows us horrors and then pulls back the curtain a little farther, letting us glimpse the horrors of which even the horrors are afraid!

An urge to increase the length and complexity of tales is not uncommon among the writers of horror stories.[12] It can be compared to the drug addict's craving for larger and larger doses—and this comparison is not fanciful, since the chief purpose of the supernatural tale is to arouse the single feeling of spectral terror in the reader rather than to delineate character or comment on life. Devotees of this genre of literature are at times able to take doses which might exhaust or sicken the average person. Each reader must decide for himself just how long a story he can stand without his sense of terror flagging. For me, all of Lovecraft, including the lengthy *At the Mountains of Madness,* can be read with ever-mounting excitement.

For it must be kept in mind that no matter how greatly Lovecraft increased the length, scope, complexity, and power of his tales, he never once lost control or gave way to the impulse to write wildly and pile one blood-curdling incident on another without proper preparation and attention to mood. Rather, he tended to write with greater restraint, to perfect the internal coherence and logic of his stories, and often to provide alternate everyday explanations for the supernatural terrors he invoked, letting the reader infer the horror rather than see it face to face, so that most of his stories fulfil the conditions set down by the narrator of "The Whisperer in Darkness": "Bear in mind closely that I did not see any actual visual horror at the end . . . I cannot even prove even now whether I was right or wrong in my hideous inference," or by the narrator of "The Shadow out of Time": "There is reason to hope that my experience was wholly or partly an hallucination—for which, indeed, abundant causes existed."[13]

IV

Strangely paralleling the development of Lovecraft's scientific realism was an apparently conflicting trend: the developement of an imaginary background for his stories, including New England cities such as Arkham and Innsmouth, institutions such as Miskatonic University in Arkham, semi-secret and monstrous cults, and a growing library of "forbidden" books, such as the *Necronomicon,* containing monstrous secrets about the present, future, and past of earth and the universe.

Any writer, even a thoroughgoing realist, may invent the names of persons and places, either to avoid libel or because his creations are hybrid ones, the qualities of many persons or places. Some of Lovecraft's inventions are of a more serious sort altogether, definitely distorting the "real" world that forms the background for many of his later supernatural tales. Not only are the *Necronomicon,* the *Unaussprechlichen Kulten* of von Junzt and other volumes presumed to have a real existence (in few copies and under lock and key, rather closely guarded secrets), but the astounding and somewhat theosophical tale they have to tell of nonhuman civilisations in earth's past and of the frightful denizens of other planets and dimensions is taken seriously by the scholars and scientists who people Lovecraft's stories. These individuals are in all other ways very realistically minded indeed, but having glimpsed the forbidden knowledge, they are generally more susceptible to cosmic terror than ordinary people. Sober and staid realists, they yet know that they live on the brink of a horrid and ravening abyss unsuspected by ordinary folk. This knowledge does not come to them solely as the result of the weird experiences in which the stories involve them, but is part of their intellectual background.

These "awakened" scholars are chiefly on the faculty of imaginary Miskatonic University. Indeed, the fabulous history of that institution, insofar as it can be traced from Lovecraft's stories, throws an interesting light on the developement of this trend in his writing.

In June 1882 a peculiar meteor fell near Arkham. Three professors from Miskatonic came to investigate and found it composed of an evanescent substance defying analysis. Despite this experience, they were highly sceptical when later on they heard of eerie changes occurring on the farm where the meteor fell and, contemptuous of what they considered folk superstitutions, they stayed away during the year-long period in which a hideous decay gradually wiped out the farm and its inhabitants. In other words, they behaved as professors are conventionally supposed to behave, intolerant of ghostly events and occult theories— and certainly showing no signs of having read the *Necronomicon,* if there was a copy at Miskatonic at that date, with any sympathy. It is significant that the story in which these events occur, "The Colour out of Space," is praised by Edmund Wilson, a generally adverse critic.

But in the course of the next twenty-five years, perhaps as an insidious result of the strange meteor fall, a change took place in Miskatonic University and in the intellectual equipment of at least some of its faculty members. For when the child prodigy Edward Pickman Derby entered Miskatonic he was able to gain access for a time to the copy of the *Necronomicon* in the library; and Nathaniel Wingate Peaslee, the political economist, during his five-year amnesia which began 14 May 1908, made indecipherable marginal notes in the same volume. Still later, a stranger who was picked up near-dead in Kingsport harbour on Christmas (in 1920, I think)[14] was allowed to view the dread book in St Mary's Hospital in Arkham.

During the 'twenties there was a wild, decadent set among the students (Miskatonic's lost generation, apparently), who were of dubious morality and were reputed to practise black magic. And in 1925 the *Necronomicon* was consulted yet again, this time by the uncouth and precocious giant Wilbur Whateley. He sought to borrow it, but Henry Armitage, the librarian, wisely refused.[15]

In 1927 (the year they were surveying for the new reservoir for Arkham) the talented young mathematician Walter Gilman also obtained temporary access to the volume. He came to a hideous end in a haunted rooming house, but not before he had presented to Miskatonic a queer, spiky image formed of unknown elements and later placed on display in the Miskatonic museum. It was not, however, the first unearthly accession to the museum, which also boasted some strangely alloyed and fantastically piscine gold jewellery from Innsmouth.

In the late 'twenties Asenath Waite, fascinating daughter of a reputed Innsmouth sorcerer, took a course in mediaeval metaphysics at Miskatonic, and we can be sure she did not lose the opportunity of prying into even more dubious branches of knowledge.

On the whole, the late 'twenties were a period particularly productive of spectral occurrences in and around Arkham; in particular the year 1928, which can in this connexion be termed "The Great Year," and in even greater particular September 1928, which may be titled "The Great Month."

We can presume that the unfortunate Gilman perished that year and that Asenath Waite was one of the student body, but those presumptions are only a beginning. Consultation of the *Journal of the American Psychological Society* shows that N. W. Peaslee then began to publish a series of articles describing his strange dreams of earth's nonhuman past. And on May sixth Albert N. Wilmarth, an instructor in literature, received a disquieting letter from the Vermont scholar Henry W. Akeley about extraterrestrial creatures lurking in his native woodlands. In August Wilbur Whateley died horrifyingly while attempting to burglarise the Miskatonic library and steal the *Necronomicon*. On September ninth Wilbur's twin brother, who took after his nonhuman father to an even greater extent, broke loose near Dunwich, Massachusetts.

On September twelfth, Wilmarth, lured by a forged letter, set out to visit Akeley in Vermont. On the same day Dr Armitage learned of the eruption of Wilbur's twin brother.

That night Wilmarth fled in horror from Akeley's farm. On the fourteenth Armitage set out for Dunwich with two of his colleagues, and next day managed to destroy the Dunwich horror.

It is startling indeed to think of two such tremendous sequences of supernatural events reaching their crisis at almost the same time. One likes to think of the frantic Armitage passing the apprehensive Wilmarth as the latter hurried to catch his train. (The most obvious explanation is that Lovecraft prepared a rather elaborate chronology for "The Dunwich Horror," written in 1928, and then made use of the same chart in laying out the plot of "The Whisperer in Darkness," written in 1930 with no tales intervening.)

After the excitement of The Great Month, almost any events seem anticlimactic. However, one should mention the Miskatonic Antarctic Expedition of 1930–31; the discovery of the secrets of the Witch House in March 1931, with further accessions to the museum; and the Australian expedition of 1935. Both expeditions included Professor William Dyer of the geology department, who also knew something of Wilmarth's dreadful experience and who can perhaps therefore lay claim to having been involved in more preternatural events than anyone else on the faculty.

One can only speculate as to why Lovecraft created and made such intensive use of Miskatonic University and the *Necronomicon*. Certainly the Miskatonic faculty constitutes a kind of Lovecraftian utopia of highly intelligent, aesthetically sensitive, yet tradition-minded scholars. As for the *Necronomicon,* it appears that Lovecraft used it as a back door or postern gate to realms of wonder and myth, the main approaches to which had been blocked off by his acceptance of the new universe of materialistic science. It permitted him to maintain in his stories at least occasional sections of the poetic, resonant, and colourful prose which he loved, but which hardly suited his later, scientifically realistic prose. It provided him with a cloud of sinister atmosphere which would otherwise have had to be built afresh with each story. It pictured vividly his Copernican conception of the vastness, strangeness, and infinite eerie possibilities of the new universe of science. And finally, it was the key to a more frightening, yet more fascinating "real" world than the blind and purposeless cosmos in which he had to live his life.

Notes

1. Two other heavily Poesque tales are "The Tomb" and "The Music of Erich Zann." —S.T.J

2. Actually, Lovecraft's greatest expression of this "human beast" concept occurs in "The Shadow over Innsmouth," where the narrator himself ultimately learns that he will become, due to his heredity, one of the half-human, half-monstrous beings that people the tale. The "human beast" idea is perhaps more broadly a reflexion of Lovecraft's concern for hereditary degeneration.—S.T.J.

3. *Collected Works,* I, p. 130.—S.T.J.

4. The relation of "Brick Row" with the *Fungi from Yuggoth* seems tenuous, since the latter was largely a recording of Lovecraft's dreams. But in both we notice Lovecraft's longing for the past, expressed poignantly in the sonnets "Nostalgia" (XXIX), "Background" (XXX), and "Continuity" (XXXVI) from the *Fungi.* In any event, Lovecraft had for years been trying to help preserve the architectural antiquities of Providence, as his letters to the editor of *The Providence Journal* for 5 October 1926 (*Collected Works,* VI, pp. 73-75) and 20 March 1929 will attest.—S.T.J.

5. *Collected Works,* II, p. 386.—S.T.J.

6. This "luck" was also involved in the earlier "The Call of Cthulhu," where Cthulhu fell back into sinking R'lyeh by mere chance.—S.T.J.

7. This is expressed clearly in *At the Mountains of Madness,* where the narrator, speaking of the alien city that he has stumbled upon, announces: ". . . above all my bewilderment and sense of menace there burned a dominant curiosity to fathom more of this age-old secret—to know what sort of beings had built and lived in this incalculably gigantic place, and what relation to the general world of its time or of other times so unique a concentration of life could have had." (*Collected Works,* II, p. 43.)—S.T.J.

8. Both *The Case of Charles Dexter Ward* and "The Haunter of the Dark" were written in the third person, and are not claimed to be documents such as are the other tales Leiber mentions. The "scholarly summing up" is actually done in "The Call of Cthulhu," in which the narrator merely compiles data and presents them to the reader.—S.T.J.

9. These are the final lines of, respectively, "Pickman's Model," "The Dunwich Horror," "The Shadow out of Time," and "The Whisperer in Darkness."—S.T.J.

10. The origin of this "orchestrated prose," as far as mere words rather than whole sections go, might have been Dunsany's tales, where intentional repetition of phrases was

used for hypnotic and emotional effect. In "Where the Tides Ebb and Flow," in *A Dreamer's Tales,* the word "mud" was successively described as "terrible mud . . . callous mud . . . dreadful mud . . . listless mud," and so on.—S.T.J.

11. It is "sleep-talking," not "sleepwalking." See *Collected Works,* II, p. 261.—S.T.J.

12. A more obvious case of this than Lovecraft is LeFanu, whose short stories were often lengthened into novels.—S.T.J.

13. *Collected Works,* I, pp. 212, 370. This is mere rhetoric on Lovecraft's part: the statements themselves are meant to imply that the horrific incidents actually occurred, and are not the result of hallucination or imagination; and they thus reveal one of the major credos in Lovecraft's aesthetic of horror: that reality is even more horrible (from the standpoint of inconsequential humanity) than the wildest dreams or imaginings. Two tales where the horrors do come from the mind of the narrators are the early "The Tomb" and "The Rats in the Walls" (where only the narrator and his cats hear the scurrying of the rats).—S.T.J.

14. Leiber is forced to include the phrase, "I think," because Lovecraft rather inconveniently fails to tell us when this story, "The Festival" (1923), took place.—S.T.J.

15. Leiber is a little off the mark here. Whateley consulted the *Necronomicon* in the winter of 1927. Cf. *Collected Works,* I, pp. 173–75.—S.T.J.

From The Supernatural in Fiction

By Peter Penzoldt

Dr Peter Penzoldt's The Supernatural in Fiction *(1952), an informal continuation of the similar studies by Dorothy Scarborough and Edith Birkhead, covers the weird work of English writers primarily; however, a large section on Lovecraft is included because he is one of the "chief representatives of . . . the Pure Tale of Horror." Penzoldt's section on Lovecraft's use of adjectives should be noted against the many claims that Lovecraft's adjectives are excessive or improper. The Penzoldt study, for all its excellence as a general appraisal, has been berated because of its superficiality.*

Today Howard Phillips Lovecraft has achieved posthumous but universal fame. I cannot pretend to give here a complete account of this extraordinary figure and his work, nor is there any need to do so, for August Derleth has honoured him in a fine critical study. Derleth's *H.P.L., A Memoir* may be considered as the standard work on the newly discovered American master.[1] It reveals the amazing and tragic story of the one author who, like LeFanu, was such as the public might imagine a ghost-story writer to be: A recluse, deeply learned in ancient and forbidden lore, living outside this century in a distant past, and quaint and ghastly to behold, when by night he would roam the streets of his native Providence.[2] Derleth's book also tells the sad tale of an author whose merits completely escaped the public's attention, until, after his death, he was suddenly hailed as a second Poe.

Indeed, during the last decade Lovecraft has been praised and overpraised. It was as if critics were trying to compensate for past neglect. In so doing they exaggerated more than a little. Perhaps scholars were somewhat amazed to find a contemporary American master in the field of weird fiction to equal English authors. But if this is the case, it seems curious that Wilbur Daniel Steele has not achieved that same glory. In many respects he is superior to Lovecraft. I am afraid that the mystery of Lovecraft's sudden fame following the complete neglect of his work must remain unsolved, but we owe much to Derleth, who more than any other was responsible for this valuable discovery.

Lovecraft's work has both great merits and great defects. He was an exceedingly cultivated and well-read man. His approach to literature and especially to weird fiction was that of a scholar as much as that of a creative artist.

Moreover his vast correspondence shows that he was a distinguished linguist and his scientific interest in language is clearly reflected by his writing. Lovecraft's tales strike us by their exceedingly rich vocabulary, verbal imagination and almost scientific research of the *mot propre;* and though his style is often somewhat artificial,[3] it is clearly that of an author with a solid background of etymological learning.

No doubt the language he wrote was not the kind that would appeal to the customary public of horror fiction. This may to a certain extent explain his failure during lifetime while he wrote for popular magazines and his sudden revival when a more refined public began to take interest in his work. We shall analyse Lovecraft's style more closely at the end of our chapter on horror fiction.

Yet Lovecraft's greatest merit was also his greatest fault. He was too well read. In his critical study "Supernatural Horror in Literature" he displays an encyclopaedic knowledge of supernatural fiction, and since he read that enormous amount of weird fiction with obvious pleasure he has been subjected to a corresponding series of influences. In fact he was influenced by so many authors that one is often at a loss to decide what is really Lovecraft and what some half-conscious memory of the books he has read. Some of the writers to whom he owes most are Poe, Machen, Bram Stoker, E. T. A. Hoffmann, H. G. Wells, Lord Dunsany, and perhaps William Hope Hodgson,[4] but there are many more.

One example is the obvious influence (of Poe) on "The Outsider." August Derleth writes of this story in his introduction to *Best Supernatural Stories of H. P. Lovecraft,* "It has been said of 'The Outsider' that if the manuscript had been put forward as an unpublished tale by Edgar Allan Poe, none would have challenged it." Another example, "Cool Air," is the story of a dead man whom will power, and a special cooling system, allow to continue life in an artificially-preserved corpse. When he finally runs out of ice the long-dead body dissolves in liquid decay. This is more than a little reminiscent of Poe's "Strange Facts in the Case of Mr. Valdemar" [sic] with the man who dies in his mesmeric sleep and dissolves when awakened. Often the structure of Lovecraft's tales also reminds one of Poe. A comparison of the opening of "Pickman's Model" with that of Poe's "Tell-Tale Heart" illustrates this.

> You needn't think I'm crazy, Eliot—plenty of others have queerer prejudices than this. Why don't you laugh at Oliver's grandfather who won't ride in a motor? If I don't like the damned subway, it's my own business; and we got here more quickly anyhow in the taxi. We'd have had to walk up the hill from Park Street if we'd taken the car.

I know I'm more nervous than I was when you saw me last year, but you don't need to hold a clinic over me. There's plenty of reasons, God knows, and I fancy I'm lucky to be sane at all. Why the third degree? You didn't used to be so inquisitive.[5]

True! nervous, very, very dreadfully nervous I had been and am; but why *will* you say that I am mad? The disease had sharpened my senses, not destroyed, not dulled them. Above all was the sense of hearing acute. I heard all things in the heaven and in the earth. I heard many things in hell. How then am I mad? Hearken! and observe how stealthily, how calmly, I can tell you the whole story.

Lovecraft's beginning is really little more than a modern form of one of the most famous openings in the history of the short story. One can understand why he was called the "modern Poe."

E. T. A. Hoffmann's influence is clearly seen in such a story as "The Music of Erich Zann,"[6] and H. G. Wells' in "The Whisperer in Darkness" and "Shadow out of Time." Discussing his own work, Lovecraft wrote: "All my stories, unconnected as they may be, are based on the fundamental lore or legend that this world was inhabited at one time by another race who, in practising black magic, lost their foothold and were expelled, yet live on outside, ever ready to take possession of this earth again."[7] But this theme is already found in Machen's "The Novel of the Black Seal," "The Shining Pyramid," and others of his tales. It can even be traced back to Bram Stoker's *Lair of the White Worm,* a story about a nameless prehuman entity that lurked beneath the foundations of an ancient castle. Lovecraft professed his admiration for Stoker's idea and regretted its imperfect handling.[8]

If one reads carefully Lovecraft's critical study on supernatural horror in literature, one is struck by his frequent remarks on how much more some authors could have made of themes they used. It seems possible that Lovecraft deliberately shaped some themes that were already known into the type of story that he considered fitted them best. Whether in fact he did this is a question that only a specialist such as Derleth could answer.

The fact remains that when Lovecraft adopted a motif which his forerunners had already used, he frequently handled it far better. His "Call of Cthulhu" and other stories on the ancient gods rank high above Machen's "Novel of the Black Seal," "The Shining Pyramid" or "The White People." His "Shadow out of Time," a novel about strange trips through time and space, and the forced exchange of human bodies with those of the mysterious prehuman "Great Race," is at once reminiscent of Wells' "The Time Machine" and of Machen's tales. It also contains many Poe-esque scenes. Yet, as a whole, the story is infinitely more poignant and convincing than either Wells' or Machen's works. The hero's

final descent into the ruined capital of the "Great Race," where he discovers his own manuscript written quadrillions of years ago, is one of the
most perfect climaxes in the history of weird fiction.

It would be unjust to say that Lovecraft's inventive powers were
limited to a better presentation of old themes. In "The Call of Cthulhu"
he created a whole mythology of his own which now and then appears in
his other tales. Later some authors borrowed the Cthulhu mythology
with Lovecraft's permission. It is a highly-evolved and completely renewed form of Machen's primitive idea. In "Pickman's Model" he had
used one of the most original ideas in the history of the weird tale. The
story is about an artist who paints ghoulish horrors with such appalling
realism that even the most callous decadents in artistic circles begin to
shun his company. Finally he has only one friend left, and him he invites
to a studio in the oldest part of Boston. This studio is connected with the
remains of some old subterranean passages where the seventeenth-
century sorcerers used to feast in company with nameless beings. The
visitor is appalled by the even greater horror and more poignant realism
of the pictures he finds in this second studio. A photograph of a suitable
background is attached to each painting, a cemetery, for instance, or a
morgue, for the artist never paints outside his studio. Later in the evening something is heard coming up through the vaults. The painter goes
out alone to meet it and chase it back into its sinister abode. He excuses
the interruption with a remark about the rats that haunt the underground
passages leading to the sea and the cemetery. But his visitor has had
enough, and leaves with a hasty excuse. For some reason he cannot explain, he had previously detached the photograph of the background
from the most appalling and ghoulish of all the pictures and put it into
his pocket. On the way home he looks at it with a sense of foreboding: It
does not show a background at all, but is a photograph, taken from life,
of the creature in the painting.

It is difficult to interpret the symbolism of Lovecraft's tales. It lies between the unconscious choice of horrible symbols as we find it in Machen
and Crawford, and the subtle intellectual perversity that makes Hartley's
"Travelling Grave" the greatest tale of its kind. Lovecraft deliberately
plays on the reader's subconscious fears as well as on his conscious repul-
sion from the scenes he is compelled to witness. While Machen and
Crawford involuntarily symbolised the problems that seem to have
obsessed them, Lovecraft keeps a certain critical distance from his work
and simply chooses the effect he wishes to produce. Moreover he was an
avowed unbeliever in the supernatural, and considered that a pure
materialist would be a better writer of supernatural tales than would
someone who believed in occult powers. "It may be well to remark here

that occult believers are probably less effective than materialists in delineating the spectral and the fantastic, since to them the phantom world is so commonplace a reality that they tend to refer to it with less awe, remoteness, and impressiveness than do those who see it an absolute and stupendous violation of the natural order.''[9]

The way in which he was influenced by so many other writers makes it very difficult to decide which symbols found an echo in his own personality, which were used for subtly calculated effect, and which arose from a more or less distinct recollection of his reading.

As it is, the most dominant motif in Lovecraft's work is the nameless, ancestral horror lurking beneath the earth, or ready to invade us from the stars; the dethroned but still potent gods of old. The symbol is a very common one and is not bound to any particular complex. It therefore strikes and horrifies more readers than would any theme having a single subconscious origin. Probably C. G. Jung's theories on the collective subconscious give the only explanation of such symbols as ''great Cthulhu,'' ''the father Yog-Sothoth.'' According to him they would symbolise very old hereditary fears. Edgar Dacqué, the famous German palaeontologist and philosopher, whose theories are somewhat different from Dr Jung's, would, strangely enough, point to a similar origin.[10] While the latter believes in an exceedingly ancient but yet subconscious origin of certain collective fears and spiritual tendencies, Dacqué suggests an equally ancient but materially existent basis for these terrors in the distant past. Perhaps such tales as ''Pickman's Model'' or ''The Call of Cthulhu'' are, after all, more than the result of purely intellectual search for effect.

Even if there is a true symbolism in Lovecraft's tales it is his realistic descriptions of pure shameless horror that strike one as the dominant feature. If any writer was able to cram his tales with more loathsome physical abominations than Crawford and Machen it is Howard Phillips Lovecraft. He delights in detailed descriptions of rotting corpses in every imaginable state of decay, from initial corruption to what he has charmingly called a ''liquescent horror.'' He has a particular predilection for fat, carnivorous, and, if possible, anthropophagus rats. His descriptions of hideous stenches and his onomatopoeic reproductions of a madman's yowlings are something with which even ''Monk Lewis'' did not disgrace fiction. I could well understand Mr Blackwood, when he once told me that to him ''spiritual terror'' seemed entirely absent from Lovecraft's tales; for if there is any, it is hidden under so much repulsive detail that the English master may well be excused for not noticing it.

I have chosen two examples from ''The Thing on the Doorstep'' at random. They are taken from the climax, which, as always in Lovecraft's tales, is placed in an excellent position and guarantees a maximum of suspense. The story is about a man whose wife, a witch, periodically forces him to exchange bodies with her. He finally gathers enough courage to kill her, but her terrible will power enables her spirit to usurp his body, and to banish his weaker mind to her "rotting carcass," now three months dead. Nevertheless, the corpse manages to "claw his way out," and claims the aid of a friend in securing vengeance. The paper he, or "it," brings to explain the whole tragedy comes between the two quoted paragraphs:

> When I opened the door into the elm-arched blackness a gust of insuffer-ably foetid wind almost flung me prostrate. I choked in nausea, and for a second scarcely saw the dwarfed, humped figure on the steps. The summons had been Edward's, but who was this foul, stunted parody? Where had Ed-ward had time to go? His ring had sounded only a second before the door opened.
>
> The caller had on one of Edward's overcoats—its bottom almost touching the ground, and its sleeves rolled back yet still covering the hands. On the head was a slouch hat pulled low, while a black silk muffler concealed the face. As I stepped unsteadily forward, the figure made a semi-liquid sound like that I had heard over the telephone—"*glub . . . glub . . .*"—and thrust at me a large, closely written paper impaled on the end of a long pencil. Still reeling from the morbid and unaccountable foetor, I seized the paper and tried to read it in the light from the doorway. . . .
>
> It was only afterward that I read the last half of this paper, for I had fainted at the end of the third paragraph. I fainted again when I saw and smelled what cluttered up the threshold where the warm air had struck it. The messenger would not move or have consciousness any more.
>
> The butler, tougher-fibred than I, did not faint at what met him in the hall in the morning. Instead, he telephoned the police. When they came I had been taken upstairs to bed, but the—other mass—lay where it had collapsed in the night. The men put handkerchiefs to their noses.
>
> What they finally found inside Edward's oddly-assorted clothes was mostly liquescent horror. There were bones, too—and a crushed-in skull. Some dental work positively identified the skull as Asenath's.[11]

But this is Lovecraft at his worst, for at times he exaggerated even more shamelessly than the lesser authors of horror tales. Yet when the details are not too ridiculous one cannot but praise his precision. There are no traces of nineteenth-century reticence left in his work. Though he sometimes speaks of "unnamable" horrors, he always does his best, and perhaps even too much, to describe them. Even if he sometimes over-shoots the mark, one may say at least that no author combined so much stark realism of detail, and preternatural atmosphere, in one tale.

It is strange how Lovecraft uses material details even if he is describing purely supernatural entities.[12] He is unable to evoke the glorious spectral and half-material shapes we find in Blackwood's tales. A presence felt, rather than perceived by the senses, is beyond his inventive powers. It is characteristic that he does not even mention Oliver Onions and Robert Hichens in his critical study; he would not have been able to appreciate such masterpeices of subtly suggested terror as "The Beckoning Fair One," or "How Love Came to Professor Guildea."[13] Nor was he able to make use of Dr James' indirect method of describing an apparition, with metaphors chosen from reality, but devoid of words directly alluding to horror. He would never have begun a climax with "It seems as if."[14] Lovecraft's monsters are usually ridiculous compounds of elephant feet and trunks, human faces, tentacles, gleaming eyes and bat wings, not to mention, of course, the indescribable foetor that usually accompanies their presence. The reader is often amused rather than frightened by the author's extraordinary surgical talents. Wells' Dr. Moreau could hardly have done better.

> "Oh, oh, my Gawd, that haff face—that haff face on top of it . . . that face with the red eyes an' crinkly albino hair, an' no chin, like the Whateleys. . . . It was a octopus, centipede, spider kind o' thing, but they was a haff-shaped man's face on top of it, an' it looked like Wizard Whateley's, only it was yards an' yards acrost. . . ."[15]

Though often slightly too long, Lovecraft's tales are nearly always perfect in structure. Suspense increases from the first page until the well-placed climax at the end is reached; only his exaggerated display of horrible details sometimes threatens to tire the reader before the end.

I do not pretend to have done justice to an author like Lovecraft in a few pages. The chief reason for discussing him here in some detail is that no study of the pure tale of horror would be complete without mention of him. It also seemed necessary that a voice should be raised in warning against too uncritical an admiration for this excellent but certainly not faultless author. [This applies less to Derieth's excellent *H.P.L.* than to a general tendency among the new generation of Lovecraft fans.] Literary history has known queer and sudden changes in posthumous fame. Convinced admirers often challenge passionate detractors and it would be a great loss to American letters if Lovecraft were to vanish from the libraries as suddenly as he has come.

As it is, these are merely a few reflexions on a subject which August Derleth has already thoroughly treated, and though I cannot fully share in his approval of the "modern Poe," his book remains the authority one would first consult.

One can reject or accept the whole group of pure horror tales, but one must admit that within the limits of the *genre* there exists a certain hierarchy of lesser and greater as in any other art. In my opinion, the pure tale of horror has the highest literary standing when it is no longer a mere outlet for neurotic tendencies but has become a sort of intellectual game. The objection may be made that a pronounced taste for horror always denotes a certain perversion. This cannot be denied, but the artistic result may be a conscious or unconscious creation. The author may, or may not, be aware of the symbolism he is using. His symbols may find no echo in his own subconscious; they may not be symbols at all, but merely skilfully calculated effects, as are some of Lovecraft's. This latter technique is usually a failure when applied to most types of short ghost-story. The horror tale is different. A fully conscious approach to the theme is likely to leave the reader with a less painful impression than a shameless display of unconscious and mostly hideous neurotic tendencies. At least one does not feel the author to be hopelessly in the grip of psychic disease. His tales are not necessarily filled with the oppressive atmosphere of a lunatic asylum.

The style of the exposition of most tales of horror does not differ greatly from the language ordinarily found in the short story of the supernatural. Machen and Crawford make frequent attempts to write in archaic language, and there are many passages of that almost biblical solemnity with the aid of which authors of the supernatural try to make incredible things credible. Indeed the greater the horror, the greater the danger of reaching the point where the reader refuses to be frightened and starts to laugh. There is, therefore, a tendency among writers of horror tales to use the most dignified and lofty style possible. Kipling, who disregarded this rule, failed utterly in his presentation of pure horror, especially in "The Mark of the Beast." The only successful exception to the rule is L. P. Hartley, who deliberately forces the reader into a pseudohumorous mood. But laughing at the author, and laughing with him, are two very different things. Hartley is probably the only English writer who successfully presented horror in a light conversational style.

But it is in the climax rather than in the exposition that the style of the horror tale differs from that of the ordinary ghost-story. The difference lies in the number and quality of words or metaphors directly describing horror.

Such single words or metaphors I shall call "descriptives." The invention of such a noun may be justified on the grounds that because grammatically the descriptives do not belong to the same order—they can be nouns, adjectives or whole phrases—there is no single word that will serve my purpose.

I propose to divide them into four or more distinct groups, (*A*), (*B*), (*C*) and (*D*).

(*A*) will consist of all descriptions containing words which, taken separately, have no especially terrible significance. For example, something may be soft, wet and cold, such as a frog, but if a soft, wet and cold hand touches you in the dark, the three adjectives become part of a phrase evoking horror. Descriptives of the type (*A*) can be defined as phrases describing horror but containing only words which would not suggest it when taken separately.

In contrast to these are descriptives of the type (*B*). Take for instance the following sentence from the climax of Machen's "The Novel of the White Powder":

> There upon the floor was a dark and putrid mass seething with corruption and hideous rottenness. . . .

Each of the words "putrid," "corruption," "hideous" and "rottenness," be it adjective or noun, denotes something horrible, even when taken from its context. Naturally such words need not stand alone, but may be combined with others that carry less unpleasant associations. For example, "dark and putrid mass" contains "dark," and "mass," neither of which taken alone suggests horror. I shall call a descriptive of type (*B*) any word that expresses horror when isolated, and any phrase or sentence that contains such a word or words. These descriptives are likely to be found in more primitive stories than type (*A*).

Type (*C*) is more closely related to (*A*) than to (*B*). But while (*A*) actually describes something horrible, (*C*) only suggests it. Type (*C*) descriptives necessarily consist of a whole sentence, or at least the entire phrase, for instance:

> . . . it seems as if Sir Richard were moving his head rapidly to and fro with only the slightest possible sound.[16]

Here the reader guesses that Sir Richard's head is really a cluster of enormous spiders, but they are suggested by something far less horrible. James gives us the onlooker's optical illusion in place of a detailed description. ". . . moving his head rapidly to and fro . . ." is the descriptive. A whole climax may contain only this type of descriptive, but its successful use demands a more highly developed technique than is required for (*A*) and (*B*).

To elucidate this point, I will try to depict the same scene, firstly using only descriptives of type (*A*) and secondly using descriptives of type (*B*). Type (*A*) would run something like this:

> On Sir Richard's pillow some creatures like enormous spiders were rapidly moving to and fro. . . .

Type (*B*) would use every adjective to make the scene as gruesome as possible.

I shall try to use words that often appear in the pure tale of horror:

> It now became clear that the filthy abominations on Sir Richard's bed were in reality some horrible spiders crawling with venomous hairy legs. . . . etc., etc.

A long description of the spiders such as only a Crawford or a Lovecraft could have imagined would naturally follow.

The fourth group of descriptives—(D)—is almost exclusively found in Lovecraft's tales. They are really no longer words at all, but are rather the phonetic transcriptions of hideous idiotic cries. Their origin appears to be a curious one. Lovecraft's great admiration for Arthur Machen is well known. Their common interest in the idea of cosmic fear and their predilection for crude physical horror is obvious. Lovecraft finds no praise too great for Machen in his "Supernatural Horror in Literature," and even mentions him in his stories, for example in "The Whisperer in Darkness."[17]

Now Machen, through the environment of his youth, was strongly influenced by Welsh folklore. This is manifest in certain details of his work as well as in his choice of themes. He seemed to regard the Welsh countryside as having a particularly mysterious atmosphere, and liked to allude to the mysteries in his tales with one or two sentences in Welsh, which he knew well. In "The Great Return," the priest celebrating the arrival of the terrible "red saints" begins the Mass of the Sangraal as follows:

> "Ffeiriadwyr Melcisidec! Ffeiriadwyr Melcisidec!" shouted the old Calvinistic Methodist deacon with the grey beard, "Priesthood of Melchizedek! Priesthood of Melchizedek!"

And he went on:

> "The Bell that is like y glwys yr angel ym mharadwys—the joy of the angels in paradise—is returned."

To those who do not know Welsh these words seem like some barbaric archaic language full of mystery, and Machen is careful to translate only part of the text, so that the rest gives one the impression of some weird runic incantation. Lovecraft probably did not know much Welsh, but he was conscious of the effect this "barbaric" language makes in a tale of horror. He therefore at times used the gaelic tongue, at times invented his own "Welsh." Usually he begins with a few comprehensible words in English or Latin and then continues with horrid exclamations of his own invention, which finally end in a series of syllabic cries:

> "Curse you, Thornton, I'll teach you to faint at what my family do! . . . 'Sblood, thou stinkard, I'll learn ye how to gust . . . wolde ye swynke me thilke wys? . . . Magna Mater! Magna Mater! . . . Atys . . . Dia ad aghaidh's ad

aodaun . . . agus bas dunach ort! Dhonas's dholas ort, agus leat-sa! . . . Ungl . . . ungl . . . rrlh . . . chchch . . ."
. . . . .
"Ygnaiih . . . ygnaiih . . . thflthkh'ngha . . . Yog-Sothoth . . ." rang the hideous croaking out of space. "Y'bthnk . . . h'ehye—n'grkdl'lh." . . .
"Eh-ya-ya-ya-yahaah—e'yayayayaaa . . . ngh'aaaaa . . . ngh'aaa . . . h'yuh . . . h'yuh . . . HELP! HELP! . . . ff-ff-ff-FATHER! FATHER! YOG-SOTHOTH! . . ."[18]

Nobody could have described the effect these words or cries produce on the reader or on the actors with whom the reader will identify himself better than Lovecraft did. The following paragraph is the prelude to the phonetic transcription quoted above. It is important to reproduce it here lest the reader should imagine that such descriptives are ridiculous. On the contrary, these meaningless words that seem to come from the mouth of an idiot and are yet supposed to allude to supernatural realities are capable of suggesting the most appalling horror when they are skilfully introduced, and appear in the climax of a perfectly constructed tale.

Without warning came those deep, cracked, raucous vocal sounds which will never leave the memory of the stricken group who heard them. Not from any human throat were they born, for the organs of man can yield no such acoustic perversions. Rather would one have said they came from the pit itself, had not their source been so unmistakably the altar-stone on the peak. It is almost erroneous to call them *sounds* at all, since so much of their ghastly, infra-bass timbre spoke to dim seats of consciousness and terror far subtler than the ear; yet one must do so, since their form was indisputably though vaguely that of half-articulate *words*. They were loud—loud as the rumblings and the thunder above which they echoed—yet did they come from no visible being. And because imagination might suggest a conjectural source in the world of non-visible beings, the huddled crowd at the mountain's base huddled still closer, and winced as if in expectation of a blow.[19]

The use of a certain type of descriptive usually involves a particular technique, but the different types appear alone as well as in manifold combinations so that the descriptive and the technique are not identical.

It is difficult to determine the exact limits of the descriptive. As they correspond to grammatical unity it is hard to say where they begin and end, especially if several occur in succession. I should say that they are complete only if, when standing alone, they still signify something horrible—provided, of course, that one knows out of what kind of story they have been taken. In other words, they are delineated by their meaning. Thus "rottenness" is a descriptive of type (*B*). But only the whole sentence: "A soft, wet, cold hand touched me" is a descriptive of the type (*A*). Type (*C*) also is almost invariably a whole sentence. But if one knows the source of the descriptive it may be complete with a particle, an adverb, and a noun like "rapidly moving head," or any other grammatical combination that does not form a complete sentence. A single word is sufficient for type (*D*). In Lovecraft's "The Thing on the Doorstep" the rotting carcass emits a "semi-liquid sound" of "glub, glub." Knowing what it implies, the reader finds this simple sound one of the most effective descriptives in the history of the horror tale.

Let us now consider the climax of H. P. Lovecraft's "The Rats in the Walls." Here at least three types of descriptives are employed:

> My searchlight expired, but still I ran. I heard voices, and yowls, and echoes, but above all there gently rose that impious, insidious scurrying; gently rising, rising, as a stiff bloated corpse gently rises above an oily river that flows under endless onyx bridges to a black, putrid sea.
>
> Something bumped into me—something soft and plump. It must have been the rats; the viscous, gelatinous, ravenous army that feast on the dead and the living. . . . Why shouldn't rats eat a de la Poer as a de la Poer eats forbidden things? . . . The war ate my boy, damn them all . . . and the Yanks ate Carfax with flames and burnt Grandsire Delapore and the secret . . . No, no, I tell you, I am *not* that daemon swineherd in the twilit grotto! It was *not* Edward Norrys' fat face on that flabby fungous thing! Who says I am a de la Poer? He lived but my boy died! . . . Shall a Norrys hold the lands of a de la Poer? . . . It's voodoo, I tell you . . . that spotted snake . . . Curse you, Thornton, I'll teach you to faint at what my family do! . . . 'Sblood, thou stinkard, I'll learn ye how to gust . . . wolde ye swynke me thilke wys? . . . Magna Mater! Magna Mater! . . . Atys . . . Dia ad aghaidh's ad aodaun . . . agus bas . . . dunach ort! Dhonas's dholas ort, agus leat-sa! . . . Ungl . . . ungl . . . rrlh . . . chchch . . .
>
> That is what they say I said when they found me in the blackness after three hours—found me crouching in the blackness over the plump, half-eaten body of Capt. Norrys, with my own cat leaping and tearing at my throat.[20]

There are many descriptives of type (*B*) as in every pure tale of horror. (*A*) is almost entirely absent, which is curious. Of course, the sentence "Something bumped into me—something soft and plump" might be considered as one or two descriptives of type (*A*), because it is revealed immediately afterwards that the soft plump things "must have been the rats." But on reading the whole paragraph we learn that it is really something quite different and far more horrible: the man whom the maniac will kill and eat. The descriptives suggest the horribly mangled body just as Dr James' "moving head" suggests the spiders. It is thus a descriptive of type (*C*), rather than (*A*). In the same way such sentences as "he lived, but my boy died!", etc., suggest the growing fury of the madman and prepare for the crazy cries of type (*D*). Yet why is type (*A*) missing? There are at least some traces of it: for example ". . . oily river that flows under endless onyx bridges. . . ." This phrase might be regarded as a descriptive of type (*A*), instead of (*B*), though "oily" hardly ever describes anything agreeable. Onyx, on the other hand, though it is used in ornaments, is the stone usually seen on the more expensive monuments in cemeteries. This analysis clearly reveals Lovecraft's strong preference for words that describe horror directly.[21]

His exceptionally rich vocabulary, which reflects his scientific interest in language, as well as his extraordinary verbal imagination, allowed him to use type (*B*) in a much less conventional manner than Crawford. At the same time it shows that even in his horror fiction he was not ready to sacrifice his literary ideals to commercial advantages. Such sentences as ". . . whilst on the masonry of that charnel shore that was not of earth the Titan thing from the stars slavered and gibbered like Polypheme cursing the fleeing ship of Odysseus," or "There is a sense of spectral whirling through liquid gulfs of infinity, of dizzying rides through reeling universes on a comet's tail, and of hysterical plunges from the pit to the moon and from the moon back again to the pit, all livened by the cachinnating chorus of the distorted hilarious elder gods and the green, batwinged mocking imps of Tartarus"[22] are powerful for all their artificiality, and could hardly have come from any other pen. But they can only be appreciated by a more cultured public.

Thus, though his lavish employment of descriptives of type (*B*) marks Lovecraft's stories as pure tales of horror, his use of every possible word or metaphor describing horror shows how more interesting these tales are than those of his predecessors.

In the light of the above discussion, it seems likely that there was some developement between Crawford and Lovecraft, but caution is necessary, for the pure tale of horror is a *genre à part,* a very well defined type of literature leaving no great scope for a highly personal interpretation, nor consequently for any great developement. There is no doubt that, as I have said, Lovecraft with his use of all four types of descriptives, is more modern than Crawford and Machen, and Machen's style is more colourful than Crawford's. But if one compares the developement of the pure tale of horror with that of any other kind of literature, it can be seen to be almost nonexistent.

Horror, though it is becoming increasingly linked with the crime story, is still to a large public a necessary feature of weird fiction. Certain authors seem to value it as a possible means of sublimating unpleasant neurotic tendencies. There will always be readers who welcome such an expression in literature of their hidden aggressiveness, or who need such reading to assure themselves that their nervous dreads correspond with little more than fictional realities.

Sometimes the pure tale of horror is shaped by the hands of a real artist, but even then it is often merely the unpleasant product of unconscious perversity and a basic crudity is noticeable even in the style. One could imagine a perfect horror tale based on true symbolism, like the best psychological ghost-stories, and written in appropriate language by an author who kept a critical distance from his work. Hartley, and sometimes Lovecraft, came very close to this ideal, but did they actually reach it? Would their tales still have been pure tales of horror if they had? As it is, Forrest Reid's statement if applied to horror fiction is still the best verdict on the genre:

> It is not the highest, but only the pedant and the prig will deny that he enjoys being thrilled, and our superior attitude towards sensational fiction is adopted largely because the blatant and the crude *fail* to produce this effect.[23]

Notes

1. See the Introductory Notes, p. 24—S.T.J.
2. This is very clearly an incomplete and in some ways misleading image of Lovecraft. Lovecraft's correspondent Robert Bloch has written: "During the four-year span of our association [1933-1937], the avowed 'recluse' sent me letters and postcards from all over the New England states, from Charleston, Richmond, Fredericksburg, Florida and Quebec. The 'sheltered and withdrawn personality' was engaged in one of the most voluminous correspondences of our times, and was welcoming the role of host to many visitors and admirers. The *revenant* from colonial times discoursed eagerly and at length upon the current political situation, modern literary ideologies, and contemporary scientific theory—doing so with such self-evident knowledgeability and discernment as to leave no doubt but that H. P. Lovecraft was very much alive in the Twentieth Century of Picasso, Proust, Joyce, Spengler, Einstein and Adolf Hitler." ("Out of the Ivory Tower," p. 174.)—S.T.J.
3. See the Introductory Notes, p. 21—S.T.J.
4. But Lovecraft did not read Hodgson until 1934 (cf. *Collected Works,* IX, p. 26), at which time his fictional career was almost over.—S.T.J.
5. *Collected Works,* I, p. 19.—S.T.J.
6. But Lovecraft had not read Hoffmann by 1921, when "The Music of Erich Zann" was written; indeed, a letter to Clark Ashton Smith dated 25 March 1923 (*Collected Works,* V, p. 214) shows that he had still not read Hoffmann even at that time.—S.T.J.
7. For the actual origin of this quote, see Prof. Mosig's "H. P. Lovecraft: Myth-Maker" (p. 109).—S.T.J.
8. Lovecraft writes in "Supernatural Horror in Literature": "Bram Stoker . . . created many starkly horrific conceptions in a series of novels whose poor technique sadly impairs their net effect. *The Lair of the White Worm,* dealing with a gigantic primitive entity that lurks in a vault beneath an ancient castle, utterly ruins a magnificent idea by a development almost infantile." (*Collected Works,* III, p. 392.)—S.T.J.
9. "Supernatural Horror in Literature," in *Collected Works,* III, p. 395.—S.T.J.
10. Cf. such works as "Urwelt, Sage und Menschheit" and "Das Verlorene Paradise."
11. *Collected Works,* I, pp. 305-07.—S.T.J.
12. Perhaps this was done in order to create the impression that these supernormal (not supernatural) beings actually exist, and are not the result of hallucination. Yet it is significant that we find no such material descriptions for the two most powerful entities in Lovecraft's myth-cycle, Azathoth and Yog-Sothoth, since these two entities and their powers are unimaginably vast. Lovecraft himself, moreover, once defended his use of material descriptives, as in this passage in *The Case of Charles Dexter Ward:* "It is hard to explain just how a single sight of a tangible object with measurable dimensions

could so shake and change a man; and we may only say that there is about certain outlines and entities a power of symbolism and suggestion which acts frightfully on a sensitive thinker's perspective and whispers terrible hints of obscure cosmic relationships and unnamable realities behind the protective illusions of common vision" (*Collected Works,* II, p. 195).—S.T.J.

13. Lovecraft, indeed, once remarked: "I have Onions's *Ghosts by Daylight.* . . . I didn't care much for the various tales." (Lovecraft to J. Vernon Shea, 14 February 1936; ms., John Hay Library, Brown University.) Hichens is at least mentioned in Lovecraft's list of celebrated "Roberts;" cf. Lovecraft to R. H. Barlow, 24 May 1935; in *Collected Works,* IX, p. 164.—S.T.J.

14. Cf. Dr James' climax of "The Ashtree."

15. From "The Dunwich Horror," in *Collected Works,* I, pp. 201–02. In the text the entire passage is italicised.—S.T.J.

16. Climax to "The Ashtree," by M. R. James.

17. Cf. *Collected Works,* I, p. 218.—S.T.J.

18. These come, respectively, from "The Rats in the Walls" and "The Dunwich Horror" (*Collected Works,* I, pp. 52, 200). Penzoldt has made slight misquotations. Lovecraft has some interesting remarks about the former tale: "That bit of gibberish which immediately followed the atavistic Latin was *not* pithecanthropoid. The first actual apecry was the '*ungl.*' What the intermediate jargon is, is *perfectly good Celtic.* . . . [I] lifted it bodily from *The Sin-Eater,* by Fiona McLeod." (Lovecraft to Frank Belknap Long, 8 November 1923; in *Collected Works,* V, p. 258.) A detailed linguistic breakdown of the passage is done by William Scott Home in "The Lovecraft 'Books': Some Addenda and Corrigenda," pp. 150–51.—S.T.J.

19. From "The Dunwich Horror," in *Collected Works,* I, p. 200.—S.T.J.

20. *Collected Works,* I, pp. 51–52.—S.T.J.

21. Cf. the following passage from "The Outsider," pp. 57–58, in *Collected Works,* I. ". . . it was a compound of all that is unclean, uncanny, unwelcome, abnormal, and detestable. It was the ghoulish shade of decay, antiquity, and dissolution; the putrid dripping eidolon of unwholesome revelation, the awful baring of that which the merciful earth should always hide."

22. Both examples quoted from "The Call of Cthulhu," in *Collected Works,* I, pp. 157–158.

23. Some of Dr Penzoldt's footnotes which in this book are inessential have been omitted. —S.T.J.

II

THE LOVECRAFT MYTHOS

The Cthulhu Mythos: A Study

By George T. Wetzel

For over thirty years, George T. Wetzel (1921–   ) has been a leading critic and scholar of Lovecraft. Most notable is his seven-volume Lovecraft Collectors Library (1952–55), containing selected essays, fiction, and poetry by Lovecraft and critical articles and bibliographies of his work. Wetzel's own main subject of research is Lovecraft's myth-cycle, and the following article, first published in 1955 and revised in 1971, amalgamates most of his critical work. Wetzel is among the leading Lovecraft bibliographers, having done invaluable work in Lovecraft's amateur publications.

When the body of Lovecraft's prose is studied, it is at once seen that there is a varied and elaborate repetition of certain concepts and supernatural actors to which the phrase "The Cthulhu Mythos" has justifiably been given. The underlying theme in his work, aside from whatever plot is manifested on the surface of individual poems and stories, is the struggle of supernatural entities to regain their mastery over the world and Man from which they were once ousted.[1] The more one studies the Mythos stories of H.P.L., the more convinced one will become as to their close unity despite their separate fictional frameworks; which brings me to conclude that the Mythos stories should actually be considered not as separate works but rather the different chapters of a very lengthy novel. When viewed this way, many series of stories using the theme of, say, "ghoul changeling" seem logical as they reveal in separate story-chapters the slow disclosure of some particular evil or horror. The gateway between the waking-world and the Hell/dreamworld of the Mythos was one such theme that is not immediately revealed in "The Statement of Randolph Carter" or in "The Temple" but only finally in

The Dream-Quest of Unknown Kadath, and similarly the nature and powers of Nyarlathotep which H.P.L. never finished, though he came close to completion in "The Haunter of the Dark." There are other half-finished concepts and still unsolved mysteries in the Mythos which only study will disclose, and some that no amount of study will ever unravel, because he died leaving some further tales unwritten which could contain the gradual unfolding of a particular mystery, as indeed would have been the fate of the "ghoul changeling" theme without the final story, "Pickman's Model."

As to why Lovecraft created the Mythos—his lengthy novel called *The Cthulhu Mythos,* if I may be permitted—evidence exists in many of his little-known philosophical articles written in amateur journals, and in some of his stories and poetry. In "The Materialist Today" he remarked: "There is no object or purpose in ultimate creation, since all is a ceaseless repetitive cycle of transitions from nothing back to nothing again . . . all is illusion, hollowness and nothingness—but what does that matter? Illusions are all we have, so let us pretend to cling to them. . . ."[2] Then there is some developement of this recurrent philosophy in the curious poem, "To an Infant" (printed in the *Brooklynite,* Oct. 1925)[3], of which the following lines give some idea:

> For dreams, as they are most precious, are most fragile
>   of all we prize,
> And the pow'rs of earth that enmesh would sear
>   them out of our eyes. . . .
> . . .They are all that we have to save us from the
>   sport of The Ruthless Ones,
> These dreams that the cosmos gave us in the voids
>   past the farthest sun. . . .

Also, passages from H.P.L.'s article, "Life for Humanity's Sake," prove his reason for creating the universe of the Cthulhu Mythos.

Other facts about his Mythos are not too well known, especially the fact that the Greek mythic ideas were formative influences in his Mythos, despite the known fact that the Dunsany stories gave him the initial push toward creation of his own Mythos. From 1917 to 1923 his poetry is full of Greco allusions and outright rhymed Greek mythic narratives. The Grecian influence in his prose is less obvious, though a quick check shows such unquestionable bits as in "The Moon-Bog," "The Tree," "Hypnos," etc. Origination of such things as the Greek-entitled *Necronomicon,* the similarity of the Mythos Hell/dreamworld to the Greek Hades, etc., prove again this contention. And in his story, "Poetry and the Gods,"[4] which is of Greek gods, one sees in Hermes the messenger, the Messenger of Azathoth named Nyarlathotep, and in the dream communication of the Greek gods with mortals the same psychic device used later by Cthulhu to contact his cult followers. In the article, "A Descent to Avernus," H.P.L. likens the cavernous earth, blighted by things suggestive of horrors in the Mythos, to the Greek Tartarus. His three poems in "A Cycle of Verse" likewise have a glimmering of the Mythos' horrors but with a Grecian taint.

Numerous other interesting facets emerge from the Mythos which a book would truly need to be written to show. Suffice it to remark on H.P.L.'s use of the terminal climax, a device used repeatedly by E. L. White, which gives to the work of both that identical quality of a nightmarish dream which likewise ends on a note of final and terrible revelation. Then H.P.L. used in a number of stories a remarkable single feverish crescendo that builds from the start to the ending, increasing without any single lessening of its fervour but instead a brilliant upsurge of fear.

Lovecraft has been called an amoralist, but in his *The Dream-Quest of Unknown Kadath* is discernible the one instance of an effective and poetic moralistic ending. Since this novel was written not long after his unfortunate New York sojourn, the conclusion that the moralistic ending, and perhaps the rest of the novel as well, is but a fragment of the spiritual autobiography is well founded.

The Necronomicon

Creation of the *Necronomicon* was one of H.P.L.'s most interesting ideas, and there is some basis for thinking that he received some of the inspiration from awareness of the similarly arcane *Book of Thoth* that occurs in Egyptian mythology. That he meant the *Necronomicon* to have some antecedents in Egyptian arcana can be shown.

I originally had translated the Greek meaning of the title as "Book of the Names of the Dead," but Donald Susan pointed out that "nom:nomos" was more correctly "region," and he interpreted the name to mean "Guide [book] to the Regions of the Dead," which does fit more logically with the character H.P.L. meant it to have in the early stories.[5]

Lovecraft, in his *History of the Necronomicon* (1936),[6] states that Alhazred, author of the Book, visited, among other places, "the subterranean secrets of Memphis" (Egypt). In the story, "The Green Meadow" (1927),[7] he tells us of an ancient Greek who had translated some awful knowledge out of an Egyptian book ". . . which was in turn taken from a papyrus of ancient Meroe" (Egypt). The well of forbidden knowledge, then, seems to have been Egypt (within the framework of the

Mythos) and Alhazred merely wrote of what he found there in the *Necronomicon.*

In "The Statement of Randolph Carter" (1919) there appeared an old and nameless book which undoubtedly was the first mention in the Mythos of the book,[8] and the fact that Harley Warren in the story used that book on his quest beneath a graveyard would indicate that it was a guide to where access would be found to the gateways between the waking world and the Hell/dreamworld of the Mythos. What he encountered below were ghouls who, according to the lines of the poem "Nemesis," guard such places or else lurk there.

Later stories such as "The Dunwich Horror" have the usage of the *Necronomicon* more as a source text of evil spells. The phenomenon of the growth that is found in other concepts and characters of the Mythos is evident in the gradual characterisation of the *Necronomicon.*

As to where and how Lovecraft first thought of the name, not the idea, of the *Necronomicon,* I can theorise from a datum found in his serialised article, "Mysteries of the Heavens," in the *Asheville Gazette-News* for 3 April 1915: "Manilius, referring to the Milky Way in his 'Astronomicon.' . . ." An erudite reader like Lovecraft, with some knowledge of Greek, well knew the translation of "Astronomicon," and when later on casting about for a suggestive name for the evil book he first had described in part in "The Statement of Randolph Carter," he hit upon the association of ideas of Astro-nomicon, necro (meaning dead), and the fact that a character in the story had used such a book to investigate the dark mysteries beneath a graveyard; and the *Necronomicon* had evolved.

Nyarlathotep

The first appearance of Nyarlathotep was a prose-poem of the same name in *United Amateur* in November, 1920,[9] and a number of clues to some understanding of him—as meant by H.P.L.—lurk in that work. The name of this god of the Mythos, if broken into "Nyarlat" and "hotep," has some significance at once. "Hotep," a suffix phrase, is Egyptian meaning "is satisfied." Lovecraft used it because it was a recurring suffix for Egyptian names and thus was a "colour" to suggest anything Egyptian.

"Nyarlat," if broken down to just the phoneme "nya," is a prefix found in the names of gods of certain African negroid tribes. One such example is the "nyankopon," the sky-god of the Ashanti.

Lovecraft spoke of Nyarlathotep as having arisen out of the darkness of twenty-seven centuries. This would place this god as having something to do with the twenty-fifth dynasty—the Ethiopian invasion of Europe. Nyarlathotep must then have been incarnate in some Ethiopian ruler of Egypt—must have been the driving power behind the Ethiopian armies that suddenly rose up and made their conquest.

But Lovecraft makes it plain that Nyarlathotep was not a negro, but a swarthy person, when he appeared in later stories. In fact, he seems to have been, in the Mythos, the embodied symbol not only of chaos and the final destruction of the world but also of darkness, as the black entity in the later "The Haunter of the Dark" (1935); likewise, the black man of the witch covens in "The Dreams in the Witch House" (1932).

Another characteristic of Nyarlathotep was his power of daemonic possession (the avatar concept used by H.P.L.) and his hinted shape-changing. In the prose-poem of 1920 it was said that he was the soul of the ultimate gods who were mindless gargoyles, which would indicate his shape-changing ability. Something of this seems likely in the black bat-like thing from the steeple in "The Haunter of the Dark;" and in this same story he attempts daemonic possession of the narrator.

"The Crawling Chaos" (1920)[10] does not mention Nyarlathotep, but the story obviously has some connexion with him, as H.P.L. refers to him in *The Dream-Quest of Unknown Kadath* (1926) as the "crawling chaos;" and "The Crawling Chaos" was about the final end of the world and probably the twilight of the Mythos' gods as well. In the *Fungi* sonnet "Nyarlathotep" (1929–30) this Ragnarok ends with "the idiot Chaos blew earth's dust away. . . ." when Chaos destroyed, crushed, what "he chanced to mould in play." As Chaos seems to have the sense of a deity, here, he must be the creator god of the Mythos, as well as its destroyer. And since Nyarlathotep has the appellation of the "crawling chaos," he must be the creator god; this conclusion is bolstered in part by the fact that he has some close connexion with the god Azathoth, who reposes in the centre of Ultimate Chaos.

The god Azathoth in the Mythos was never quite developed (though if the fragmentary story "Azathoth" were ever completed, more might be known as to what his eventual characterisation was) but in the prose existing, he does seem to have some connexion with Nyarlathotep. Collate the similar spellings of the Mythos god, Azathoth, and the alchemic term, Azoth, meaning "the primogenic source-essence of life." The god existing at the centre of Chaos which in the Mythos seems to have been the centre of the universe and life, then consider that chaos was a god in the sonnet "Nyarlathotep" and consider the epithet given Nyarlathotep as "the crawling chaos": what is seen is a part of the Mythos still not quite formed but in the slow process of gestation.

The Hell of the Mythos

It is in the novel, *The Dream-Quest of Unknown Kadath* (1926), that the Hell of H.P.L.'s Cthulhu Mythos is fully described and made the locale of a story. Though H.P.L. does not identify this curious *sinisterra* of dream as the Mythos' Hell, it is so nevertheless and can be shown to be so upon study. The most outstanding proof of this is the similarity to the two-fold Hell of Greek mythology.

In *Dream-Quest* H.P.L. wrote of King Kuranes that "he could not go back to these things in the waking world because his body was dead."[11] King Kuranes was then the soul of a man, dead in the outside world; making the locale of *Dream-Quest* the otherworld of the dead, Heaven, the Elysium of the Greeks.

But this pastoral aspect or Elysium of the Mythos' underworld had contiguous regions that corresponded to the Tartarus of the Greeks, wherein a number of fearful entities might be encountered—like the domain of the gugs or the mountain peak of Inquanok[12] where Carter meets the shantak-birds.

Curiously enough, the Hell of the Mythos was also the dream-world wherein a slumberer's psyche existed during sleep. Carter's own perception of the Mythos' Hell was because he entered it in sleep. As sleepers have both pastoral and nightmarish dreams, H.P.L. was able to make his conception of the dream-world coincide with the likewise twin concept of the otherworld of the dead.

When boiled down, H.P.L.'s Mythos' Hell was a commingled otherworld of the dead and the world of dream.

The dream-world part of this Hell concept was further developed in another way; those adventures therein that the dreamer Carter had, like his meetings with the night-gaunts, were not the peaceful visions of dreams but the dark side, its nightmares. There is a possible suggestion in *Dream-Quest* of such dark entities of this Hell's dream-world aspect, such nightmares gaining access to the waking world (a contemplated story at some time?) and creating havoc. By such horrors running amok in the waking world, certain hideous daemons and human monsters and ghouls in the Mythos would be explained.

In the dream-novel there were several places where the waking world was touched upon by some of the *sinisterra* of the Mythos' Hell, places where these embodied nightmares could enter the waking world, giving rise to tales among men of daemons, and possibly explaining also why gargoyles atop cathedrals bore resemblance to the ghouls of this place. Where these entrances touched the waking-world from the wood of the zoogs, there shone the phosphorescence of fungi; there was a phosphorescent shining abyss in the story "The Nameless City" (1921) and in the drowned temple in the story, "The Temple" (1920).

There were some fearsome gates to this Hell—through the burrow of the ghouls beneath graveyards, as finally revealed in the dream-novel; when Carter visits the ghouls he notes that he is very near the waking-world which the appearance of grave-stones and funeral urns strewn about indicates all too clearly. The line, "Through the ghoul-guarded gateways of slumber," from the early poem "Nemesis" (1918), which prefigured some of this, takes on a disturbing meaning.

Harley Warren, in "The Statement of Randolph Carter," obviously came to his doom at the hands of such ghouls when exploring burrows under a graveyard.

In this concept of entering the Mythos' Hell not only in dream or even at certain earthly abysses but also under a graveyard or, more specifically, *through* a grave, H.P.L.'s awareness of Greek beliefs again was used for imaginative and inventive purposes. "Grave" was sometimes used in the New Testament as a synonym for "Hell," and the entrance to Hell (the Elysium and the Tartarus) was through a grave. Lovecraft utilised this idea in brilliant fashion in his Mythos concept.

The Ghoul-Changeling

In Lovecraft's hands, many supernatural concepts that were handled by other writers in orthodox fashion, and close to their traditional outlines, became transmuted into something original and refreshingly new. Like the manner in which he elaborated and developed the ghost theme into something not like its traditional presentation and like the manner in which he treated the avatar theme with similarly original presentations, so he did with the ghoul theme, changing some of it from its appearance in ethnic lore. With it, he embodied the changeling concept, a totally different ethnic belief (the changeling idea being Celtic, the ghoul theme, Persian), so that a new supernatural actor or character was invented. By such inventions he gave not only to his own prose a freshness, but also bequeathed to supernatural fiction—already threadworn with overly familiar supernatural actors—a new lease on life, a new source of plot and character material. This, along with the fusing of science-fictional concepts to the supernatural, is what makes his work so interesting.

Who has not puzzled over the identity of the narrator in Lovecraft's "The Outsider"? Even "The Rats in the Walls" has several unanswered questions posed within its fictional framework. The mystery produced in these two stories and other tales is found only by their careful study in conjunction with the clue furnished by a later title, "Pickman's Model."

To my mind, the start of this mystery was the earlier "The Picture in the House" (1920). Here, an ancient countryman possessed a book containing pictures of a hideous butcher shop of the Anzique cannibals, and he himself was cursed with a cannibalistic craving.

Then in 1921 was created the nebulous and Poe-esque horror of "The Outsider." Many explanations as to the nature of the narrator have been put forth by readers of this tale, although it is significant that Lovecraft very obviously refrained from any. Even the climactic discovery of the narrator that a monstrous creature which appalls him is his own mirrored reflexion does not completely reveal his nature. Beyond the fact that he has existed in a subterranean place below a graveyard, all is vague.

The horrendous "The Rats in the Walls" (1923) was next to appear. Herein the motifs in the two tales named above reiterate and are further developed. In the grotto beneath Exham Priory a ghastly butcher shop is found. There are cases of fratricide in the family history of the de la Poers, the owners of the place, for the implied reason that the secret of their character, or their true nature, has occasionally been revealed. But most significant is the fact that the passage between the priory cellar and the dreadful grotto was chiselled *upward* through the foundation rock.

All these evil adumbrations reach a peak in "Pickman's Model" (1926). The protagonist of this story is degenerating, and a ghoulish trend is strongly hinted. Richard Pickman speaks authoritatively of ghouls who kidnap human children, leaving their own daemon offspring in their stead. Old graveyards, he says, are frequently inhabited by ghoulish things that burrow through the earth.

Piecing these clues together gives us a single common theme. The decadent countryman in "Picture" now assumes the character of a ghoul-changeling. The tomb-dweller in "The Outsider" is a kidnapped human who has dim memories of some teacher similar to the ghoulish mentors painted by Pickman in his picture, "The Lesson." The fratricides in "Rats" were perhaps necessitated by discovery that family members were ghoul-changelings; certainly the evidence of the subterranean passageway bespeaks close connexion of some sort between the human beings and the underground creatures.

Where Lovecraft got the central idea of his story, "The Outsider," was apparently a passage in Hawthorne's "The Journal of a Solitary Man," from which the following is quoted as evidence:

I dreamed one bright afternoon that I was walking through Broadway, and seeking to cheer myself with warm and busy life of that far famed promenade. . . . I found myself in this animated place, with a dim and misty idea that it was not my proper place, or that I had ventured into the crowd with some singularity of dress or aspect which made me ridiculous. . . . Every face grew pale; the laughter was hushed . . . and the passengers on all sides fled as from an embodied pestilence. . . . I passed not one step farther but threw my eyes on a looking-glass which stood deep within the nearest shop. At first glimpse of my own figure I awoke, with a horrible sensation of self-terror and self-loathing . . . I had been promenading Broadway in my shroud!

In his *Commonplace Book* Lovecraft recorded the germ idea of "The Outsider" and placed after "Identity" a question-mark.[13] Even though he may have only had a subconscious idea of the human identity of the character, the source of the story seems evident. The leaving of loose threads in a story (which he eventually tied together in a later story) is akin to Edward Lucas White's style in that this author gave a true nightmarish quality to his prose by such vague and still partially outlined horrors at his terminal climaxes.

Lovecraft recorded in his *Commonplace Book* seven ideas obtained from Hawthorne's *American Notebooks* and some of his prose. However, five such borrowed germ ideas have relevance to the ghoul theme variations of H.P.L. just considered. To begin with, there is this idea copied directly from Hawthorne's book: ". . . a defunct nightmare which had perished in the midst of its wickedness and left its flabby corpse on the breast of the tormented one, to be gotten rid of as it might."[14]

Lovecraft jotted down, besides this quote from Hawthorne, a variation of it. When one considers the descriptions and habitations of Lovecraft's ghouls—that is, the facts that they lingered near dream-gates and were perhaps the embodied nightmares of such a realm—it is quite possible that Lovecraft modified the Hawthorne ideas in this fashion.

Though the foregoing is not conclusive but slightly speculative, this note in the *Commonplace Book*—"Man lives near graveyard—how does he live? Eats no food."—is not equivocal. Lovecraft obtained it directly from Hawthorne's *Dr. Grimshawe's Secret.* Its ghoulish hints are too obvious for comment.

There is one more idea, borrowed from Hawthorne, and its variation in the *Commonplace Book.* The original in Hawthorne's own words is found dated 6 December 1837, as follows: "Stories to be told of a certain person's appearance in public, of his having been seen in various situations, and of his making visits in private circles; but finally, on looking for this person, to come upon his grave and mossy tombstone." For comparison, here are Lovecraft's words: "Visitor from tomb—stranger at some public concourse followed to graveyard where he descends into the earth." But the variation of this that Lovecraft jotted elsewhere in his book concerning in essence "a man observed in public with features and jewellery belonging to a dead man" was used in H.P.L.'s "The Festival."

In 1918 Lovecraft wrote "Nemesis" which was one of the most important poems he penned, adumbrating the concept of the dream-gate and its nearby lurkers. But besides that, "Nemesis" foreshadows bits of the Poe-esque underground landscapes of "The Outsider;" particularly these lines:

> I have peered . . .
> At the many-roofed village laid under
> The curse of the grave-girdled ground. . . .

The degenerating painter in "Pickman's Model" had a chilling genius in the painting of faces, which Lovecraft wrote could be compared in their hellishness only to the gargoyles of Notre Dame. This comparison was reiterated in the dream-novel when Carter, climbing a ladder, "saw a curious face peering over it as a gargoyle peers over a parapet of Notre Dame."

The gargoyle theme is also found in Lovecraft's *Commonplace Book* in two entries which, I contend, were inspired by passages in George MacDonald's *Phantastes*. Compare H.P.L.'s "unspeakable dance of the gargoyles—in morning several gargoyles of old cathedral found transposed" with Chapter XIV of the MacDonald book, reading in part:

> I became conscious at the same moment that the sound of dancing had been for some time in my ears. I approached the curtain quickly and lifting it, entered the black hall. Everything was still as death . . . but there was something about the statues that caused me still to remain in doubt. As I said, each stood perfectly still upon its black pedestal, but there was about every one a certain air, not of motion but as if it had just ceased from movement. . . . I found all appearances similar only that the statues were different and differently grouped.

Compare as well from the *Commonplace Book* "Ancient cathedral—hideous gargoyle man seeks to rob—found dead—gargoyle's paw bloody" the following from MacDonald's Chapter XV:

> . . . But I saw in the hands of one of the statues close by me a harp. . . . I . . . laid my hand on the harp. The marble hand . . . had strength enough to relax its hold and yield the harp to me.

And finally, knowing Lovecraft's penchant for quaint humour, I suspect the reason gargoyles were considered by him descriptive of ghouls was because "gargoyle" suggested the homophonic "gar-ghoul" (gar—fish; ghoul—necrophagi).

"Pickman's Model," according to Mrs Muriel Eddy, an old friend of Lovecraft's, was inspired by a trip he once took to Boston. That story itself is doubly interesting in that it is the only story upon which he lavished so much background research and local colour.[15] The tunnels used by the ghouls in this story have, or had, their real counterparts in that city.

In 1840 excavators in Boston's old North End, when digging foundations for houses on the east side of Henchman Street, found part of a subsurface arch which, up to at least 1900, could still be seen in part of the cellar of one house there. Subsequent researchers traced a tunnel to the house of Sir William Phipps abutting the Copps Hill Burying Ground in the same neighbourhood. Some antiquarians said this tunnel was built by a Captain Grouchy, a later owner of the Phipps house, during the French Wars for smuggling purposes.

Another such tunnel was found extending from the William Hitchinson house on North Street opposite the old Hancock Wharf near Fleet Street.

The narrator of "Pickman's Model" has a fear of the Boston subway, which minor incident Lovecraft undoubtedly developed from knowledge about the tunnels in Boston's South End—an over-all area, incidentally, of about one mile if the tunnel area of the North End is included. One such South End tunnel ran between Province Court and Harvard Place, issuing on Washington Street. A passage branched off this one and extended under the Providence House and the front highway eastward toward the sea, its outlet apparently somewhere near Church Green between Summer and Bedford Streets. These two tunnels were closed off in later years by construction of the Washington Street Subway.

In *Dream-Quest of Unknown Kadath* Lovecraft resorted again to actual lore of Boston when he has Carter notice the ghoul possessing two grave-stones, one from the Granary Burying Ground atop Copps Hill in Boston, the other from a Salem graveyard. The pilfering of grave-stones for use as doorsteps, chimney tops and window ledges by Bostonians 150 and more years ago is true. Lovecraft, in this passage in the dream-novel, speaks of the ghoul that was Pickman sitting on such a grave-stone "stolen" (as Lovecraft says) from the Granary Burying Ground. Apparently he shunned the known historical human culprits and blamed such prankish pilfering on the ghouls—which goes to prove that H.P.L. had a dry, even quaint sense of humour.

Ghosts and Avatars

The psychic possession theme and the ghost theme, in a Lovecraft story, are altogether different from their more orthodox presentation in the work of others. In the Mythos, both these themes are at times interwoven so that there emerges a concept particularly Lovecraftian. Thus the reason for considering both under one section. For purposes of simplicity, I allude to the psychic possession theme as the avatar theme in the Mythos.

H.P.L. embodied both themes in "The Tomb" (1917), wherein a restless spirit seeks consecrated burial and thereby peace by possession of a man's body and soul. It is very likely that this story was suggested to him by de la Mare's novel *The Return,* which is similar in part.[16] In H.P.L.'s story the memories and personality of the dead man are infused into the living body of the narrator, sharing with him a common soul—this latter delineation appears in the later stories of the Mythos; there is also some mention of the wandering of the narrator's dream-soul, another significant point in other later stories.

In "The Tree" (1920) the metempsychosis of the dead artist's personality into an olive tree occurs. "Herbert West—Reanimator" (1921-22) deals with reanimated dead—as does the story "In the Vault"—but by scientific resurrection and is reminiscent of the putrescent horror of Poe's "The Facts in the Case of M. Valdemar."[17]

"The Hound" (1922) is a story where the ghost concept borders on the classification of a daemon entity. An amulet is stolen by two diabolists from the grave of a ghoul; it is carved with a picture of a winged hound, the lineaments of which were "drawn from obscure supernatural manifestations of the souls" of ghouls. This idea that the souls of the dead have terrifying shapes Lovecraft elaborated upon in the later story, "The Unnamable." In "The Hound," the winged hound is the visual shape of the dead ghoul, which shape kills one of the diabolists and recovers its amulet. When the survivor opens the grave of the ghoul, there comes from the jaws of the ghoul's corpse "a deep, sardonic bay as of some gigantic hound," and the corpse is again wearing its amulet.

"The Unnamable" (1923) portrays in fuller detail H.P.L.'s idea that the psychic emanation (ghost) of a dead man is a grotesque distortion, and since in this story the corpse was extemely hideous in life, being half-human and half-animal, this rendered its ghost so much more grotesque that it could be described by a character in the story as "unnamable." The ghost of such a biological anomaly once living is what attacks the two men in the story.

"The Shunned House" (1924) is a fuller elaboration of the Lovecraftian ghost concept. The shunned house was built over a graveyard where a vampire had been buried. (In "The Unnamable" Lovecraft had remarked of the graveyard's retaining the intelligence of generations.) Some of the source material of this story can be very definitely traced. In an unpublished ms. which Lovecraft sent to Wilfred Talman, titled "Who Ate Roger Williams?",[18] there is much of this story's plot. Somewhat more of the same is to be found in "The Green Picture" contained in Charles Skinner's *Myths and Legends of Our Land,* Vol. I, p. 76;[19] in fact, much of the same general description in the Skinner opus appears in the Lovecraft work as comparisons will show. It is interesting to note that fungus actually will grow atop the ground in which there has been a burial. Lovecraft also embodied another source, verbatim, of the vampire Roulet from the account given by John Fiske in his *Myths and Myth-Makers.* In this H.P.L. story the ghost of the dead vampire hovers about in a luminous vapour (the special Lovecraft idea of a grotesque ghost is not prominent here)[20] and invades the minds and bodies of its victims. They share its memories and also the same common soul.

"In the Vault" (1925) is the closest Lovecraft ever came to the usual form of a ghost-story and significantly enough when it was printed in *Tryout,* November, 1925, Lovecraft prefaced it thus: "Dedicated to C. W. Smith from whose suggestion the central situation is taken."

Ghosts appeared in other Lovecraft ghost-stories such as "The Evil Clergyman," "The Festival," and "He" (this last being of dead Indians). One of the curiosities in the Mythos stories was the ghost of King Kuranes in the dream-novel, whose body lay dead in the waking-world but whose ghost frequented the dream/underworld of the Mythos.

The avatar concept has been shown to be interwoven with the ghost concept by H.P.L., but he also wrote other stories in which other beings than ghosts possessed a living person. These other stories were of humans with strange magical powers who performed possession or even mind exchange, or of *outré* life forms who did the same, or even the gods, the most notable being Nyarlathotep.

In "The Festival" (1923) he makes quite obvious what it is that shares a common soul—"the soul of the devil-bought hastes not from this charnel clay but fats and instructs *the very worm that gnaws;* till out of corruption horrid life springs. . . ."[21]

The thing in "The Colour out of Space" (1927) absorbs all in a fungoid blighted area in its own substance, even humans and their minds —again the common soul idea. In *The Case of Charles Dexter Ward* (1926–27)[22] the invading entity completely ousts the original soul; whereas in "The Shadow out of Time" and "The Challenge from Beyond"[23] there is mind-exchange as in "The Thing on the Doorstep." "Beyond the Wall of Sleep" is of an alien mind existing simultaneously in the mind of an earthman.

The most interesting, however, is "The Haunter of the Dark" (1935) where the sentient blackness from the steeple was the avatar of Nyarlathotep that briefly daemonically possessed the mind and body of Robert Blake. This may require some further proof as follows: In this story Nyarlathotep is mentioned as "in antique and shadowy Khem taking the form of man," which indicates that god's power of psychic possession; also, in the passage from which the above quote comes (at the story's end) it is apparent the thing from the steeple is being referred to. In the same passage it is written: "Roderick Usher—am mad or going mad—I am it and it is I."[24] This points out the common soul and possession of Blake's mind. The reference to Roderick Usher seems unrelated until H.P.L.'s remarks on Poe's "The Fall of the House of Usher" are recalled. "*Usher* . . . displays an abnormally linked trinity of entities at the end of a long and isolated family history—a brother, his twin-sister, and their incredibly ancient house all sharing a single soul and meeting one common dissolution at the same moment."[25]

When the lightning strikes the black thing, the fatal bolt is transferred to Blake, since he shares a common soul with it, and he is killed. The aspect of blackness is peculiar to Nyarlathotep; in this story it is evident and it also occurs in the prose-poem "Nyarlathotep" and in the form of the Black Man in "The Dreams in the Witch House." Since black was a symbol of evil in ethnic tales, H.P.L. obviously meant this god to be the physical embodiment of evil.

Closing Notes on Influences on H.P.L.

An acquaintance to whom H.P.L. was indebted for a few story ideas was the late Edith Miniter of North Wilbraham, Mass., who, though interested in folklore, did not care to write supernatural prose herself. The blasted heath of "The Colour out of Space" (1927) and another such spot in "The Dunwich Horror" (1928) had a physical prototype near her home which H.P.L. commented upon in a memoir of her.[26]

In that memoir he likewise reminisced about an antiquarian trip on which he had accompanied her to Marblehead, during which she supplied him with the local belief that window-panes absorbed and retained the likenesses of those who habitually sat by them year after year. This idea is part of the plot of "The Unnamable" (1923). Likewise, Charles Fort documented the phenomenon in his book *Wild Talents* (1932) as happening in 1870 in Lawrence, Mass.

That whippoorwills were psychopomps and of a sinister gathering of fireflies—those were ideas H.P.L. learned from her when he visited her farm in 1928. They were both incorporated into "The Dunwich Horror." There was one story given him which he never lived to write. It concerned a damp, dark street near her farm and the tenants of the houses on its hillward side who had gone mad or killed themselves. A corresponding state of affairs in "The Rats in the Walls" would presuppose that ghoul-changelingism was behind the mystery this new idea displayed.

Another contemporary who influenced H.P.L. was Jonathan Hoag, to whom H.P.L. dedicated a number of his own poems. Cooperatively with a friend he published the collected poems of Hoag and H.P.L. wrote a preface. In that preface he expressed his admiration for the awesome grandeur of nature Hoag so artistically caught in his poetry.[27] H.P.L. in that preface quoted a line from Hoag's "To the Grand Canyon of Colorado" (1919) where in black caves "vast nameless satyrs dance with noiseless feet." When H.P.L. came to write *At the Mountains of Madness* (1931) he referred in chapter five to that quoted imagery of Hoag's. (See also H.P.L.'s story "The Transition of Juan Romero" for the same imagery.)

In Hoag's poems "Immortality" (1918) and "Life, Death and Immortality" (1919) he used the phrase "beyond the walls" as a euphemism for death. Lovecraft picked up and used the same poetic image in his "Ex Oblivione" (1921). The phrase itself appears in the title, "Beyond the Wall of Sleep" (1919), in which story its symbolism is somewhat baffling until certain scattered remarks of H.P.L.—that life is a dream, a sleep and that death is an awakening—are collated.

Despite such grim, morose tendencies (which saw their fullest expression in "The Horror in the Burying Ground" [1937])[28], a pessimistic philosophy and evidences of a death wish in some of his writing, H.P.L. was not without a balancing sense of humour.

His mock elegies "The Dead Bookworm" (1919) and "On the Death of a Rhyming Critic" (1917), in verse and slightly autobiographical, prove he was no stuffed-shirt and didn't take himself too seriously, because in them he made uproarious jibes at his own idiosyncrasies. In both he gives himself a facetious lecture for a top-heavy diet of books. He scandalises himself with derogatory lines about being a "scribbling pedant," "a temperence crank" and more. In his story "The Tomb" (1917) he dynamites his prohibitionist views with the uproarious line, "Better under the table than under the ground."

His anglophilism was said to be an affectation by some. But as he was the grandson in direct line of a British subject not naturalised in the U.S., Lovecraft could claim under British law to be a British subject. His strong pro-British feelings could then be viewed as patriotic fervour.

H.P.L.'s interest in astronomy can be traced primarily to his maternal grandmother, Rhoby Phillips, who studied it thoroughly in her youth at Lapham Seminary and whose collection of old astronomical books started him on the subject. His interest for things Grecian was stimulated when he read of the Grecian figures in the constellations. But after failing to find their literal silhouettes, he was sadly disappointed.

Of all the constellations, he admired those of winter. This was remarkable and speaks volumes of his constant observation of night stars, for to know the stars of winter one must study them often in bitter cold weather, and we know that he was incapacitated at times by even mildly cold air, being unacclimated to low temperatures due to thin blood and too much indoor seclusion.

Notes

1. This is somewhat untenable. The supernormal entities are not at all interested in regaining control over man or the world, since both are of such inconsequence cosmically.—S.T.J.
2. In *Something about Cats and Other Pieces,* pp. 158-59.—S.T.J.
3. Also in *The Arkham Collector,* 4 (Winter 1969), 113.—S.T.J.
4. Written in collaboration with Anna Helen Crofts.—S.T.J.
5. Although William Scott Home ("The Lovecraft 'Books': Some Addenda and Corrigenda," p. 141) has also attempted a reconstruction of the roots in the word *Necronomicon,* Lovecraft's own derivation was as follows: "*nekrós,* corpse; *nómos,* law; *eikón,* image—An Image [or Picture] of the Law of the Dead;" cf. Lovecraft to Harry O. Fisher, [late February 1937]; in *Collected Works,* IX, p. 418. The brackets are Lovecraft's.—S.T.J.
6. Actually written in late 1927.—S.T.J.
7. Written in collaboration with Winifred V. Jackson in 1918 or 1919, though first published in 1927.—S.T.J.
8. Scott Connors disagrees: "Wetzel . . . says that the book Harley Warren carried with him into the tomb was the *Necronomicon.* But H.P.L., in 'Through the Gates of the Silver Key' [*Collected Works,* II, p. 402], mentions that the book was in the same characters as the parchment found in the box where Carter found the Silver Key, and that it was in the R'lyehian [*Collected Works,* II, p. 427]. Thus, if anything at all, it would be the *R'lyeh Text.*" (Letter to the Editor, *Nyctalops,* II, 4-5 [April 1976], 46.) Moreover, it is implied in "The Statement of Randolph Carter" that the book was *not* written in Arabic, as the *Necronomicon* was, but "in characters whose like [Carter] never saw elsewhere" (*Collected Works,* II, p. 285). William Fulwiler has pointed out to me, however, that the actual title *R'lyeh Text* was invented, not by Lovecraft, but by August Derleth.—S.T.J.
9. Included in Lovecraft's *Writings in The United Amateur,* pp. 128-29.—S.T.J.
10. Written in collaboration with Winifred V. Jackson.—S.T.J.
11. *Collected Works,* II, p. 336.—S.T.J.
12. All texts of the novel print the name as "Inquanok;" but in the manuscript (at the John Hay Library, Brown University) it is written "Inganok."—S.T.J.
13. The full entry in the *Commonplace Book* reads: "Fear of mirrors—memory of dream in which scene is altered and climax is hideous surprise at seeing oneself in the water or mirror. (Identity?)" Cf. *The Shuttered Room and Other Pieces,* p. 102.—S.T.J.
14. *Ibid.,* p. 104.—S.T.J.
15. Actually, both *The Case of Charles Dexter Ward* and "The Shunned House" have as much or more local colour as "Pickman's Model." Note also "The Whisperer in Darkness" and "The Shadow over Innsmouth."—S.T.J.
16. But Lovecraft did not read de la Mare until 1926, for he announces to Frank Belknap Long (20 May 1926) that "I have not yet read [de la Mare's] prose lucubrations;" by June, however, he has written to Long (11 June 1926) that "De la Mare can be exceedingly powerful when he chooses." It is possible, therefore, that de la Mare's *The Return* influenced not "The Tomb" but *The Case of Charles Dexter Ward,* which also concerns psychic possession.—S.T.J.

17. "Cool Air" (1926) also concerns the reanimated dead, and is conceptually far more similar to the Poe story than "Herbert West—Reanimator," for whose derivation we probably need look no farther than Mary Shelley's *Frankenstein.*—S.T.J.
18. It has now been determined that Talman himself wrote "Who Ate Roger Williams?". In any case, it was written after the penning of "The Shunned House."—S.T.J.
19. Excerpts of this are printed in Ronald J. Willis' "Possible Sources for Lovecraftian Themes."—S.T.J.
20. On the contrary, it is very prominent: at the conclusion of the tale it is discovered that the curious "cloudy whitish pattern on the dirt floor" of the cellar, which comprises the physical remains of the vampire, is, although the "patch bore an uncanny resemblance to a doubled-up human figure," merely the "titan *elbow*" of the entity. Cf. *Collected Works,* II, pp. 225, 246.—S.T.J.
21. *Collected Works,* III, p. 195.—S.T.J.
22. The novel was written completely in the early months of 1927.—S.T.J.
23. Written in collaboration with C. L. Moore, A. Merritt, Robert E. Howard, and Frank Belknap Long (1935).—S.T.J.
24. *Collected Works,* I, p. 120.—S.T.J.
25. Cf. "Supernatural Horror in Literature," in *Collected Works,* III, p. 378.—S.T.J.
26. "Mrs. Miniter—Estimates and Recollections." Lovecraft saw the blasted heath in July 1928, at which time "The Colour out of Space" had already been written; cf. Prof. Dirk W. Mosig's review of *The Californian: 1934-1938, The Fossil,* 220 (October 1977), 10.—S.T.J.
27. Lovecraft actually revised a large amount of Hoag's poetry, though to what extent is unknown.—S.T.J.
28. Ghost-written by Lovecraft for Hazel Heald probably in 1933.—S.T.J.

Some Notes on Cthulhuian Pseudobiblia

By *Edward Lauterbach*

Prof. Edward S. Lauterbach boasts critical work in three genres: mystery fiction, horror fiction, and science-fiction. His articles have been published in The Armchair Detective, The Dark Brotherhood Journal, Extrapolation, *and elsewhere. The following article continues the studies of Lin Carter, T. G. L. Cockcroft, William Scott Home, and others who have analysed the mythical "books" of occult lore invented by Lovecraft and his colleagues, noting here several invented tomes which have gone unnoticed by previous commentators. The work of Lauterbach, a Professor of English at Purdue, testifies to the increasing interest in Lovecraft's work by academicians, both here and abroad, that has occurred in this decade.*

I

One of the more fascinating aspects of the Cthulhu mythos is the creation of imaginary books by H. P. Lovecraft and his followers. The first terrible book described by Lovecraft was the *Necronomicon* of the mad Arab, Abdul Alhazred. Lovecraft followed the *Necronomicon* with such tomes of forbidden lore as the *Pnakotic Manuscripts,* the *Book of Dzyan,* the *R'lyeh Text,* the *Dhol Chants,* and the *Seven Cryptical Books of Hsan.* Lovecraft's friends and fellow-writers soon added to the Cthulhu library. Clark Ashton Smith created the *Book of Eibon,* also known by its alternative title *Liber Ivonis.* Robert Bloch contributed *De Vermis Mysteriis* by Ludvig Prinn. Robert Howard offered von Junzt's *Unaussprechlichen Kulten.* And August Derleth added two more titles: the Comte d'Erlette's *Cultes des Goules* and the *Celaeno Fragments.* The creation and use of these imaginary books of occult lore, with titles hinting at daemonic, unspeakable horrors described within their covers, became an integral part of the Cthulhu mythos, especially during the 1930's and 1940's. As the Cthulhu tradition has continued, more recent bibliographical contributions include the *Revelations of Glaaki,* created by J. Ramsey Campbell, the *Cthaat Aquadingen* and the *G'harne Fragments,* unearthed by Brian Lumley, and the *Zanthu Tablets* and the *Ponape Scripture* added by Lin Carter.

By far the best known of all these volumes of eldritch lore is Lovecraft's original creation, Abdul Alhazred's *Necronomicon*. This book has the most detailed provenance and can be traced in several editions. Among collectors of supernatural fiction the *Necronomicon* has taken on near-corporality. Many bibliophiles have attempted to find actual copies of the *Necronomicon* in any edition and have plagued numerous book dealers to be on the lookout for this tome. As a group of occult books, all the volumes in the Cthulhu library form a magnificent collection of magical literature suitable for the use of any warlock.[1]

The purpose of Lovecraft and his collaborators in creating this library of imaginary titles was to give a feeling of verisimilitude to their stories. Most of these titles have a proper classical, even pedantic, flavour and sound as if they originated in the ancient Orient or in the Mediaeval and Renaissance worlds of learning. The pseudo-Latin, French, and German of many of the titles can easily be translated to hint at the forbidden contents. Such titles seem to echo lists of actual alchemical and occult treatises from the days of early printing, and the ability to quote passages of magical lore from such books, sometimes intermixed with actual occult titles, allowed a writer to add great authenticity to fictional supernatural narratives. One suspects, too, that Lovecraft and his fellow Cthulhuians delighted in creating titles for the delectation of each other and for their readers who loved to collect books. It is pleasant to dream of titles that never existed, titles that would be delightful to hold in one's hands. Such imaginary titles are a minor form of *world of if* fantasy in which book collectors often indulge.

There was also a certain amount of humour involved in the creation of such titles. Not quite hoax or forgery, many of the titles in the Cthulhu library suggest the type of rare book which pedants discourse about and cultists pretend contains all the secrets of the cosmos. There is, of course, an obvious pun on Derleth's name in the imaginary writer Comte d'Erlette, author of *Cultes des Goules*. Furthermore, Robert Bloch has stated that he and Lovecraft created Ludvig Prinn's *De Vermis Mysteriis* and its publication history "tongue-in-cheek."[2] Here, at least, are two examples of Cthulhu writers who saw the humour of inventing imaginary titles, even though their subject is dreadful, terrifying horror. But such humour should not be unexpected. Humour also lay in the mind of H. P. Lovecraft himself when he prepared his history of the *Necronomicon*. Derleth called Lovecraft's bibliographical descriptions of various editions of the mad Arab's book "whimsical" and "obvious spoofing."[3] Since the titles in the Cthulhu library obviously deal with occult phenomena such as ghosts, spirits, and daemons, and since these titles are actually nonexistent, they can surely be described as "bibliographical ghosts," with both the occult and the bibliographical connotations of "ghost" being appropriate.

II

When Phil Stong published his outstanding anthology of science-fiction, fantasy, and horror stories, *The Other Worlds,* his introductory note to Part III of his collection, devoted to "Horrors," was somewhat humorous and satiric in describing stories by Lovecraft and his followers. However, Stong did praise Lovecraft's achievement and was serious when he said, ". . . almost any weird tale editor reading a script from any of twenty writers, will glance at a reference to Arkham or Yuggoth or the 'Book of Eibon' or the 'Unausspreklicken [*sic*] Kulten' and pass it without further notice, as being completely intelligible to his audience."[4] Stong emphasised that the writers contributing to the Cthulhu mythos and to Cthulhuian pseudobiblia were "personal friends as well as literary acquaintances of Lovecraft."

But there were other writers outside the main Lovecraft group who were also fascinated by Lovecraft's cosmos of horror and the imaginary Cthulhuian books. Perhaps because the Cthulhu stories were popular in pulp magazines, chiefly *Weird Tales,* other writers may have wished to cash in, to sell a story to pulp editors, by using references similar to those of the Lovecraft school, thus appealing to the Lovecraft audience. Or, possibly, writers using such materials, including titles of imaginary books, did so in simple admiration of Lovecraft's success. The idea of imaginary titles may have caught a writer's imagination, or pleased his humour, and he too wished to join in the game of creating Cthulhuian pseudobiblia. Stanley G. Weinbaum and Charles R. Tanner, both remembered best as science-fiction writers, added interesting but little-known titles to the Cthulhu library.

Stanley G. Weinbaum wrote notable science-fiction during the 1930's as evidenced in the two stories in *The Black Flame* ("Dawn of Flame" and "The Black Flame"), in the collection *A Martian Odyssey,* and in the novel *The New Adam.* Weinbaum is not usually associated with the Cthulhu mythos, with the Lovecraft circle, or with supernatural horror stories.[5] But he was familiar with Lovecraft's work and in *The New Adam* created his own Cthulhuian title, even though this addition to the Cthulhu library is generally overlooked.[6]

The New Adam is one of Weinbaum's most interesting pieces of writing.[7] It is a superman story about Edmond Hall, a man born with two individual minds. Hall is a forerunner of the next developement in *homo sapiens,* a race destined to supplant men with only one brain. *The New Adam* has philosophical overtones, and it gives Weinbaum's view of American life in the 1920's and 1930's. There are parts of the book that remind a reader of the sweet-sad world of F. Scott Fitzgerald.

Despite the fact that Edmond Hall is superior to ordinary men and women, he marries Evanne Marten, a beautiful 1920's-style girl, nick-named Vanny. Among Hall's eccentricities is his delight in the skull of a dead pet monkey mortised over his fireplace—a nice gothic touch. Since he is superior to ordinary men, Hall tastes sin, evil, and forbidden knowledge with impunity. His private library, it is revealed, contains some strange and daemonic books, which mildly interest him.

Weinbaum carefully develops Hall's study of evil and the unspeakable in only a few, brief scenes. The first hint of this interest in evil is given when Hall hires a friend, Paul Varney, to show him how ordinary men and women take their pleasures in life. Paul wants to be an author and shows Hall an effort at writing a poem. Hall in turn composes a poem, orally, that shocks Varney. Edmond Hall's knowledge of evil is well established in this episode.

Hall's knowledge of forbidden books is emphasised later in scenes with Evanne Marten, his wife. In her marriage Evanne leads an ecstatic, nearly dream-like existence. She is never capable of comprehending her husband, a man with two minds. One morning she finds Hall reading:

> . . . "What's that you're reading, dear?"
> Edmond leaned back in the chair. "The only surviving volume of the work of Al Golach ibn Jinnee, my dear. Does the name mean anything to you?"
> "Less than nothing!"
> "He was an apostate monk, turned Moslem. His work is utterly forgotten; no one save me has read these pages for nearly five centuries."
> "Ooh! What's it about?"
> Edmond translated the page before him; Vanny listened almost incredulously. "Gibberish," was her first thought, but an eerie shadow made her tremble. Little of the mad blasphemy was clear to her, yet there was an aura of horror cast about her by the words.
> "Edmond! Stop!" (p. 107)

Here is a strange book written by a man with an Arabian name, a book filled with blasphemies and one that induces a feeling of horror. The alert reader may see similarities to Lovecraft's *Necronomicon* by Abdul Alhazred. In any event, the book is so horrible that it causes an ordinary girl like Vanny to shudder and to retreat to her kitchen.

Edmond Hall and Vanny find they cannot exist as man and wife. They separate but, eventually, return to living together despite the danger that each will destroy the other. Though Hall tries hard to be kind to Vanny and protect her from undue shock, one day she comes across another strange book in his library and again is badly shaken by what she finds in it:

> The terrible things of their former days together were forgotten by Vanny, and Edmond guarded carefully against the vision of the inexpressible, marshaling his thoughts into selected channels lest she sense implications dangerous to her tense little mind. He was not always successful. One afternoon he returned to the library to find her trembling and tearful over a very ancient French translation of the *Necronomicon* of the Arab. She had gathered enough of the meaning of that blasphemy colossal to revive the almost vanished terrors of her old thoughts. Edmond soothed her by ancient and not at all superhuman means, but later she noticed that half a dozen volumes had been removed from the library, probably to his laboratory. One of these, she recalled, was the *Krypticon* of the Greek Silander in which Edmond had once during the old days pointed out to her certain horrors, and another was a nameless little volume in scholastic Latin by one who signed himself Ferus Magnus. With the removal of these books, an oppressive atmosphere vanished from the library and the room seemed lighter. Vanny spent more of her time there, reading, listening to music, keeping her household accounts or simply day-dreaming. Even the skull of Homo above the fireplace had lost its sarcastic leer, and grinned as foolishly as any dead monkey. (pp. 169–70)

Here Weinbaum includes Lovecraft's *Necronomicon* by name in his science-fiction novel. In addition he creates "a very ancient French translation," an edition not generally listed by commentators on Cthulhu books in bibliographies of the *Necronomicon* (see Derleth, "Cthulhu Mythos," p. x). Furthermore, Weinbaum follows the Cthulhu tradition of inventing new titles of forbidden lore, the *Krypticon* by the Greek Silander, and another book, untitled by one Ferus Magnus.

Surely a title such as the *Krypticon,* with its connotations of "secret" and "hidden," is as inventive and imaginative a book of occult lore as the better known ones described in so many stories of the Cthulhu mythos. Here is Weinbaum's contribution to Cthulhu pseudobiblia, and it is worthy to be listed in any catalogue of a Cthulhu library.

III

In a short story relying heavily on Lovecraft material, the science-fiction writer Charles R. Tanner contributed another title to Cthulhu pseudobiblia that is also worth noting. Tanner became popular with his story "Tumithak of the Corridors," which appeared in the January 1932 issue of *Amazing Stories,* and its sequel, "Tumithak in Shawm" (*Amazing,* June 1933) was "greeted with enthusiasm."[8] Tanner published a third Tumithak story, "Tumithak of the Towers of Fire," in the November 1941 issue of *Super Science Stories,*[9] and a few other science-fiction stories in various magazines.

Tanner's "Out of the Jar"[10] is a somewhat minor supernatural horror story that shows distinctly the influence of Lovecraft and his school. James Francis Denning, a collector of antiques and *objets d'art,* purchases an earthenware jar, which is tightly closed. Denning puts the jar on his mantle, where it remains until a specialist in occult lore, Edward Barnes Halpin, sees it. Halpin wishes to buy the jar, because he recognises that it has been sealed by the Seal of Solomon and guesses that it imprisons a Jinn. Halpin insists on owning the jar, and when Denning refuses, he returns after several weeks to steal it. When Denning catches Halpin in his theft, Halpin drops the jar, allowing a monstrous figure to materialise. Halpin demands a wish from the entity—"the Elder One, demon, or angel or whatever it was"—in the best *Arabian Nights* tradition. His wish is: "All my life I have been a student, seeking—and learning nothing. And now—I want to know the why of things, the cause, the reason, and the end to which we travel. Tell me the place of man in the universe, and the place of this universe in the cosmos!" (p. 52). The entity grants Halpin's wish, and when Halpin looks into a dimensional window created by the entity he has a mental breakdown: ". . . he suffered the stroke which made him the listless, stricken thing that he is today" (p. 43).

Tanner's story is complete with references to the Lovecraft type of horror tale, as for example: "Halpin, at this time, was still under thirty, yet he had become already a recognized authority in this country of that queer borderland of mystic occult story that Churchward, Fort, Lovecraft and the Miskatonic school represent" (p. 45). And, "To be sure, Denning was no student, he had probably never heard of the Cabala, nor of Abdul Alhazred" (p. 46). And, " 'There are old Arabian and Hebrew legends, Jim, that speak of a group or class of beings called Jinn. . . . Probably they were the same things that other legends have called the Elder Ones, or the Pre-Adamites!' " (p. 49). Both editors and readers would easily recognise these references, and Tanner added one more title to the ever-growing list in the catalogue of Cthulhuian pseudobiblia. In his description of Halpin, already partly quoted, Tanner says, "His article on some of the obscure chapters of d'Erlette's 'Cultes des Goules' has been accepted favorably by American occult students, as well as his translation of the hitherto expurgated sections of the Gaelic 'Leabhar Mor Dubh' " (p. 45).

Tanner's contribution, then, to the list of forbidden books was *Leabhar Mor Dubh,* a volume of Gaelic lore. Translated, the title means *Large Black Book,* or even better because of alliteration, *Big Black*

Book. It might also be possible to translate this title as *The Book of Great Blackness*. These are appropriate titles for a tome of the occult because they may refer to the size of the book, the colour of the binding, the horrid blackness of the necromantic knowledge contained within its pages, or all. Weinbaum's *Krypticon* and the *Leabhar Mor Dubh* are worthy to be included in any list of such Cthulhuian books. However, most commentators have overlooked both the *Krypticon* and *Leabhar Mor Dubh*. The process of discovering such Cthulhuian pseudobiblia is ongoing. Who knows what titles are still to be found in lesser known stories in files of pulp magazines of the 1930's and 1940's, or what new titles of imaginary books of occult horror are still to be created by the follower of H. P. Lovecraft?

Notes

1. For further discussions of the books, imaginary and real, in the Cthulhu mythos, see Lin Carter, "H. P. Lovecraft: The Books," *The Shuttered Room and Other Pieces,* pp. 212–49; T. G. L. Cockcroft, "Addendum: Some Observations on the Carter Glossary," *Shuttered Room . . .,* pp. 268–77, especially pp. 268–70; William Scott Home, "The Lovecraft 'Books': Some Addenda and Corrigenda," *The Dark Brotherhood and Other Pieces,* pp. 134–52; August Derleth, "The Cthulhu Mythos," *Tales of the Cthulhu Mythos* (New York: Beagle Books, 1971), I, ix–x; Lin Carter, "The Cthulhu Mythos," *The Spawn of Cthulhu* (New York: Ballantine Books, 1971), p. 3; Lin Carter, *Lovecraft: A Look Behind the "Cthulhu Mythos,"* pp. 89–92, 95, 109–10, 114, 119, 121, 182. Also see the large number of stories related to the mythos in R. E. Weinberg and E. P. Berglund, comps., *Reader's Guide to the Cthulhu Mythos,* 2nd rev. ed. Derleth in "Cthulhu Mythos" gives the title of the Smith book as "*Ivoris*"; Carter in "Cthulhu Mythos" gives it as "*Ivonis*" and in *Lovecraft* as "*Ivonie.*"
2. Carter, *Lovecraft,* p. 110.
3. H. P. Lovecraft and August Derleth, "History and Chronology of the *Necronomicon,*" *The Arkham Sampler,* I, 1 (Winter 1948), 15–19. Imaginary libraries and imaginary titles are found at least as early as 1533 in Rabelais' *Gargantua and Pantagruel*. For a discussion of imaginary libraries and titles, usually with the purpose of humour and/or satire, see Edwin H. Carpenter, Jr, *Some Libraries We Have Not Visited* (Pasadena, Calif.: Ampersand press, 1947).
4. Phil Stong, ed., *The Other Worlds* (New York: Funk, 1941), pp. 328–30.
5. For a discussion of Weinbaum's science-fiction see Sam Moskowitz, "Dawn of Fame: The Career of Stanley G. Weinbaum," *Explorers of the Infinite: Shapers of Science Fiction,* pp. 296–312. Weinbaum is not among the Lovecraft group listed by Kenneth W. Faig, Jr, "The Lovecraft Circle: A Glossary," *Mirage,* 10 (1971), 27–40.
6. Weinbaum's work is not found in the standard lists of Cthulhuian pseudobiblia, note 1, above.
7. Stanley G. Weinbaum, *The New Adam* (Chicago: Ziff-Davis, 1939; rpt. New York: Avon Books, 1969), pp. 61–63; subsequent citations are from the Avon edition with page numbers in parentheses.
8. Isaac Asimov, ed., *Before the Golden Age: A Science Fiction Anthology of the 1930's* (Garden City, N.Y.: Doubleday, 1974), pp. 210, 344. Asimov describes his delight in

Tanner's science-fiction, pp. 210, 261, and reprints these stories, pp. 211–61 and 345–413. Tanner's work is not among the Cthulhuian pseudobiblia in the works listed in note 1, above, nor in Faig's "Lovecraft Circle."

9. Asimov, p. 413. An example of a supernatural story by Tanner is "Angus MacAuliffe and the Gowden Tooth," *Other Worlds Science Stories,* III (March 1951), 62–79; rpt. in Groff Conklin, ed., *The Supernatural Reader* (New York: Collier Books, 1962), pp. 148–67. I wish to thank Frank D. McSherry Jr for calling my attention to the publication data of Tanner's stories.

10. *Stirring Science Stories,* I, (February 1941), 101–08; rpt. in *Zacherley's Vulture Stew,* ed. anon. (New York: Ballantine Books, 1960), pp. 43–53; subsequent citations are from *Stew* with page numbers in parentheses.

H. P. Lovecraft: Myth-Maker

By Dirk W. Mosig

Prof. Dirk W. Mosig (1943–) is among the world's leading Love-craft scholars. The following article, first published in Italy and subse-quently appearing in American, French, and German journals, is an important critical article on Lovecraft, revealing many of the misconcep-tions that August Derleth imposed on Lovecraft's work and, especially, on the myth-cycle. Prof. Mosig is co-editing a book of Lovecraft essays for publication in Italy and is currently writing a book on Lovecraft for Twayne's United States Authors Series. His articles have achieved world-wide publication.

"The oldest and strongest emotion of mankind is fear, and the oldest and strongest kind of fear is fear of the unknown," wrote H. P. Love-craft in "Supernatural Horror in Literature."[1] But although it is obvious from even a cursory examination of his works that Lovecraft himself ful-ly understood the meaning and implications of his assertion, it is amaz-ing to note how little the same was appreciated by others who, as August Derleth and, more recently, Brian Lumley, decided to "expand" the Lovecraft *ouevre* by adding to it their own inferior and unimaginative pastiches, almost invariably marred by over-explanatory naiveté.

In his essay "Notes on Writing Weird Fiction," Lovecraft provided a series of guidelines and helpful advice which should have been seriously pondered by all prospective weird fictioneers, and in particular by those interested in adding to Lovecraft's own mythopoeic conceptions. This has not been the case—they seem to have been noticed by few, and followed by even less.

But most Lovecraft imitations fall short not merely on the account of poor writing. There is a deeper underlying problem, namely a serious misconception of the basic ideas and philosophical undercurrents per-meating the Lovecraft *oeuvre*. And the principal culprit seems to have been Lovecraft's disciple and correspondent, August Derleth. Despite his role in the preservation and propagation of his mentor's writings, Derleth was apparently unable or unwilling to understand the essence of Lovecraft's dynamic pseudomythology. Promulgating his own elucidation of the same as obvious fact and dogma, Derleth succeeded in disseminating an extremely distorted interpretation of what he termed Lovecraft's "Cthulhu Mythos." His version was not only blindly followed by other writers, but uncritically accepted by most readers and critics—the results were disastrous.

To restore the proper perspective, it is necessary first to examine Lovecraft's philosophical stance. H. P. Lovecraft was a "mechanistic materialist," in the philosophical sense of the words, totally devoid of any dualistic belief in religion or the supernatural. Possessing a bright scientific mind, already manifest in his childhood interest in chemistry and astronomy, he clearly perceived man's abysmal insignificance and meaninglessness in the vast mechanistic and purposeless cosmos, governed by blind, impersonal ("mindless") streams of force. A believer in the inexorable action of causality, he stated as early as 1921, in a letter to R. Kleiner: "Determinism—what you call Destiny—rules inexorably; though not exactly in the personal way you seem to fancy. We have no specific destiny against which we can fight—for the fighting would be as much a part of the destiny as the final end. The real fact is simply that every event in the cosmos is caused by the action of antecedent and circumjacent forces, so that whatever we do is unconsciously the inevitable product of Nature rather than of our own volition. If an act correspond with our wish, it is Nature that made the wish, and ensured its fulfillment."[2]

Contrary to what is assumed by many, Lovecraft did not conceive the cosmos as basically inimical *or* beneficial to man. He stated in a letter to J. F. Morton, dated 30 October 1929: ". . . I am . . . an *indifferentist*. . . . I do not make the mistake of thinking that the resultant of the natural forces surrounding and governing organic life will have any connexion with the wishes or tastes of any part of that organic life-process. . . [The cosmos] doesn't give a damn one way or the other about the especial wants and ultimate welfare of mosquitoes, rats, lice, dogs, men, horses, pterodactyls, trees, fungi, dodos, or other forms of biological energy."[3]

Lovecraft was pessimistic with respect to man's ability to cope with the realisation of his own meaninglessness and insignificance in an indifferent universe. The first paragraph of "The Call of Cthulhu" reflects his doubts about man's capacity to preserve his precarious sanity in a confrontation with bleak and unpalatable reality: it is only "the inability of the human mind to correlate all its contents"[4] which prevents our mental disintegration when we come across dissociated bits of knowledge about our frightful position in the black seas of infinity that surround us. Notice that here Lovecraft is *not* deploring knowledge, but rather, *man's inability to cope with it.*

Lovecraft's fiction, and in particular his pseudomythology (which I prefer to call the Yog-Sothoth Cycle of Myth, to differentiate it from the distorted version labelled "Cthulhu Mythos" by Derleth) was *not* a reaction *against* his austere and parsimonious materialistic philosophy, but instead formed the natural outgrowth of the same. Lovecraft wrote primarily to give himself "the satisfaction of visualising more clearly and detailedly and stably the vague, elusive, fragmentary impressions of wonder, beauty, and adventurous expectancy which [were] conveyed to [him] by certain sights . . . , ideas, occurrences, and images encountered in art and literature," as he stated in "Notes on Writing Weird Fiction," and chose weird stories "because they suit[ed his] inclinations best—one of [his] strongest and most persistent wishes [having been] to achieve momentarily the illusion of some strange suspension or violation of the galling limitations of time, space, and natural law which for ever imprison us and frustrate our curiosity about the infinite cosmic places beyond the radius of our sight and analysis."[5] Inclined to write *weird fiction,* Lovecraft's rationalistic intellect could conceive no weirder or more bizarre happening than a dislocation of natural law—not ghosts, daemons, or the supernatural, but the suspension of the laws of Nature.

Predisposed to write imaginative fiction by temperament and environmental contingencies, Lovecraft became also aware of the fact that supernatural themes were rapidly losing their ability to evoke the emotion of fear needed to "create a convincing picture of shattered natural law or cosmic alienage and 'outsideness' ",[6] at least among the more educated and sceptical readers. Consequently he turned to the unplumbed abysses of space and the unknown and unknowable spheres of alien dimensions (as well as to the tortuous depths of the unconscious) for the source of horror in his tales. As George T. Wetzel and Fritz Leiber have pointed out, he developed the concept of the "mechanistic supernatural," and was, in a sense, a "literary Copernicus,"[7] producing a body of *cosmo-centred* fiction unlike most of the anthropocentred writings of his predecessors and, regrettably, of most of his successors. Being a materialist, Lovecraft created the materialistic tale of supernatural horror. Far from implying an unconscious rejection of his philosophy, it was highly consonant with the same—it was the only kind of fiction he could have written, in view of his intellectual genius, his *Weltanschauung,* and his aesthetic inclinations!

In a letter to F. B. Long, dated 27 February 1931, Lovecraft stated: "It is inevitable that a symbolic aesthetic outlet will be demanded . . . under all phases of cosmic interpretation, as long as a sense-chained race of inquirers on a microscopic earth-dot are faced with the black, unfathomable gulph of the Outside, with forever-unexplorable orbs and its virtually certain sprinkling of utterly unknown life-forms. A great part of religion is merely a childish and diluted pseudo-gratification of this perpetual gnawing toward the ultimate illimitable void. Superadded to this simple curiosity is the galling sense of *intolerable restraint* which all sensitive people (except self-blinded earth-gazers like little Augie Derleth) feel as they survey their natural limitations in time and space as scaled against the freedoms and expansions and comprehensions and adventurous expectancies which the mind can formulate as abstract conceptions."[8] (Well did H.P.L. realise the limitations of his pupil!)

Lovecraft did not envision the various mythopoeic conceptions that were going to become integral parts of his *oeuvre* at the start of his writing career. Instead, the various elements involved in his pseudomythology gradually evolved and constantly changed during his lifetime. The Yog-Sothoth Cycle of Myth centres around a certain group of alien entities from "Outside"—from beyond the sphere of conscious human experience: the unplumbed abysses of space, other dimensions, other universes, and the nightmare depths of the unconscious. The main ones are Azathoth, Yog-Sothoth, Nyarlathotep, Cthulhu, and Shub-Niggurath, and these are known with the generic name of "Old Ones" (although it does *not* follow that they are related or belong to a similar "species;" with the possible exception of Cthulhu, each seems to be unique). These Old Ones *were, are,* and *will be.* They are *not* mere symbols of the power of evil, although they may appear to be inimical to man, in the same way that man would appear to be inimical to ants, should these get in his way. The Old Ones are above and beyond mankind—they transcend man, and care no more for him than he does for ants.

As the result of occasional and more or less fortuitous contacts between man and those forces from Outside which he could not control nor comprehend, cults, superstitions, legends, and books of forbidden lore (such as the *Necronomicon*) emerged. Several of Lovecraft's stories record the consequences of attempts to use such forbidden knowledge to meddle with the powers from Outside—man, essentially helpless and impotent in his encounters with the Unknown (although at first often unaware of the extent of his own helplessness), does not fare well. In the few instances in which he escapes annihilation or insanity, it is ironically due, not to his own efforts, but to some accident beyond his control (e.g. the second sinking of R'lyeh).[9] And what could be more terrifying for man than the realisation of his own impotent insignificance face to face with the Unknown and the Unknowable?

From the above sketch it should be readily obvious that there is *no* real parallel between the Christian Mythos and Lovecraft's pseudomythology, despite Derleth's assertions to the contrary. The "Elder Gods," as benign deities representing the forces of good, were entirely Derleth's invention. The expression "Elder Gods" does appear in H.P.L.'s *The Dream-Quest of Unknown Kadath* and in "The Strange High House in the Mist," but only to denote the "weak gods of the earth." It also occurs in *At the Mountains of Madness,* but only as a label for one of the extraterrestrial species which inhabited the earth aeons before man. Nowhere did Lovecraft use the expression to refer to any powerful benign deities which might intercede for man—in Lovecraft's indifferent universe, man cannot expect such outside help in his confrontations with the Unknown.

August Derleth, perhaps in part due to his Catholic background, was unable to share Lovecraft's bleak cosmic vision, and conceived instead an anthropocentred universe, wherein benevolent Elder Gods and malevolent Old Ones would engage in ludicrous battles for the sake and welfare of man, much in the same way as the Judaeo-Christian God and his angels confronted Lucifer and his daemonic hordes. While Lovecraft's hapless protagonists were left alone and defenceless in their chilling confrontations with an incomprehensible Reality, Derleth supplied his heroes with ridiculous star-stone amulets which played the role of garlic and the crucifix in the hackneyed vampire tale,[10] not to mention interventions by rescuing Elder Gods which arrived with a timing reminiscent of the U.S. Cavalry in cheap Western films. (Although star-shaped stones are mentioned in *At the Mountains of Madness,* their power as talismans was entirely Derleth's unimaginative contribution.)

Not satisfied with perpetuating his own myopic pastiches, Derleth attempted to force his interpretation on the Lovecraft *oeuvre,* prefacing major collections of Lovecraft's tales with expositions of his own views presented as dogmatic and self-evident truths. One of his favourites was the contention that the main entities in Lovecraft's Yog-Sothoth Cycle of Myth represented *elementals,* a notion clearly refuted by Richard L. Tierney in his critical essay, "The Derleth Mythos." Derleth viewed Cthulhu as a water elemental, not realising that the presence of wings, the extraterrestrial origin of Cthulhu and his kin, and the fact that he was *imprisoned* or *trapped* in his watery grave, the sunken city of R'lyeh, all militated against the hypothesis that Cthulhu is an aquatic being! (And although Cthulhu is described as only a "cousin" of the Old Ones in the *Necronomicon* included in "The Dunwich Horror,"[11] and is perhaps one of the weakest and least important of the main entities involved in the Yog-Sothoth Cycle of Myth—save for his immediacy—Derleth became strangely enamoured with him, bestowing upon Lovecraft's pseudo-mythology the singularly inappropriate sobriquet "Cthulhu Mythos,"[12] and writing countless pseudo-Cthulhuoid pastiches, collected in *The*

Mask of Cthulhu and *The Trail of Cthulhu.*) In a similar way, the contention that Nyarlathotep is an earth-elemental is indefenceable, for this entity is in no way restricted to subterranean activities, appearing under various guises in eight Lovecraft tales (including revisions), as well as in the celebrated sonnet-sequence, *Fungi from Yuggoth.* Hastur (a name appearing in R. W. Chambers' "The Yellow Sign")[13] was mentioned by Lovecraft in his fiction only twice, in "The Whisperer in Darkness," but without giving any indication of its being aerial, cosmic, a "half-brother to Cthulhu," or even an entity at all . . . much less an air elemental! All such meaningless categorisations were strictly Derleth's.

Lovecraft wisely allowed his fictional entities to remain mysterious and nebulous—the strongest emotion of mankind being fear of the unknown, the entities were to play the role of the Unknown and the Unknowable. Not so Derleth and his disciples. By their systematic attempts at categorisation and over-explanation, they committed the cardinal sin of any writer of weird tales—the over-explained and dissected Unknown ceases to be mysterious and terrifying, becoming merely absurd and ridiculous. Nothing could illustrate this point better than the Derleth collections mentioned above, and Brian Lumley's more recent *The Burrowers Beneath* and *The Transition of Titus Crow.*

One of the main "proofs" or arguments advanced by August Derleth to push his interpretation of the Old Ones as powers of evil that were expelled in the same way that Satan was expelled from Eden, was the following quotation (allegedly from a Lovecraft letter), which regrettably has received more attention and diffusion than any other single paragraph attributed to H.P.L., both here and abroad: "All my stories, unconnected as they may be, are based on the fundamental lore or legend that this world was inhabited at one time by another race who, in practising black magic, lost their foothold and were expelled, yet live on outside, ever ready to take possession of this earth again." Which doesn't sound like Lovecraft at all—particularly that allusion to "black magic." Instead, it sounds like something one would have expected from Derleth himself! Naturally, this "quotation" did not go unchallenged, but when R. L. Tierney requested that Derleth produce the Lovecraft letter containing such paragraph, the latter became angry and refused. After Derleth's death in 1971, and as the result of the heightened interest in H. P. Lovecraft and his works in recent years, several researchers examined Lovecraft's unpublished letters at Brown University's John Hay Library and elsewhere, including L. Sprague de Camp (author of the highly opinionated biography of Lovecraft released by Doubleday in 1975). De Camp arrived at the conclusion that the famous paragraph simply *did not exist* in any of Lovecraft's letters to Derleth, or in any of the Lovecraft letters at the John Hay Lovecraft collection! Instead, this is what Lovecraft wrote to Farnsworth Wright on 5 July 1927: *"All my tales are based on the fundamental premise that common human laws and interests and emotions have no validity or significance in the vast cosmos-at-large. . . . To achieve the essence of real externality, whether of time or space or dimension, one must forget that such things as organic life, good and evil, love and hate, and all such local attributes of a negligible and temporary race called mankind, have any existence at all."*[14] Which sounds very much like Lovecraft, indeed![15] It is of course possible that the famous "black magic" paragraph was paraphrased by Derleth from memory of something he had read, but was now unable to locate (he never supplied any reference to the origin of the same, other than to say that it was a Lovecraft letter), but it is also possible that the most reprinted paragraph attributed to H.P.L. was a hoax, a fabrication by his ardent but misguided disciple, "self-blinded earth-gazer" August Derleth. The suspicion is strengthened by the realisation that the controversial paragraph seems to fit with Derleth's anthropocentred conception of the so-called "Cthulhu Mythos" better than anything within the Lovecraft *oeuvre.* The reader must judge by himself.[16]

Parenthetically, it should be pointed out that Lovecraft of course *did* write about the various struggles and conflicts that took place among the different races of extraterrestrial beings preceding man on this planet—these were detailed in two grandiose and separate accounts, *At the Mountains of Madness* and "The Shadow out of Time," with their vast scope of cosmic nemesis and history. Nevertheless, none of these conflicts resembled in the least the Derlethian battle between cosmic (or should that be *comic?*) Good and Evil, between the "Elder Gods" and the Old Ones.

Another point which deserves clarification is that the Yog-Sothoth Cycle of Myth (or YSCOM, and I propose that the inadequate label "Cthulhu Mythos" be permanently discarded) refers to various alien entities, cults, books, and places, but the tales themselves—whether by Lovecraft, Derleth, or anyone else—do not, and cannot "belong" to the myth-cycle! Practically all of Lovecraft's stories are loosely connected by common themes, locales, legendry, and philosophical undercurrents, but to state that some of these tales "belong to the Cthulhu Mythos" and others don't is largely meaningless and misleading. Instead, it would be correct to state that in some of the tales elements of the Yog-Sothoth Cycle of Myth are of pivotal importance, while in others they assume a marginal role, or are absent. With this criterion in mind, a careful examination of the Lovecraft *oeuvre* reveals a dozen stories and novelettes in which the pseudomythological elements form the core of the narrative. These are: "The Nameless City," "The Festival," "The Call of Cthulhu," *The Dream-Quest of Unknown Kadath,* "The Dunwich Horror," "The Whisperer in Darkness," "The Shadow over Innsmouth," *At the Mountains of Madness,* "The Dreams in the Witch House," "The Shadow out of Time," "The Haunter of the Dark," and the collaboration "Through the Gates of the Silver Key" (with E. Hoffmann Price). This list differs in some respects from the ones provided by Derleth and others. "The Colour out of Space," in my opinion Lovecraft's masterpiece, is not included because it does not contain any explicit YSCOM elements, while such elements are only of marginal importance in *The Case of Charles Dexter Ward* and "The Thing on the Doorstep." On the other hand, pseudomythological entities appear in prominent roles in the *Dream-Quest* (in which Lovecraft succeeded in connecting many of his previous tales), and in "Through the Gates of the Silver Key."

It should also be pointed out that Lovecraft *did* encourage some of his friends and correspondents to incorporate Yog-Sothoth Myth-elements into their own works, and in return mentioned some of the others' contributions in a few of his own tales, notably in "The Whisperer in Darkness." There was nothing wrong with such procedure, of course, and tales written by old and new aspiring writers including Lovecraftian pseudomythological elements can be interesting and entertaining, particularly if they stop short of servile imitation, and do not *misuse* or *distort* Lovecraft's ideas beyond recognition. Regrettably, with some very few happy exceptions, such misuse, distortion, and slavish imitation have been the rule in the past, in part due to the misinterpretation of the Lovecraft *oeuvre* popularised by Derleth. How many would-be Lovecraft pastichists inadvertently wound up imitating Derleth's own inferior imitations! Hopefully the trend will be reversed in the future, now that the facts are out in the open.

Once all the distortions and misconceptions superimposed by Derleth on Lovecraft's work (and perpetuated by uncritical "fans" and disciples) are removed, what remains is a work of genius, a cosmic-minded *oeuvre* embodying a mechanistic materialist's brilliant conception of imaginary realms and frightful reality "beyond the fields we know," a literary rhapsody of the cosmos and man's laughable position therein, which is likely to appeal to new generations of readers all over the world, for many years to come. The Lovecraft *oeuvre* can be regarded as a significant contribution to world literature—may it be remembered without the "adornments," "embellishments," and "improvements" contributed by his "self-blinded, earth-gazing" imitators!

Notes

1. *Collected Works,* III, p. 347.—S.T.J.
2. H. P. Lovecraft to Rheinhart Kleiner, 13 May 1921; in *Collected Works,* V, p. 132.—S.T.J.
3. *Collected Works,* VII, p. 39.—S.T.J.
4. *Collected Works,* I, p. 130.—S.T.J.
5. *Marginalia,* p. 135.—S.T.J.
6. *Ibid.*—S.T.J.
7. See Wetzel's "The Mechanistic-Supernatural of Lovecraft" and Lieber's "A Literary Copernicus."—S.T.J.
8. *Collected Works,* VII, p. 295.—S.T.J.
9. Cf. "The Call of Cthulhu," in *Collected Works,* I, pp. 130-59.—S.T.J.
10. This Derlethian feature occurs especially in the "posthumous collaboration," "Witches' Hollow" (*The Watchers out of Time and Others,* pp. 294-307).—S.T.J.
11. *Collected Works,* I, p. 175.—S.T.J.
12. Derleth's naming Lovecraft's myth-cycle "the Cthulhu Mythos" was apparently "because it was in 'The Call of Cthulhu' that the myth-pattern first became apparent." —See Derleth and Wandrei, preface to *The Outsider and Others,* p. xii.—S.T.J.
13. The name "Hastur" was originally created by Ambrose Bierce, who, in "Haïta the Shepherd," depicted the entity as a god of the shepherds. Chambers, like Lovecraft, only mentions Hastur in "The Yellow Sign" ("We spoke of Hastur and of Cassilda. . . ."), and never deems it as any sort of entity.—S.T.J.
14. *Collected Works,* VI, p. 150.—S.T.J.
15. Incidentally, although L. Sprague de Camp included the above information in the corrected third printing of his *Lovecraft: A Biography,* he is definitely in error when he contends that Derleth "apparently misquoted" the letter to Wright, obtaining the famous "black magic" paragraph given above. The 1927 letter to Wright was printed in the "Eyrie" of the February 1928 issue of *Weird Tales,* and Derleth was very much aware of the exact text of it, for he reprinted the letter in *Marginalia* [pp. 305-06] and in *Selected Letters II.* Furthermore, shortly after Lovecraft's death, an article by August Derleth appeared in Ben Abramson's *Reading and Collecting,* titled "A Master of the Macabre," where Derleth stated: "In one of his letters, Lovecraft says:"—here follows the often quoted "black magic" paragraph—"which will be recognised as being basically similar to the Christian mythos regarding the expulsion of Satan and the constant power of evil. In another letter, he adds . . ."—and here follows the relevant quote from the letter to Wright! But not all of it . . . Derleth conveniently left out the sentence which starts: "To achieve the essence of real externality . . ." since it obviously was incompatible with the Christian mythos-parallel hypothesis!
16. Prof. Mosig conducted, after writing this article, some further research into the origin of this quotation: "While reading the [Harold S.] Farnese letters to H. P. Lovecraft, I came across the following thought-provoking passage, which may have been the genesis of the apocryphal 'black magic' paragraph: 'If I comprehend your work correctly, I take from it the suggestion of an outer sphere (may I call it) of Black Magic, at one time ruling this planet but now dispossessed, awaiting "on the outside" a chance for a possible return.' (From Farnese's second letter to Lovecraft, dated 3 September 1932, in which he replied to H.P.L.'s missive of August 30th.) Lovecraft's reply must have been dated around Sept. 25, for on Sept. 24 Farnese mailed a letter expressing concern at not having received an answer to his previous one, and on Sept. 28 prepared another epistle indicating that he had at last received the reply whose previous lack had prompted the Sept. 24 enquiry. . . . There is no doubt that Derleth had copies of the Farnese letters . . . , and I cannot help but wonder if consciously or unconsciously he might have paraphrased Farnese in composing that most famous 'quotation' attributed to H.P.L., while adding a slight twist that lent credence to his own dogmatic but myopic approach to the Lovecraft *oeuvre.*" ("Random Notes," *The Miskatonic,* V, 2 [1 May 1977], [5].)—S.T.J.

III
LITERARY INFLUENCES

On the Literary Influences
Which Shaped Lovecraft's Works

By J. Vernon Shea

*J. Vernon Shea (1912–   ), correspondent of Lovecraft's from 1931
to Lovecraft's death, has long been an astute critic of his associate's life
and work. Shea has expressed many lively and controversial opinions
about Lovecraft (particularly in his memoir, "H. P. Lovecraft: The
House and the Shadows"), and this comprehensive article is no different. In its massive scope this essay should lay the foundation for
future work in the literary influences upon Lovecraft, as Shea suggests
many authors and titles whose similarities to Lovecraft's fiction have
been overlooked by critics. The essay has been slightly abridged.*

Some literary masterpieces are so fresh and original, so completely
unique, that they foster the illusion that their authors were never consciously influenced by the writings of anyone else. But that, of course, is
not true: a writer tends to read a great deal, and his mind is the repository
of many ideas culled from his reading. When he goes to write his own
stuff he is selective, and tends to mould his efforts after the writings he
has admired the most, or at least the kind of writing he suspects he can
imitate most easily.

That H. P. Lovecraft was influenced by a great many other writers is
readily apparent from his works. Some critics tend to look down upon
him for that reason and call his work "derivative," and ask where are the
writings which might be labelled wholly Lovecraftian. Lovecraft himself,
acutely (and perhaps unnecessarily) conscious of his own literary short-
comings, once wrote in a letter that there were his "Poesque" tales, and
his "Dunsanian" tales, but where were his "Lovecraftian" stories?[1]

Possibly part of Lovecraft's dilemma rose from the fact that he was insufficiently endowed with egotism. Unlike August Derleth or Ernest Hemingway, he never consciously set out to become a Great Writer, but fell into fiction-writing almost by accident. True, he had written some stories at a remarkably early age, but these were forms of self-gratification which he never took seriously, and in later years he destroyed most of them. As he grew toward adolescence his interest in fiction was supplanted by an ever-growing fascination with the natural sciences, and he was writing columns on astronomy as a teenager. In his twenties he turned to amateur journalism, and his fiction for such journals developed merely as a sideline, an attempt to broaden his range; he was far more interested in writing poetry, which he considered his "proper" literary medium. (His mother had always told him that he was destined to become a great lyric poet.)[2] It was largely, or perhaps only, because the other amateur journalists of that period wrote glowingly of his fictional attempts that he turned serious attention to stories.

He considered himself remarkably ill-equipped for the writing of fiction. At the time of his first published writings he had scarcely set foot away from his native New England, and because of his insulated childhood and reclusive early manhood he had known very few people; as it happened, he also had a tin ear for dialogue. He was ill-at-ease with modern mainstream fiction, so much concerned with matters he had no interest in, and realised very well that he could never compete in the literary marketplace with such writers; and so he turned to the kind of writing which had enchanted him as a child: the classical mythology, the curious old books, the *Arabian Nights,* etc. which he had found in his grandfather's library.

Thus his earliest stories are full of references to classical mythology and Grecian and Roman history, stories like "Hypnos" and "The Tree" and "Celephais." Indeed, George Wetzel claims classical mythology was the genesis of his later Mythos stories, and possibly they *are* an extension or outgrowth of such myths; but the stories in which classical mythology plays a prominent part are usually among the weakest of Lovecraft's tales.

More to the point, it was probably from classical mythology—or possibly from Doré's illustrations to Dante's *Inferno*—that Lovecraft got his abiding interest in subterranean horrors, one of the basic *motifs* of his fiction. One thinks immediately of Orpheus' descent into the underground and the Minotaur story, which Lovecraft later used in his revision of Kenneth Sterling's "In the Walls of Eryx." His interest in mysterious passageways leading into the bowels of the earth was reinforced by Poe's tales, with their cemetery vaults and putrescent corpses and people buried alive, and by the reading of John Uri Lloyd's neglected literary curiosity *Etidorhpa,* which he recommended enthusiastically to his correspondents.[3] But one suspects that even without Poe he would have written of cemeteries, for the ones on College Hill fascinated him so.

It was undoubtedly the memory of the *Arabian Nights* of his boyhood reading which resulted in the Oriental place-names of so many of his stories. (He never bothered to learn any Arabic whatsoever, as that linguistic horror "Abdul Alhazred" attests.) He would have written so-called "Dunsanian" stories even if he had never encountered Lord Dunsany's works, and in fact did so in the case of "Polaris." Though apparently he tried to imitate Dunsany's style later, he never quite succeeded, for he could not master Dunsany's grace and Irish lyricism. It was the lack of these same qualities which mars his poetry.

Yet Lord Dunsany very obviously became a great influence upon his fiction. His title, *At the Mountains of Madness,* comes from Dunsany's *A Dreamer's Tales.* From another of the stories in that collection, "Idle Days on the Yann," he took the idea of the throne carved from a *single* piece of ivory in "The Doom that Came to Sarnath." The title of his favourite Dunsany story, "Bethmoora," became one of the established place-names of his Mythos.

These Dunsanian "imitations," however, are usually considered to be among Lovecraft's weakest stories, and many readers find them rather tedious. Certainly if all his stories had been in that vein he would never have acquired any posthumous fame. But "The White Ship" and "The Cats of Ulthar" are surely among the best of these stories, and some readers are also entranced by "Beyond the Wall of Sleep," "The Silver Key," "The Quest of Iranon," and *The Dream-Quest of Unknown Kadath.*[4] It is debatable whether or not "The Music of Erich Zann," one of Lovecraft's very best stories, should be considered "Dunsanian" also; it was one of the earliest stories of his adulthood, and Lovecraft himself always had a high regard for it, ranking it second only to "The Colour out of Space" of all his stories. It is possible also to regard the story as one of his Poe-esque creations, and its Parisian setting is reminiscent of "The Murders in the Rue Morgue."

A case might be made, however, that Thomas Burke's collection *Limehouse Nights,* which also has Oriental characters and which Lovecraft presumably read before he came upon Dunsany, may have had some influence upon the so-called "Dunsanian" tales.

Lovecraft devotes so much space in his "Supernatural Horror in Literature" to the Gothic novelists that presumably they must have influenced his writings at least to some extent; but except for the Gothic trimmings such influences are not too readily apparent. It is true that the protagonist of Charles Brockden Brown's *Wieland,* who is incarcerated in a mental institution, is a quite recognisable figure to Lovecraftians; and the anti-religious sentiments expressed in Matthew Lewis' *Monk* are echoed throughout Lovecraft's writings. (*The Monk* obviously influenced Montague Rhodes James when he came to write "Count Magnus" and "An Incident of Cathedral History;" and a case might be made that Lovecraft's dream-story, "The Evil Clergyman," may have been derived from it also, although it would seem to owe more to Poe's "William Wilson.") Horace Walpole's *Castle of Otranto,* with its ancestral paintings whose eyes followed the proceedings in the castle, also must have influenced Lovecraft to some extent; there are many old castles in Lovecraft's stories, as in "The Outsider" and "The Moon-Bog." But, of course, an ancient castle is an integral part of almost all the Gothic novels; one cannot imagine *Frankenstein* or *Dracula* or the like without one. But Mrs Radcliffe's novels, with their "realistic" explanations for the apparently supernatural occurrences, certainly did not seem to influence Lovecraft's work noticeably, nor did the novels of the Brontë sisters. (If one were to cite *Jane Eyre* as the genesis of "The Shuttered Room," one would be told, of course, that that story was purely of Derleth's devising, not of Lovecraft's.)

The so-called "Byronic" hero of these Gothic novels, perhaps best exemplified by Heathcliff in *Wuthering Heights,* obviously was not to Lovecraft's liking, and he never used him. To do so, of course, would have necessitated bringing in a heroine for him, and Lovecraft always avoided writing about women as much as possible.

Nathaniel Hawthorne was almost as influential in shaping Lovecraft's stories as Poe was, but that fact is not recognised by most Lovecraftian scholars because Hawthorne is so little read today. Whereas Poe's scholarship was largely bogus, Hawthorne's was quite genuine; despite Hawthorne's old-fashioned style and moralistic strictures, he had a fine mind very much like Lovecraft's. Whereas Poe dealt frequently with a decadent Southern aristocracy of whom Lovecraft had no immediate knowledge, or placed his tales in some vague Never Never Land, Lovecraft was quite at home in Hawthorne's New England, and it was presumably Hawthorne's example which turned Lovecraft's attention to writing about the places and the houses which he knew intimately.

The themes of a family curse and a tainted ancestry, although first adumbrated in Walpole's *Castle of Otranto,* received their most exemplary literary expression in Hawthorne's *House of the Seven Gables,* a novel which foreshadowed Lovecraft's reworking of the themes in stories like *The Case of Charles Dexter Ward,* "The Shadow over Innsmouth," "Facts concerning the Late Arthur Jermyn and His Family," and "The

Moon-Bog.'' Hawthorne, too, because of his ancestor Judge Hathorne's involvement with the witchcraft trials, dealt with witches in stories like "Young Goodman Brown" and "Feathertop," and, like Lovecraft, could never quite rid himself of the Puritan ethos; the presence of evil was to him almost a palpable thing. As Philip A. Shreffler points out in his *H. P. Lovecraft Companion,* Hawthorne's work was very congenial to Lovecraft, who wrote of Hawthorne in his "Supernatural Horror in Literature" thus:

> The degree of American weirdness was his to a most intense degree, and he saw a dismal throng of vague spectres behind the common phenomena of life.[5]

Despite Shreffler's assertion to the contrary, however, Lovecraft was little interested, as Hawthorne was, in writing moral allegories, even though he fully agreed that the transgressor should be punished, as witness his early tales "The Tree" and "In the Vault." Shreffler asserts that "The White Ship" "is a moral allegory, pure and simple, based on *Pilgrim's Progress* and possibly on Hawthorne's 'The Celestial Railroad' ", a statement I find highly questionable. Lovecraft was not enamoured of Bunyan's piece, and "The White Ship" would seem to owe more to A. Merritt's *Ship of Ishtar* and to Poe's "Descent into the Maelstrom," possibly even to the *Odyssey.*

The famous Witch House, of which Hawthorne wrote, was of course also used by Lovecraft in his "Dreams in the Witch House;" and some scholars feel that Hawthorne's little anecdote of a man's walking down the street and being regarded with horror by passersby (because he was wearing a shroud) was the genesis of "The Outsider," but that tale would seem to owe much more to Poe. A detailed examination of Hawthorne's stories in the *Twice-Told Tales* would probably elicit more examples of possible influences upon Lovecraft.

While Hawthorne's stories provided the *physical* backgrounds for many of Lovecraft's works, it was in the tales of Edgar Allan Poe that Lovecraft found his spiritual home. Poe's influence upon Lovecraft has perhaps been overstated; while of course it looms very large in Lovecraft's early stories, Lovecraft seems to have made a conscious effort to eradicate it to a very great extent in his Mythos tales, which were far more influenced by Machen. Of the Mythos stories, only *At the Mountains of Madness* owes much of a debt to Poe unless one accepts "The Hound" as part of the Mythos. (One rather wishes, however, that Lovecraft had never read "The Tell-Tale Heart," for that "They tell me that I am mad" opening was reprised to death by Lovecraft.)

Back in 1966 I made the statement that "The Outsider" could easily pass as a "lost" story of Poe's because in it Lovecraft had aped Poe's style and subject matter so assiduously;[6] and ever since then other writers have followed my lead. Poe's overwrought style has been both praised and damned by critics; Poe himself seems to have been conscious of its imperfections, for in his later *Narrative of A. Gordon Pym* he modified it considerably. But the young Lovecraft apparently was enchanted by that style and imitated it to the point of absurdity.

Part of the reason for Lovecraft's unpopularity with the literary critics of his day lay in the fact that mainstream literature, following Sherwood Anderson's and Hemingway's leads, was turning more and more toward simple sentences and action-packed narration. Hemingway would go through his manuscripts and vigorously excise any adjectives. It was felt that verbs and adverbs were much more vivid than adjectives and carried the story along better.

But Lovecraft preferred to write description rather than narration; he thought that the essential part of a story was its mood or atmosphere rather than its story-line or even its *dénouement,* which was sometimes given away at the very beginning of his tale; and so he peppered his tales with adjectives to heighten the mood. His choice of adjectives was not always the best, and some of them—like the ubiquitous *eldritch*—have been ridiculed by critics. Unfortunately, Lovecraft was never good at finding the unexpected simile or metaphor which brings the reader sharply to attention, as writers like Ramsey Campbell do; and after an extended dip into his tale his adjectives become wholly *predictable.* But in this matter he was merely following the established literary traditions; he was following Poe.

It takes no great acumen to point out the stories of Lovecraft's which were influenced by Poe; they cry out "Poe!" very plangently. Some of the most easily detectable ones are "Cool Air," practically a rewriting of "The Facts in the Case of M. Valdemar;" "The Outsider," with its patent borrowings from both "The Masque of the Red Death" and "William Wilson;"[7] *At the Mountains of Madness,* an acknowledged sequel to *Pym*; and "The Hound," with its many references to Poe's tales. But it was the style and technique of the early tales, rather than their plot elements, which clearly stamp them "Poe-esque;" they were like a composer's student exercises written "in the manner of" some other composer.

H. P. Lovecraft's famed *critique,* "Supernatural Horror in Literature," is practically a guidebook to his own literary influences; as one reads casually in it about some fantaisiste who, one would have thought, had little discernible influence upon Lovecraft's writings, one is caught up short by some reference which immediately brings one of Lovecraft's own tales to mind.

Lovecraft's reading in the *genre* was very wide, whereas most of the modern Lovecraftian scholars, albeit they have studied the master's works minutely, would seem to have little knowledge of the infinite spectrum of fantasy and have therefore concentrated largely upon such very obvious influences as those of Poe, Dunsany, and Machen. But it is quite likely that literally dozens of writers contributed directly or indirectly to the formation of that master of supernatural horror we know as H. P. Lovecraft.

Let me cite some examples. Sir Edward Bulwer-Lytton is very little read today, regrettably, for Lovecraft was quite right in proclaiming "The House and the Brain" as "one of the best short haunted-house tales ever written."[8] It was possibly the first story in which the house itself is wholly malignant and works its will upon its occupants, a theme much exploited in modern times in tales like Robert Bloch's "The Hungry House" or in novels like Jay Anson's *The Amityville Horror* or in such films as *Burnt Offerings, The Evil, The Sentinel, The Legend of Hell House,* and *The House of Dark Shadows.* Lovecraft himself was to use this theme, of course, in "The Shunned House."

But Lovecraft considered Bulwer-Lytton's masterpieces to be his novels *Zanoni* and *A Strange Story,* especially the latter. According to Lovecraft, *Zanoni* "introduces a vast unknown sphere of being pressing on our own world and guarded by a horrible 'Dweller of the Threshold' who haunts those who try to enter and fail"—surely a Lovecraftian theme if there ever was one! There is also in the novel a "brotherhood kept alive from age to age," but Lovecraft qualifies that statement by calling the brotherhood "benign," a term far more Derlethian than Lovecraftian.

Although Lovecraft deplores the melodramatic claptrap of *A Strange Story,* he tells us that:

> . . . again we have the mysterious user of life's elixir in the person of the soulless magician Margrave, whose dark exploits stand out with dramatic vividness against the modern background of a quiet English town and the Australian bush; and again we have shadowy intimations of a vast spectral world of the unknown in the very air about us—this time handled with much greater power and vitality than in *Zanoni.* One of the two great incantation passages, where the hero is driven by a luminous evil spirit to rise at night in his sleep, take a strange Egyptian wand, and evoke nameless presences in the haunted and mausoleum-facing pavilion of a famous Renaissance alchemist, truly stands among the major terror scenes of literature. Just enough is suggested, and just little enough is told.

Very curiously, in the continuation of Lovecraft's *critique* upon *A Strange Story,* we come upon this passage, which surely suggests the

Mythos to come, with its strange incantations to the gods of Lovecraft's pantheon:

> Unknown words are twice dictated to the sleep-walker, and as he repeats them the ground trembles, and all the dogs of the countryside begin to bay at half-seen amorphous shadows that stalk athwart the moonlight. When a third set of unknown words is prompted, the sleep-walker's spirit suddenly rebels at uttering them, as if the soul could recognise ultimate abysmal horrors concealed from the mind.[9]

By the time he came to the writing of "Supernatural Horror in Literature" Lovecraft had already established in his mind his own artistic credo. For instance, he deplores the school of fantastic writing exemplified by such authors as LeFanu, Wilkie Collins, Haggard, Conan Doyle, H. G. Wells, and Stevenson (all of whom can be shown to have influenced Lovecraft's writings to some extent) by writing that to this school:

> . . . clearly belong such of our contemporary horror-tales as specialise in events rather than atmospheric details, address the intellect rather than the impressionistic imagination, cultivate a luminous glamour rather than a malign intensity or psychological verisimilitude, and take a definite stand in sympathy with mankind and its welfare. It has its undeniable strength, and because of its "human element" commands a wider audience than does the sheer artistic nightmare. If not quite so potent as the latter, it is because a diluted product can never achieve the intensity of a concentrated essence.

Such writing, of course, is precisely what editors, and perhaps most readers, are looking for; this passage, in essence, is what many of Lovecraft's critics cavil at. But a writer must write according to his own lights; a present-day writer cannot be faulted for not writing like Shakespeare any more than Lovecraft can be blamed for not writing like Seabury Quinn.

But I have strayed a bit from my citing of writers who possibly influenced Lovecraft. Of the Brontë sisters, Charlotte became the most famous, but her *Jane Eyre* was much less to Lovecraft's taste than Emily's *Wuthering Heights*. Lovecraft refers to the latter's "epically cosmic setting." What he has to say of Heathcliff suggests Kaspar Hauser and the changelings of his own tales:

> Heathcliff, the modified Byronic villain-hero, is a strange dark waif found in the streets as a small child and speaking only a strange gibberish till adopted by the family he ultimately ruins. That he is in truth a diabolic spirit is more than once suggested.

One is reminded of the opening passages of "The Outsider," and even more of the film *The Omen*. It is, of course, possible, considering the fact that both of Lovecraft's parents would end up in mental institutions, that Lovecraft may have entertained at one time or another the fantasy that he himself was a changeling.

Even such an unlikely weird tale as *Undine,* by Friedrich Heinrich Karl, Baron de la Motte Fouque, may have been a literary influence upon Lovecraft. Lovecraft refers to "the malicious waterfall-spirit Kuhleborn" in it; and Kuhleborn is a name not too far removed from Cthulhu. Undine, the heroine, daughter of a water-spirit, "was exchanged by her father as a small child for a fisherman's daughter, in order that she might acquire a soul by wedding a human being." This sexual traffic with water-creatures brings to mind the characters of "The Shadow over Innsmouth;" and a later reference by Lovecraft to "the haunted wood with its gigantic snow-white man and various unnamed terrors" suggests the Abominable Snowman and is perhaps an intimation of *At the Mountains of Madness.*

Theophile Gautier's *One of Cleopatra's Nights,* with its rather flippant title, might also be cited as a possible literary influence. Consider this passage:

> Gautier captured the inmost soul of aeon-weighted Egypt, with its cryptic life and Cyclopean architecture, and uttered once and for all the external horror of its nether world of catacombs, where to the end of time millions of stiff, spiced corpses will stare up in the blackness with glassy eyes, awaiting some awesome and unrelatable summons.

That reference to "stiff, spiced corpses" is Lovecraft's dry wit at its best; but the passage also suggests "Imprisoned with the Pharaohs" and a number of other tales with a "nether world of catacombs."

Baudelaire was, of course, far more of a literary influence upon Clark Ashton Smith, who translated his poems, than upon Lovecraft, but Lovecraft's reference to Baudelaire as one of the "artists in sin" reminds one of the two protagonists of "The Hound."[10]

Maupassant's influence upon Lovecraft seems to have been largely overlooked. Surely the mentioning of "the imminence of nameless terrors and the relentless dogging of an ill-starred individual by hideous and menacing representatives of the outer darkness" could apply to almost any of Lovecraft's tales, with especial pertinence perhaps to "The Haunter of the Dark." In his last years, as his mind was besieged by the darkness of encroaching insanity, Maupassant wrote some frenetic tales which sound almost Lovecraftian, especially his famous "Horla." "The Horla" 's invisible monster is not wholly original—it had been preceded by Fitz-James O'Brien's "What Was It? A Mystery" and, perhaps, by Bierce's "Damned Thing"—but when one reads Lovecraft's description of "an invisible being who lives on water and milk, sways the minds of others, and seems to be the vanguard of a horde of extraterrestrial organisms arrived on earth to subjugate and overwhelm mankind" one is immediately reminded of a number of Lovecraftian tales, especially "The Dunwich Horror." Invisible monsters seem to have fascinated Lovecraft: remember the fate of the poor author of the *Necronomicon*; recall "The Invisible Monster," the Sonia Greene story revised by Lovecraft; think of the invisible whistling octopoid creatures of "The Shadow out of Time." And, of course, the reference to the "extraterrestrial organisms arrived on earth to subjugate and overwhelm mankind" is reminiscent of the Mi-Go of "The Whisperer in Darkness."

Lovecraft never employed so obvious a fantastic theme as a werewolf (albeit he suggested to H. Warner Munn that a good werewolf tale might be written from the *werewolf's* point of view)[11], but in writing about "The Man-Wolf," by the collaborators Erckmann-Chatrian, he said that "a transmitted curse works toward the end in a traditional Gothic-castle setting," which reminds one of "The Moon-Bog" and, perhaps, of *The Case of Charles Dexter Ward*; and his description of their " 'Invisible Eye,' where a malignant old hag weaves nocturnal hypnotic spells which induce the successive occupants of a certain inn chamber to hang themselves on a crossbeam" clearly evokes "The Dreams in the Witch House."

Lovecraft has often been accused of anti-Semitism, but he was quite aware of the Jewish legacy to weird fiction. In "Supernatural Horror in Literature" he writes quite sympathetically of the Jewish tradition, which has counterparts in his own fiction:

> Cabbalism itself, so prominent during the Middle Ages, is a system of philosophy explaining the universe as emanations of the Deity, and involving the existence of strange spiritual realms and beings apart from the visible world in which dark glimpses may be obtained through certain secret incantations. . . . Jewish folklore has preserved much of the terror and mystery of the past, and when more thoroughly studied is likely to exert considerable influence on weird fiction. . . .[12]

which of course has come true in the writings of Bernard Malamud and especially Isaac Bashevis Singer. Lovecraft goes on to describe the famous Jewish work *The Dybbuk,* with Prague's "ancient ghetto with its spectral, peaked gables" (more suggestive, perhaps, of Hawthorne than of Lovecraft) and its "possession of a living body by the evil soul of a dead man," a theme adumbrated in both "The Evil Clergyman" and *The Case of Charles Dexter Ward,* but used with singular power in "The Thing on the Doorstep."

Those critics who are convinced that Lovecraft was a student of the occult and used it in his fiction may get some corroboration in the passage on cabbalism cited above; yet very frequently both in his correspondence and in "Supernatural Horror in Literature" Lovecraft rails at writers overly concerned with occult "manifestations": he writes with apparent distaste of William Godwin's *St. Leon* with its "Rosicrucian" elements and Bulwer-Lytton's over-fondness for "Rosicrucianism" and "his amusingly serious occult studies."

The New England tradition is the key element to Lovecraft's fiction. Without the magical evocation of its frequently forbidding atmosphere Lovecraft's stories might have been little better than the work of his *Weird Tales* confrères. Lovecraft was quite aware that New England was his own especial fictional milieu. In "Supernatural Horror in Literature" he wrote:

> This additional fund proceeded . . . first from the keen spiritual and theological interests of the first colonists, plus the strange and forbidding nature of the scene in which they were plunged. The vast and gloomy virgin forests in whose perpetual twilight all terrors might well lurk; the hordes of coppery Indians whose strange, saturnine visages and violent customs hinted strongly of infernal origin; the free rein given under the influence of Puritan theocracy to all manner of notions respecting man's relation to the stern and vengeful God of the Calvinists, and to the sulphureous Adversary of that God, about whom so much was thundered in the pulpits each Sunday; and the morbid introspection developed by an isolated backwoods life devoid of normal amusements and of the recreational mood, harassed by commands for theological self-examination, keyed to unnatural emotional repression, and forming above all a mere grim struggle for survival—all these things conspired to produce an environment in which the black whisperings of sinister grandams were heard far beyond the chimney corner, and in which tales of witchcraft and unbelieveable secret monstrosities lingered long after the dread days of the Salem nightmare.[13]

This rather perfervid passage, which may have caused Lovecraft to wince in later years, provides clues to some of his own writings. Surely he maligned the Indians, without whose assistance and knowledge of nature the colonists would soon have perished, but this exaggerated portrait of them is echoed in his own story "He." Although he cast aside at the age of six the theological trimmings, Lovecraft himself was never to escape wholly from the Puritan tradition with its "unnatural emotional repression," especially inasmuch as his own upbringing, despite the pampering, was essentially just as grim a lot as those of the colonists he wrote about here. The "secret monstrosities" to be found behind the respectable facades of the New England houses were to be expressed in many of his tales like "The Picture in the House" and "The Terrible Old Man" and "The Dunwich Horror." The theme of witchcraft runs like a *leitmotif* through tales like *The Case of Charles Dexter Ward* and "The Dreams in the Witch House."

It is exceedingly curious that in the entire length of "Supernatural Horror in Literature" no mention is made of America's two top writers, Mark Twain and Herman Melville, although both wrote fantasies which may or may not have influenced Lovecraft's own writings. Melville was especially masterful at depicting a New England background, even more so perhaps than Hawthorne, and his *Moby-Dick,* with its sulphurous sermons, its background of village superstitions, and its depiction of people who depended for their livelihood upon the sea but lived always in fear of it, would seem to be a novel which had much in common with "The Shadow over Innsmouth." Perhaps Lovecraft was put off by Melville's purposeful ambiguities; for instance, in that horror masterpiece "Benito Cereno" the situation turns out to be completely different from what the reader at first is led to believe; and perhaps Lovecraft thought that Melville wasted too much time upon characterisation and dialogue, which concerned him very little.

But surely Mark Twain's works would seem to have been much more to Lovecraft's taste. They shared a distaste for religion, and in *The Mysterious Stranger* Twain anticipated by decades the Fortean theme of "We are property"—in the novella a youth creates some homunculi, or little men, and then cruelly and capriciously destroys them (obviously Twain's feeling about God). (A suggestion here, perhaps, of "The Terrible Old Man"?) *A Connecticut Yankee in King Arthur's Court* should have delighted Lovecraft, for in it a New Englander goes back into time (much as the protagonist of Lovecraft's favourite film, *Berkeley Square,* did) and defeats the manipulations of King Arthur's courtiers by his Yankee shrewdness. And surely "Those Extraordinary Twins," a story which was later metamorphosed into the novel *Pudd'nhead Wilson,* should have intrigued Lovecraft with his love for "monstrosities," for the tale was inspired by Twain's having seen a circus poster of the Tocci brothers, a pair of Siamese twins who were joined completely from the sixth rib downward, "having not merely a single anus and penis, but only two legs"—being topheavy, they were unable to walk.

But "the dark Puritan age" was expressed better in Hawthorne's work in Lovecraft's viewpoint than in either Twain's or Melville's, even though Hawthorne's tales seemed to lack "the cosmic malignity" of Poe. One is rather amused reading Lovecraft's account of a tale which Hawthorne never got around to writing, "The Ancestral Footstep," "of an ancient and accursed line whose members left footprints of blood when they walked," for it reminds one of the glowing handprints left by Boris Karloff in *Die, Monster, Die!* (the film version of "The Colour out of Space"); and one wonders where the accursed family got all that blood! Another of Hawthorne's never-to-be-written tales was to have "an especially vivid plot . . . concerning a baffling stranger who appeared now and then in public assemblies, and who was at last followed and found to come and go from a very ancient grave," which hints at some of Lovecraft's own tales, especially of "The Outsider."

From Hawthorne "Supernatural Horror in Literature" skips quite a few decades to the work of the Irish-American Fitz-James O'Brien, whose "What Was It? A Mystery" was the progenitor of all the tales of invisible monsters, and then to Ambrose Bierce. Bierce's influence upon Lovecraft has been somewhat neglected by Lovecraft's critics, for of course Bierce was essentially a writer of *contes cruels,* tales of physical rather than of supernatural horror; yet Lovecraft owed a considerable debt to him. The kind of sardonic humour of which Lovecraft was so fond was clearly derived from Bierce, who wrote chapter headings like "One Does Not Always Eat What Is on the Table," referring to a corpse in a morgue; and one of the opening sentences of Bierce's tales could pass very readily for a Lovecraft opening. However, Bierce's style was usually quite flat and prosaic, to point up the unexpectedness of the horror to come—an example which Lovecraft, of course, did not follow.

"The Death of Halpin Frayser" was Lovecraft's favourite of all Bierce's tales; one is tempted immediately to write that this tale of a doting mother who, after her death, becomes a mindless ravening monster intent upon destroying her son would seem to have peculiar relevance to Lovecraft's own case. It may have influenced the writing of "The Thing on the Doorstep." "The Spook House," with its "strange subterranean room," in which the protagonist is enclosed within a vault and never seen again, suggests a number of Lovecraft's tales; its grisly humour would seem to be the progenitor of "In the Vault," whose unscrupulous undertaker, one of Lovecraft's few attempts at vivid characterisation, seems very much in the Biercian mood.

One is rather surprised that *The Turn of the Screw,* one of the great masterpieces of American literature, receives so little attention from Lovecraft, who seems to have missed its psychological implications. He wrote that Henry James was "too much addicted to subtleties of speech," not apparently realising that the great subtlety here was the subtlety of the characterisation of the governess; all the ghostly elements of the tale, of course, occur just in the governess' mind. Lovecraft has rightly been lauded for his discernment in the case of "The Fall of the House of Usher" (he was the first to point out that Usher, his sister, and the house all shared a common soul); but his discernment apparently failed him when he came to *The Turn of the Screw,* which he dismissed as just a ghost-story, a *genre* for which he had no great liking. Henry James, unfortunately, seems to have had little or no influence upon

Lovecraft, who could have used some of James' consummate ability at technique and characterisation. Like many readers, Lovecraft seems to have been rather put off by James' literary style, although it was much simpler in *The Turn of the Screw* than it was in the later novels. *The Turn of the Screw* has been dramatised and filmed several times, most splendidly in *The Innocents,* a film which Lovecraft of course never got to see.

F. Marion Crawford's tales are likewise rather scamped in "Supernatural Horror in Literature." " 'The Dead Smile,' " Lovecraft wrote, "treats of family horrors in an old house and an ancestral vault in Ireland"—a theme which would seem to suggest "The Moon-Bog;" and of "For the Blood Is the Life," he wrote of "a case of moon-cursed vampirism near an ancient tower," which would also seem to have pertinence to some of Lovecraft's own tales. Crawford, however, is most famous for his ghost-stories like "The Screaming Skull" and "The Upper Berth;" the latter belongs on any list of best ghost-stories. It may have influenced the writing of M. R. James' "Count Magnus," one of Lovecraft's great favourites.

A considerably lesser writer, Robert W. Chambers, who usually wrote just popular slush, seems to have struck a much deeper chord in Lovecraft. Indeed, there is considerable evidence to point to *The King in Yellow* as the genesis of Lovecraft's own *Necronomicon:* "a series of vaguely connected short stories having as a background a monstrous and suppressed book whose perusal brings fright, madness, and spectral tragedy." The best of these stories, "The Yellow Sign," is one of the great influences upon the Mythos tales; the Yellow Sign itself is mentioned frequently in the tales, and Lovecraft derived one of the principal gods of his pantheon in "the accursed cult of Hastur."[14] Today it is impossible to take "The Yellow Sign," with its jaunty journalism and wretched style, as seriously as Lovecraft apparently did. As Lovecraft himself pointed out, "it is worth observing that the author [Chambers] derives most of the names and allusions connected with his eldritch land of primal memory from the tales of Ambrose Bierce."

Other writers whom Lovecraft mentioned in this chapter—Mary E. Wilkins Freeman, Charlotte Perkins Gilman, and Ralph Adams Cram—do not appear to have influenced him at all, though they *did* influence August Derleth; and so we skip to a more modern writer, Irvin S. Cobb. Cobb, a Southerner of the old school, had what we today would term racist elements in his tales. For instance, in "Black as Sin" the reader is supposed to be horrified by the discovery that a white man's mistress, who goes heavily veiled throughout the story, is black; and this dependence upon a veil as a plot device may have influenced the writing of "Facts concerning the Late Arthur Jermyn and His Family," even though veils were very popular with Victorian writers, as in Dickens' "Black Veil." Another story, "The Unbroken Chain," is "the tale of hereditary memory where a modern man with a negroid strain utters words in African jungle speech when run down by a train under visual and aural circumstances recalling the maiming of his black ancestor by a rhinoceros a century before"—such tales of atavism, of reversal to a Jungian ancestral memory, were popular with Lovecraft and seem to have influenced his own writing. More to the point, an early tale of Cobb's, "Fishhead," with "its portrayal of unnatural affinities between a hybrid idiot and the strange fish of an isolated lake," clearly evokes "The Shadow over Innsmouth." Cobb, usually regarded as a humourist, wrote a number of highly effective horror tales like "The Belled Buzzard," "The Escape of Mr. Trimm," and "Faith, Hope and Charity," and would seem to be due for a revival.

Another work dealing with ancestral memory, *The Dark Chamber,* by Leonard Cline, has elements suggestive of "The Hound": "He calls for madder music and takes stranger drugs" and "In the end he takes to the woods, howling at night beneath windows." Even more reminiscent of Lovecraft's work is Herbert S. Gorman's novel, *The Place Called Dagon,* "which relates the dark history of a western Massachusetts backwater where the descendants of refugees from the Salem witchcraft still keep alive the morbid and degenerate horrors of the Black Sabbat."

Edward Lucas White had in common with Lovecraft the fact that his "themes arise from actual dreams." White's story "The Snout" suggests an actual dream of Lovecraft's himself as related to Robert Bloch in his *Selected Letters IV.*[15] Curiously, Lovecraft does not mention "Amina," which is the only story I know of which has a *female* ghoul; and he makes only passing mention of White's other tales, including his most famous one, "Lukundoo," which was probably inspired by H. G. Wells' *Pollack and the Porrah Man.*

Most readers seem unaware that "Lukundoo" appeared first in *Weird Tales,* the pulp magazine which was to figure so largely in Lovecraft's own literary career. The only other *Weird Tales* writer mentioned by Lovecraft in "Supernatural Horror in Literature" (aside from his quoting one of Frank Belknap Long's poems) is Clark Ashton Smith, and the paragraph he devotes to Smith's poetry and tales sounds a bit like a plug to spur Smith's flagging finances. Smith himself would seem to have had little influence upon Lovecraft's own writings—it was the other way around—albeit he added some new names to the Mythos.

One suspects that Lovecraft may have purposely eschewed mention of *Weird Tales* in case his *critique* found a wider audience than that of amateur journalism; he realised full well that the elitist literary critics of his day would have questioned the value of any critical work which mentioned pulp magazines, considered then beyond the bounds of literary respectability. Yet *Weird Tales* and its writers unquestionably helped to shape his own tales; throughout the volumes of *Selected Letters* he rails at Farnsworth Wright[16] and his magazine for exerting a deleterious through largely unconscious effect upon his own style and technique. And it is easy to pick out stories from the magazine which may have influenced his own writings: for example, "In Amundsen's Tent," by John Martin Leahy, a possible prototype for *At the Mountains of Madness;* "The Floor Above," by M. L. Humphries; "Beyond the Door," by J. Paul Suter; "Back to the Beast," a tale of atavism by Manly Wade Wellman; "Ooze," by Anthony M. Rud; and, of course, "The Shambler from the Stars," by Robert Bloch, which directly inspired the writing of a "sequel," "The Haunter of the Dark." Some of the stories which Lovecraft rewrote for his revision clients were very definitely meant to fit the *Weird Tales* pattern.

The discussion of modern American fantaisistes ends quite abruptly with Clark Ashton Smith, although there were obviously other contemporaries whom Lovecraft could or should have mentioned: Gouverneur Morris, whose "Back There in the Grass" has a decided kinship with "The Curse of Yig;" Stephen Vincent Benét; James Branch Cabell; Edith Wharton; Conrad Aiken; F. Scott Fitzgerald; John Russell; Ellen Glasgow; Zona Gale; Gertrude Atherton; W. C. Morrow, and others, some of whom Lovecraft may not have read.

Writers whom Lovecraft *did* read but did not mention in his treatise, possibly because their works appeared first in another pulp magazine, *Argosy,* were Edgar Rice Burroughs and A. Merritt. Rather recently articles have appeared which purport to show the great influence Burroughs and Merritt had upon Lovecraft. Burroughs' Pellucidar novels have been cited at considerable length as an influence upon the writing of *At the Mountains of Madness,* although another subterranean novel which preceded Burroughs' works, John Uri Lloyd's *Etidorhpa,* may have wielded even more influence. From Burroughs, however, Lovecraft presumably took the word "shoggoth." Burroughs produced such a vast quantity of writing that sooner or later he touched upon most of the fantasy and science fiction themes, and it *is* possible that Lovecraft may have taken some of his ideas from him.[17]

Merritt's supporters, however, would seem to have a much better case. Lovecraft frequently expressed his great admiration for the original novelette version of "The Moon Pool," and the beautiful but monstrous Shining One rather obviously had something to do with Lovecraft's conception of Yog-Sothoth, albeit in the sequel, *The Conquest of the Moon*

Pool, the Shining One is reduced almost to the dimensions of a pet of the villainess. The frog footmen of the sequel would seem to have something in common with Innsmouth's hybrid inhabitants. "The Moon Pool" was Merritt's masterpiece, and it conveys a horror of the sea which was to be surpassed only by William Hope Hodgson's works. The sequel, however, geared more to the popular taste of the time, was a considerable diminution in literary quality.

In common with the stories of Lovecraft which were written in Brooklyn, a favourite device of Merritt's was to begin his stories or novels in a New York City setting the better to contrast it with the fantastic events to follow. Like Lovecraft, Merritt had a style which was immediately recognisable: a pseudopoetic style which seems quite beautiful at first but becomes ultimately cloying. It is a style much better suited to a dreamlike fantasy like *The Ship of Ishtar* than to a more realistic tale. *The Ship of Ishtar* may have inspired the writing of "The White Ship."[18] Other stories which conjure up Lovecraftian visions are *Through the Dragon Glass, The People of the Pit,* and *The Face in the Abyss,* although Merritt seems to have returned the compliment by imitating Lovecraft in a much later novel, *The Dwellers in the Mirage.*

When, in "Supernatural Horror in Literature," Lovecraft turns to relatively more modern British writers, he pauses only briefly to recognise the talents of Rudyard Kipling, Lafcadio Hearn, Oscar Wilde, M. P. Shiel, and Bram Stoker, none of whom would seem tó have had a great influence upon his works. However, the ending of Wilde's novel *The Picture of Dorian Gray,* commented upon by Lovecraft, must have "inspired" the quite similar ending of Machen's "Novel of the White Powder," a story which *did* influence Lovecraft's stories markedly; and Stoker's *Lair of the White Worm,* just a skeletal synopsis of a novel never fully developed, must have had some bearing upon "The Shunned House," as it deals with a "gigantic primitive entity that lurks in a vault beneath the ancient castle." M. P. Shiel's "House of Sounds," whose very title suggests some relationship with "The Music of Erich Zann," was a story greatly admired by Lovecraft. He wrote of it:

> It tells of a creeping horror and menace trickling down the centuries on a sub-arctic island off the coast of Norway; where, amidst the sweep of daemon winds and the ceaseless din of hellish waves and cataracts, a vengeful dead man built a brazen tower of terror.

Shiel's idea of a window looking out into the infinity of space was employed by Lovecraft not only in "The Music of Erich Zann" but also in "He" and in "The Dreams in the Witch House."

Then Lovecraft goes on to Francis Brett Young's novel *Cold Harbour,*

"in which an ancient house of strange malignancy is powerfully delineated"—a theme which was a favourite of Lovecraft's, possibly best por-
trayed in the crumbling houses which surrounded Innsmouth Harbour.

John Buchan's fantasies are little noted today, for he is best remembered for novels like *The 39 Steps.* The fantasies have marked flaws; for
instance, American readers are put off *Witch Wood* because of its abun-
dance of Scottish dialect. But the novel impressed Lovecraft, who wrote
of it that it "depicts with tremendous force a survival of the evil Sabbat
in a lonely district of Scotland" and who admired its "description of the
black forest with the evil stone, and . . . the terrible cosmic adumbrations
when the horror is finally extirpated," words which suggest some kinship
with the Mythos. Lovecraft was always fascinated by tales of African
witchcraft, like Buchan's "Green Wildebeeste" and, of course, any tale
of an "awakening of dead Britanno-Roman horrors," like Buchan's
"Wind in the Portico." Buchan's "Skule Skerry" impresses the reader
at first with its atmosphere that has "touches of sub-arctic fright," but
he is greatly put down by the ending, in which the "monster" is revealed
to be just a seal.

In his letters to me Lovecraft listed as the greatest modern fantaisistes
Blackwood, Machen, Dunsany, M. R. James, and Walter de la Mare—
to which list he later added Hodgson—but in "Supernatural Horror in
Literature" he rather scamped de la Mare's writings, devoting to them
just a single long paragraph. This was to do an injustice to de la Mare,
whose work can be shown to have influenced Lovecraft's writings to a
considerable extent. Possibly Lovecraft was somewhat put off by the
subtlety and occasional obscurity of de la Mare's style, which would
never have passed muster with Farnsworth Wright. De la Mare was much
more attuned to mainstream literature than the others on Lovecraft's
list, and, from the literary standpoint, possibly rates higher than they do,
albeit his fantasies *per se* are somewhat less noteworthy.

Lovecraft does not even mention such a masterpiece as de la Mare's
Memoirs of a Midget, which was not in his own line, and says of "The
Listeners," a poem which surpasses any of Lovecraft's, only that it
"restores the Gothic shudder to modern verse." De la Mare's poems and
tales for children, like *Broomsticks,* are dismissed as "sheer whimsical
phantasy of the Barrie order." (Sir James M. Barrie was quite capable of
chilling effects, as in his short play *Shall We Join the Ladies?*) That remarkable little tale of de la Mare's, "The Riddle," is passed over completely. Such effective *contes cruels* as "An Ideal Craftsman" and "In
the Forest" are not mentioned either.

What Lovecraft *does* mention are the indubitable masterpieces like the
novel *The Return,* in which "we see the soul of a dead man reach out of

its grave of two centuries and fasten itself upon the flesh of the living, so that even the face of the victim becomes that which long ago returned to dust" (the relationship here to both *The Case of Charles Dexter Ward* and "The Evil Clergyman" should be obvious); the much-anthologised vampire tale "Seaton's Aunt;" and "All-Hallows," one of the finest ghost-stories ever written, and a possible influence upon "The Haunter of the Dark." Lesser tales cited by Lovecraft include "The Tree" (a title also used by Lovecraft), "which tells of a frightful vegetable growth in the yard of a starving artist" (a hint perhaps of the weird vegetation of "The Colour out of Space," although the tree here is symbolic); "Out of the Deep," "wherein we are given leave to imagine what thing answered the summons of a dying wastrel in a dark lonely house when he pulled a long-feared bell-cord in the attic of his dread-haunted boyhood" ("The Outsider" springs to mind)[19]; "A Recluse," who is much like the sequestered old men of Lovecraft's own tales; and most especially "Mr. Kempe." The coincidence of their being two writers thousands of miles apart who are writing essentially the same story unbeknowst to one another is not a rarity in literary history. De la Mare managed to get *his* story published first, and Lovecraft read it apprehensively, but was relieved to discover that there were enough differences between it and "The Whisperer in Darkness" not to invalidate his own tale.

The late E. F. Benson, better known for his mainstream work, had several volumes of fantastic tales published, of which "Negotium Perambulans" is the most celebrated. But Lovecraft seems to have been more influenced by "The Man Who Went Too Far," which "breathes whisperingly of a house at the edge of a dark wood" (as in "The Whisperer in Darkness") "and of Pan's hoof-mark on the breast of a dead man," and by "The Horror-Horn," "through which lopes a terrible half-human survival dwelling on unvisited Alpine peaks." The latter story was perhaps the first tale to treat of the Abominable Snowman legend.

At this point in Lovecraft's treatise H. G. Wells and Sir Arthur Conan Doyle are mentioned somewhat tangentially again. However, Wells' *The Time Machine,* which goes into the grim far future much as "The Shadow out of Time" did, is not noted because of its science-fiction trimmings, nor is "In the Abyss," whose deep sea horrors certainly have a close relationship with Lovecraft's own tales of sea monsters. Some of Wells' early stories were fantasies rather than science-fiction and some of their themes were exploited by fantaisistes.

Conan Doyle, as has been mentioned before, had a decided influence upon Lovecraft's writings. His "Lot No. 249," with its revived mummy theme, is regrettably little known today; Derleth wanted to use it in one of his anthologies, but considered the permission fee too high. Lovecraft notes "The Captain of the Pole-Star," "a tale of arctic ghostliness," but ignores "The Maracot Deep," which has a theme similar to Wells' "In the Abyss." The Professor Challenger novels, even *The Lost World,* surprisingly get no notice here, although the professor himself is much like Lovecraft's own academicians. The Conan Doyle influence sifted down into Edgar Rice Burroughs' novels, so it is a moot point as to whose influence was the more predominant upon Lovecraft.

Other writers cited by Lovecraft here include E. M. Forster, whose "Story of a Panic" is similar to Machen's "Great God Pan," although of course a science-fiction masterpiece as "The Machine Stops" receives no mention; John Metcalfe, the atmosphere of whose "Bad Lands" is marvellously evocative; Sir Hugh Walpole, whose *Old Ladies* influenced Derleth much more than it did Lovecraft—just as Bradbury's *forte* is malevolent children, Walpole specialised in evil old women; and May Sinclair, reproved by Lovecraft for her dependence upon occultism.

Before he came to the evaluation of Machen's works Lovecraft permitted himself a little breather, mentioning casually Joseph Conrad (whose masterpiece *The Heart of Darkness* was ignored) and some of the Irish writers. One would have expected far more space to have been devoted to William Butler Yeats, whom Lovecraft considered the greatest living poet and who was also the author of some poetic and haunting plays.

The influence of Arthur Machen has perhaps been overstressed by Lovecraft's commentators. His most famous story, but hardly his best one, was "The Great God Pan." Victorian readers were scandalised that a writer could write so beautifully of such vile things. One is amused today by the prudish distaste Dorothy Scarborough, in her study *The Supernatural in Modern English Fiction,* displayed for the story; obviously she considered it inexcusable. Machen, a rather naive former actor, was absolutely fascinated by the thought of depravity; a *voyeur* only in spirit, he welcomed the assignment of translating the *Memoirs of Casanova,* even though he had little command of Italian and depended largely upon dictionaries.[20] Just as "The Hound" hinted at orgies Lovecraft would have been hard-pressed to describe in detail (a film like *Behind the Green Door* would have nauseated Lovecraft completely), "The Great God Pan" describes with sophomoric relish the adventures of Helen Vaughan. Lovecraft's account of those adventures is unconsciously hilarious: she "is finally discovered to be a frequenter of the lowest dens of vice in London, where even the most callous degenerates are shocked at her enormities."

"The Great God Pan" had a theme which was almost an obsession with Machen, for he returned to it again in both "The White People" and "The Novel of the Black Seal." A young woman is subjected to brain surgery and becomes an idiot in consequence, dying a year later. But before she dies she gives birth to a child, Helen Vaughan, who had "no mortal father"—she is the daughter of the Great God Pan. The story is vitiated by its melodramatic content and absurd coincidences; so Machen tried to improve upon it in "The White People." The latter story was Lovecraft's favourite of all Machen's tales, but it has never been very popular, for it is overlong and nothing much ever seems to happen in it.

That seeming eventlessness, however, is an illusion, as the tale is very subtly told. As Lovecraft noted, its "central portion purports to be the diary or notes of a little girl whose nurse has introduced her to some of the forbidden magic and soul-blasting traditions of the noxious witch-cult." The story remained unique in literature until Shirley Jackson used a similar technique in her novel *We Have Always Lived in the Castle* and Robert Aickman penned "Pages from a Young Girl's Journal," in which the young diarist is gradually introduced to vampirism. The ending of "The White People" is so subtle that its significance is still a matter of dispute amongst readers; according to Lovecraft's version, the 13-year-old child is impregnated by Pan, "but she poisons herself in time."

Machen's obsessive theme becomes much more explicit in "The Novel of the Black Seal," one of the episodes of a curious hybrid novel entitled *The Three Imposters.* Here we have "a strange idiot son born to a rural mother after a fright in which her inmost faculties are shaken"—which was, of course, the inspiration for the quite similar episode in "The Dunwich Horror" in which the serving wench gives birth to the two monstrous Whateleys. (The father, of course, is not Pan but Yog-Sothoth.)

It is easy to demonstrate that "The Novel of the Black Seal," although not one of Machen's best tales, was the genesis of Lovecraft's own Mythos. To most people, the "Little People" of Gaelic mythology—the leprechauns and the fairies and the like—are merely creatures of whimsy, and are treated as such in films; but Machen imbued them with the most frightening hideousness, and it is ironic that they were transmuted in Lovecraft's mythology into a pantheon of gigantic gods. Lovecraft's description of the ending of the tale could be applied to almost any of his own Mythos stories.

> Professor Gregg knew the stark frenzy of cosmic panic in its darkest form. He knew the abysmal gulfs of abnormality that he had opened, and went forth into the wild hills prepared and resigned. He would meet the unthinkable "Little People"—and his document ends with a rational observation: "If

unhappily I do not return from my journey, there is no need to conjure up
here a picture of the awfulness of my fate.''

One suspects that a psychoanalyst might say that Machen's obsession
with the "Little People" smacked of paranoia; and, indeed, another portion of *The Three Imposters,* "The Novel of the White Powder," has
frequently been called "a masturbatory fantasy," which surely demeans
the tale. Its ending has been "borrowed" by a great many writers since,
even by Lovecraft in "Cool Air" and "The Thing on the Doorstep."
Almost all the elements of the story have reappeared in Lovecraft's own
tales. In it the quite innocent protagonist, "nervously worn out by seclusion and overwork," goes to have the prescription for a sedative filled;
but the careless apothecary has let his drugs stand on his shelves too long,
so that the substance given the young man has been changed into the
vinum sabbati, the powder used during the orgies of the Witches' Sabbat
to effect startling transformations. The protagonist seems at first to have
benefitted from the drug, but gradually he realises that he is changing
horribly. "Servants report that food left at the locked door is no longer
touched." At the conclusion of the tale the doctor breaks down the door
and what he sees lying upon the floor makes him "strike again and again
with an iron bar at the blasphemous semi-living thing he finds there."
"The Novel of the White Powder" is one of Machen's best known tales,
but he seems to have taken the effect of the drug from Stevenson's *Dr.
Jekyll and Mr. Hyde.*

Machen returned to the "Little People" in minor tales like "The Red
Hand" and "The Shining Pyramid." Another exceedingly minor tale
was "The Bowmen," a story which received such wide circulation during
World War I that many people are still convinced of the "truth" of the
legend. But Machen is best remembered for the extraordinary beauty of
his style, which Lovecraft never hoped to emulate, and for his largely
autobiographical novel *The Hill of Dreams,* which had only one chapter,
which gave the book its title, which was fantastic. Lovecraft apparently
was not influenced by an excellent novella of Machen's, *The Terror,*
although it inspired a number of stories and films in which birds and
animals rebel against mankind.

Lovecraft's commentators tend to forget that he ranked Algernon
Blackwood even higher as a fantaisiste than Machen:

Less intense than Mr. Machen in delineating the extremes of stark fear, yet
infinitely more closely wedded to the idea of an unreal world constantly pressing upon ours is the inspired and prolific Algernon Blackwood, amidst whose
voluminous and uneven work may be found some of the finest spectral literature of this or any age. . . . Of the quality of Mr. Blackwood's genius there can
be no dispute; for no one has even approached the skill, seriousness, and

minute fidelity with which he records the overtones of strangeness in ordinary things and experiences, or the preternatural insight with which he builds up detail by detail the complete sensations and perceptions leading from reality into supernormal life or vision. . . . He is the one absolute and unquestioned master of weird atmosphere.

As atmosphere is precisely what is most notable about Lovecraft's own fiction, it is evident that a close examination of Blackwood's stories would well repay Lovecraft's critics. Blackwood's influence upon Lovecraft is not so plangently obvious as that of Machen, and among Blackwood's stories it is rather difficult to put one's finger upon stories linked with Lovecraft's own, although "The Willows," which Lovecraft considered the greatest weird tale ever written, is clearly related to "The Colour out of Space." Part of the trouble in tracing Blackwood's influence upon Lovecraft resides in the fact that his finest collection, *Incredible Adventures,* is exceedingly hard to obtain today. Lovecraft lent me his own copy, and I recall with especial vividness such stories as "A Descent into Egypt" (which may have laid the framework for Lovecraft's own subterranean tales) and "The Regeneration of Lord Ernie." Most of Blackwood's readers today know him principally through *John Silence, Physician Extraordinary,* tales of a "psychic detective," which, though splendid enough in their way (and "Ancient Sorceries" is much more than just "splendid"), are not usually to be considered among his best writings. The anthologists have contented themselves usually with minor examples of Blackwood's work, and such a collection as *The Doll and One Other,* which Arkham House circulated, was clearly just a product of his tired old age.

Blackwood had his faults, of which a rather graceless prose style, repetitiousness, and too firm an adherence to occultism are most apparent; and some of his ghost stories, like "Keeping His Promise" and "A Woman's Ghost Story," are quite ordinary. However, "The Wendigo" ranks perhaps second among his tales, and was an influence upon Lovecraft but much more so upon Derleth; and in his treatise Lovecraft also singles out such remarkable works as "An Episode in a Lodging House," in which "we behold frightful presences summoned out of black space by a sorcerer" and "The Listener," which "tells of the awful psychic residuum creeping about an old house where a leper died," a tale perhaps related to "The House and the Brain." Such almost forgotten novels as *Jimbo* and *The Centaur* are dream-like in substance and may have had some bearing upon the writing of Lovecraft's own dream tales.

Of the three writers Lovecraft sought most to emulate—Poe, Machen, and Dunsany—he was least successful in imitating Edward John Moreton Drax Plunkett, the eighteenth Baron Dunsany. Unlike Poe or

Machen, or Lovecraft himself, Lord Dunsany was a man of the world, a veteran of the wars, born to the aristocracy. Unlike Poe or Machen, he was well aware of the motivations of people; Lovecraft observes in "Supernatural Horror in Literature" that "humour and irony, too, are often present to impart a gentle cynicism." Some of Dunsany's works are very close to mainstream literature.

Lovecraft seems to have understood Dunsany much less than he did either Poe or Machen; in "Supernatural Horror in Literature" he over-stresses some of Dunsany's qualities and underestimates others. For instance, he writes:

> Inventor of a new mythology and weaver of surprising folklore, Lord Dunsany stands dedicated to a strange world of fantastic beauty, and pledged to eternal warfare against the coarseness and ugliness of diurnal reality. His point of view is the most truly cosmic of any held in the literature of any period.

Surely Lovecraft is overstating the case for Dunsany here.

Conversely, Lovecraft seems rather blind to Dunsany's strong points. He writes of his "simple lyric style based on the prose of the King James Bible," which conveys little or nothing of Dunsany's verbal magic, of which Lovecraft himself possessed very little. He notes, rather imperceptibly, that "beauty rather than terror is the keynote of Dunsany's work." Beauty in itself soon becomes cloying—a woman who possesses great beauty and little else is soon recognised to be dull; Dunsany was very careful to impart an underlying sense of terror to his tales and plays, and some of the things which happen in them, as in "Two Bottles of Relish" and *The Gods of the Mountain* and *A Night at an Inn,* are very nasty indeed.

One suspects rather that it was the dream-like quality of Dunsany's works, their sense of far times and places, which enchanted Lovecraft most, and which he sought to copy in his own tales. Some of the works of Lord Dunsany which apparently influenced Lovecraft have already been mentioned in the earlier part of this essay. "In *The Laughter of the Gods* there is a domed city at the jungle's edge, and a ghostly lutanist heard only by those about to die," Lovecraft wrote (perhaps a suggestion of "The Music of Erich Zann"). Another play, *The Queen's Enemies,* would seem to have been the inspiration for Tennessee Williams' only story for *Weird Tales,* but *A Night at an Inn,* in which there are jewel thieves, may be related to "The Terrible Old Man."

The final writer treated in "Supernatural Horror in Literature," Montague Rhodes James, who specialised in ghost stories, apparently had only a peripheral influence upon Lovecraft, although elements of some of the tales were very much to Lovecraft's liking. He may have drawn upon the hideous "Count Magnus" for his dread ancestor in *The Case of Charles Dexter Ward;* the "curious toad-like carving" in "The Treasure of Abbot Thomas" evokes memories of "The Moon-Bog;" and surely the spectral cathedral to be encountered in "The Stalls of Barchester Cathedral" and "An Episode of Cathedral History" are very like the old churches in Lovecraft's own tales, especially the one in "The Haunter of the Dark."

"Supernatural Horror in Literature" ends a bit abruptly, as if Lovecraft had wearied of his self-imposed assignment, and it does not include many other writers who, if one is to judge by his letters, must have provided some fictional inspiration. The (mostly) nonfictional writer Charles Fort, in a series of books which list some very curious natural phenomena, suggested eventually that we are perhaps just the "property" of extraterrestrials, a theme which of course plays a large part in the Mythos. Lovecraft used just such phenomena to build up the atmosphere of some of his tales like "The Colour out of Space" and "The Whisperer in Darkness."

Marcel Proust, of course, was not a fantaisiste, but in one of his letters to me Lovecraft remarked that no other writer understood the nature of time and the changes it brings so well as Proust did; and time was a theme which fascinated Lovecraft endlessly, as can be seen in "The Shadow out of Time" and many other stories.

Franz Kafka gets no mention whatsoever in "Supernatural Horror in Literature," yet he employed themes very similar to Lovecraft's: the hideous transformation and sense of alienation of the protagonist of *The Metamorphosis;* the feeling of helpless buffeting and the incomprehensibility of the horror of a malign universe displayed in *The Trial* and *The Castle;* the cruelty which was just routine for the Inquisitor in *In a Penal Colony;* the bewilderment of a "promised land" turned sour in *Amerika.* It may well be, of course, that Lovecraft was put off a bit by the religious symbolism implicit in Kafka's work, its suggestion that the individual *is* important, after all, that he should *not* be just a cosmic plaything. Yet Kafka's characters come to ends just as horrifying in their own way as any of Lovecraft's.

Sir Richard Burton, who died the year Lovecraft was born, was an influence completely overlooked by Lovecraft's commentators. It was his translation of the *Arabian Nights,* discovered in his grandfather's library, which first turned the enchanted child in the direction of fantasy. Several times in the course of our correspondence Lovecraft urged me to read Burton's great travel book, *Arabia Deserta,* a book which may well have influenced the writing of stories like *The Dream-Quest of Unknown Kadath.*

Science-fiction was outside the scope of Lovecraft's treatise, and consequently receives very little mention therein; but surely the basic themes of science-fiction, the reachings out into time and space, had very much to do with the body of his work. Poe was one of the pioneers in the *genre*, and his influence upon *At the Mountains of Madness* has been noted. I have not read Jules Verne's sequel to Poe's *Arthur Pym, The Sphinx of the Ice-Fields,* and so do not know if Lovecraft employed any of Verne's ideas in his own sequel to the work. Lovecraft rightly condemned the usual run of science-fiction of his day, but it would seem that the staggeringly cosmic conceptions of W. Olaf Stapledon's novels like *Last and First Men* and *Starmaker* would not have been lost upon him. At the time of Lovecraft's death the science-fiction writers were just beginning to exploit Fortean themes. J. D. Beresford, Stapledon, and A. E. Van Vogt all explored the concept of the supernormal man harried by a hostile environment, a theme also adumbrated by "Beyond the Wall of Sleep." So many of Lovecraft's tales touched upon themes to be found in science-fiction that Sam Moskowitz quite mistakenly classified Lovecraft as primarily a science-fiction writer!

Despite his copious borrowings from other writers, Lovecraft's literary world was very much of his own making. The derivative plot elements are really a minor consideration; one reads Lovecraft much more for mood and atmosphere than for his sometimes transparent plots. Just as we recognise that Shakespeare took his themes from other sources, so in spite of some hackneyed literary devices we soon find ourselves falling under Lovecraft's spell.

One wishes, however, that Lovecraft had not taken so many bad writers as literary models. As this essay has attempted to suggest, very few of the writers who influenced him decidedly were first-rate from the highest literary standards; their limitations tend to be repeated in Lovecraft's tales.

Notes

1. Cf. Lovecraft to Elizabeth Toldridge, 8 March 1929; in *Collected Works,* VI, p. 315.—S.T.J.
2. Cf. W. T. Scott's "His Own Most Fantastic Creation," in *Exiles and Fabrications,* p. 60.—S.T.J.
3. Cf. Lovecraft to Alfred Galpin, 26 January 1918; in *Collected Works,* V, pp. 54-55.—S.T.J.
4. "Beyond the Wall of Sleep" is not usually classified as "Dunsanian," and may be so only in its incorporation of dreams, a technique used often in Dunsany.—S.T.J.
5. *Collected Works,* III, p. 381.—S.T.J.
6. Cf. Shea's "H. P. Lovecraft: The House and the Shadows," p. 91.—S.T.J.

7. While the borrowings from these two tales by Poe are in terms of plot and theme, the stylistic impetus for "The Outsider" seems to have been "Berenice": the opening paragraphs of the two tales reveal startling similarities in phraseology.—S.T.J.
8. *Collected Works,* III, p. 367.—S.T.J.
9. *Ibid.,* pp. 367-68.—S.T.J.
10. Baudelaire is also quoted as the epigraph for "Hypnos;" cf. *Collected Works,* III, p. 160.—S.T.J.
11. In a letter to the editor of *Weird Tales,* published in the issue for March 1924.—S.T.J.
12. *Collected Works,* III, pp. 373-74.—S.T.J.
13. *Ibid.,* p. 380.—S.T.J.
14. Actually Lovecraft, on the few times that he mentions Hastur, does not even declare that it is an entity; cf. note 13 to Mosig's "H. P. Lovecraft: Myth-Maker."—S.T.J.
15. Cf. *Collected Works,* VIII, p. 242.—S.T.J.
16. The editor of *Weird Tales* from 1924 to 1940.
17. Cf. William Fulwiler's "E.R.B. and H.P.L.," *ERB-dom,* 80 (February 1975), 41, 44.—S.T.J.
18. It is unlikely that Lovecraft read *The Ship of Ishtar* so early as 1919, the time of the writing of "The White Ship."—S.T.J.
19. But Lovecraft did not read de la Mare until 1926, by which time "The Outsider" had long been written.—S.T.J.
20. Casanova's memoirs were written in French.—S.T.J.

THROUGH HYPERSPACE WITH BROWN JENKIN

Lovecraft's Contribution to Speculative Fiction

By Fritz Leiber, Jr

In the following article Fritz Leiber (1910–   ) has written a compre-hensive study of Lovecraft's work in the field of science-fiction; especially relevant are his appraisals of "The Whisperer in Darkness," "The Col-our out of Space," and "The Dreams in the Witch House." The con-cluding section, however, where Leiber outlines the history of the solar system as expressed in Lovecraft's tales, curiously parallels Lin Carter's earler article, "HPL: The History" (1950). Like Poe, Lovecraft's posi-tion in the history of science-fiction is important, though it is doubtful whether he wrote "science-fiction" itself.

Beginning with "The Call of Cthulhu" and "The Colour out of Space," speculative science played a larger part in Lovecraft's fiction: hibernating races and travel through space, hyperspace, and time. That those two tales were written very soon after *Amazing Stories* was found-ed in 1926 and the second published in that magazine is at least sug-gestive.

Amazing Stories began with reprints of Wells and Verne, giving hopes of at least a moderately high literary level—hopes largely dashed, which may account for Lovecraft veering away from that market after his first sale.

In more than half his subsequent fiction, however, monsters raised by black magic and thwarted by white are replaced by extraterrestrial or even extracosmical beings who sojourned on earth in the past and may secretly reside among us today. The *Necronomicon* largely ceases to be used for its spells of exorcism, but remains a sourcebook on the habits and history of these more realistic monsters.

True, Lovecraft said in "Some Notes on a Nonentity," "I doubt if I could ever succeed well in the ordinary kind of science fiction,"[1] while in "Some Notes on Interplanetary Fiction" he gloriously lambasted "dime-novel theatricalism," "stock romance," and such cliches as "over-facile language-learning . . . weddings with beautiful anthropomorphic princesses . . . stereotyped Armageddons with ray-guns and space-ships . . . court intrigues and jealous magicians . . . hairy ape-men of the polar caps,"[2] and advised writers to concentrate on describing realistically, thoughtfully, and with emotional power and proper awe the take-off from earth, the trip through space, and the landing on the strange planet.

Here clearly Lovecraft is excoriating Buck Rogers, the Martian novels of Edgar Rice Burroughs, and similar extravaganzas; the *Weird Tales* stories which Farnsworth Wright described with wonderful precision as pseudoscientific or weird-scientific (electric space-ships leaping about the cosmos, battles of anthropomorphised angels and devils, carnivorous plants, murderous scientists, grey fungoid plagues, mysterious serums from tropic blooms, giant spiders); and the magazine speculative fiction of what Isaac Asimov called the Gernsback Era (1926-1938)—stories fairly long on science but fairly short on all literary qualities and further enfeebled by Gernsback's idealistic dictum that "scientifiction" should be sugar-coated science education.

When stories of any literary merit appeared, he was quick to recognise them. He said of the tales of Stanley G. Weinbaum, "I saw with pleasure that someone had at last escaped the sickening hackneyedness in which 99.99% of all pulp interplanetary stuff is engulfed. Here, I rejoiced, was somebody who could think of another planet in terms of something besides anthropomorphic kings and beautiful princesses . . . etc."

Lovecraft also asserted, "Social and political satire are always undesirable."[3] Here perhaps even more clearly he seems to be thinking of the crude anti-religious element in Burroughs and perhaps of such books as Bellamy's *Looking Backward* and Jack London's *The Iron Heel.* He could hardly be referring to *Gulliver's Travels* or to such novels by H. G. Wells as *The First Men in the Moon,* or to Olaf Stapledon's *Last and First Men.*

The fact is that Lovecraft barely but completely missed the beginning in America and the rekindling in Britain of literate speculative fiction. He died in 1937. In that year was published William Sloane's *To Walk the Night,* a novel written in a lively but solid modern style and with almost excessive restraint about the sojourn of an extraterrestrial being on earth—and which also arouses a quite Lovecraftian mood of awe, puzzlement, and cosmic dread. In the same year Karel Capek's *War with the Newts* was published in an English translation. Still farther in the future lay C. S. Lewis' *Malacandra* (or *Out of the Silent Planet*), an interplanetary novel which reads as if it had been written to satisfy Lovecraft's criteria. Literate writers like Robert Heinlein, Norman Knight, Don Stuart, Isaac Asimov, and Lovecraft's protegé Henry Kuttner were still to appear in *Astounding Stories* and that magazine under the editorship of John Campbell to begin to work toward the research realism in speculative writing which Lovecraft desired. While it would be a decade or two before the publication of such outstanding novels of speculative fiction as Edgar Pangborn's *A Mirror for Observers,* Theodore Sturgeon's *More Than Human,* Arthur Clarke's *Childhood's End,* Philip Dick's *The Man in the High Castle,* Kurt Vonnegut's *Cat's Cradle,* John Hersey's *The Child Buyer,* Philip Wylie's *The Disappearance,* Gore Vidal's *Messiah,* Ward Moore's *Greener Than You Think* and *Bring the Jubilee,* Judith Merril's *Shadow on the Hearth* and *The Tomorrow People,* Ray Bradbury's *Fahrenheit 451,* George Orwell's *1984,* Frederick Pohl's and Cyril Kornbluth's *The Space Merchants,* Frank Herbert's *The Dragon in the Sea,* Herbert Best's *The 25th Hour,* Clifford Simak's *Way Station,* Robert Heinlein's *Beyond This Horizon,* Hal Clement's *Mission of Gravity,* James Blish's *A Case of Conscience,* and Robert Graves' *Watch the North Wind Rise* (in England *Seven Days in New Crete*).

But during the very Gernsback era he detested, Lovecraft made his own contribution to speculative fiction, in addition to the critical item already noted. Both worked, along a horror story side track, toward the maturation of the field.

These contributions were largely in the direction of paying proper attention to cosmology, astronomy, and geology and to impressing on the reader the vast size and duration of the cosmos. Lovecraft's extraterrestrials were never stock humanoid figures (such as the appealing yet ridiculous oviparous princesses of Burroughs' Mars), but beings with a wholly nonhuman morphology and biology, and with languages, architectures, industries, and cultures wholly their own.

Lovecraft did his best to get writers to stop using obvious English roots in devising the names of earth-aliens—"Tarko," say, or "Akor"—and instead try to imagine nonhuman sounds and then render them phonetically. While some of his biological creations are masterful feats of imagination: the appearance of a specimen of the Old Ones, as described by Lake in *At the Mountains of Madness,* is chillingly real—if the reader will make the effort to visualise the being as described in dry scientific language. If Lovecraft had been able and willing to put such a being *into action* in one of his tales, he would doubtless have won many new readers. But for reasons in part aesthetic he never took this step. Perhaps he was tempted to and his hesitation fully to abandon supernatural horror for less restrictive speculative fiction was one of the reasons for his creative slow-down during his last years.

Certainly Lovecraft helped lead the way toward greater realism in subsequent speculative fiction.

It must be admitted, however, that Lovecraft devoted very little attention to novel inventions, to scientific speculations for their own sake, and to extrapolations from present-day society into the future—aside from a general conviction that human affairs would get worse, at least from the viewpoint of a lover of traditions and of social stability. After all, his chief artistic interest was in creating backgrounds for horror stories; graveyards and homely ghosts were losing interest, while cosmic outsideness was gaining, and in one way he simply followed this trend—to the point of seeing both *At the Mountains of Madness* and "The Shadow out of Time" published in *Astounding Stories.*

However, what scientific speculations the Old Gentleman did make were very clever indeed and most of them were carefully researched. His scientists and their paraphernalia—their personalities and mannerisms and daily professional work—were convincingly presented; Lovecraft was always good on the scholarly type.

Moreover, in his cosmic speculations Lovecraft was following not only an outward trend, but a deep inward passion, as shown by a statement he makes in a latter to Clark Ashton Smith (17 Oct. 1930): "The true function of phantasy is to give the imagination a ground for limitless expansion, and to satisfy aesthetically the sincere and burning curiosity and sense of awe which a sensitive minority of mankind feel toward the alluring and provocative abysses of unplumbed space and unguessed entity which press in upon the known world from unknown infinities and in unknown relationships of time, space, matter, force, dimensionality, and consciousness. I *know* that my most poignant emotional experiences are those which concern the lure of unplumbed space, the terror of the encroaching outer void, and the struggle to transcend the known and established order."[4]

Hibernating Races: Cthulhu's "House at R'lyeh" is really a sort of time-capsule—a sunken city whose extraterrestrial inhabitants are held in suspended animation until the city appears again above the surface of the sea. The full functioning of the beings also depends on the stars "being right," when they can plunge from planet to planet and exercise other tremendous powers. Cthulhu himself is a shape-changer: he can rearrange his molecules into their original pattern, when they have been disrupted, and surely this would make it easier for him to space-travel. The architecture of R'lyeh suggests that its builders had a knowledge, working rather than theoretical, of non-Euclidean geometries.

Also in "The Call of Cthulhu" the background of professional archaeology and anthropology is most authentically presented, particularly at an imagined meeting of the American Archaeological Society in 1908.

Space-travel: the Plutonian beings or Mi-Go in "The Whisperer in Darkness" are able to fly through space "on clumsy, powerful wings which have a way of resisting the ether."[5] This notion was good speculative fiction back in the 1920's when the ether was still a fringe-fashionable science concept, and today the notion of sailing or perhaps even winging through space is back in speculative style again, light pressure taking the place of ether. A very patient sailor could even tack in from Pluto on these photonic winds, braving storms in the solar plasma, and perhaps find tail winds in one of the hydrogen bands streaming through the cosmos or in some steady gust of cosmic wavicles.[6] Had he lived, we can be sure that Lovecraft would have made great use of the new astronomy in his fiction; World War Two, culminating in its world-changing discoveries in atomics and rocketry, would have worked at least as powerfully on him as it did on other imaginative writers.

Most of Lovecraft's monsters were equipped to live indefinitely in the thinness of space: by having extremely tough tissues, by suspended animation, or by having shape-changing powers like Cthulhu and perhaps travelling between planets and stars as a cloud of independent molecules, like Stapledon's Martians. If an animal were tough as a space-ship, there's no reason he mightn't be able to travel as efficiently as one—he could carry his fuel like a camel carries his water.

"The Whisperer" also has the charmingly friendly touch of the Mi-Go carrying about with them through space in small canisters—tucked under their wings or clutched in their maternal pincers—the living brains of beings so unfortunate as not to be able to travel space embodied. In the story this is effectively presented as a horror, but on second thought such immortality has great appeal.

The folklore and anthropology background of "The Whisperer" is well handled. The authors Akeley lists to prove his competence in those fields are a nice selection.[7]

The centipedal beings which Lovecraft devised to provide a rationale for the round-robin story "The Challenge from Beyond" broadcast by rocket throughout the galaxy small encapsulated send-receive telepathy stations which enable them to exchange minds with any being who finds one of the stations and starts to listen in. It is noteworthy that it was Lovecraft who provided the scientifically plausible explanation in this story rather than any other of the authors: C. L. Moore, A. Merritt, Robert E. Howard, and Frank Belknap Long. The same method of space-travel by exchange of minds is used in "The Thing on the Doorstep," but for shorter trips.

The beings in "The Colour out of Space"—it is a moot point whether these were intelligent—travelled by meteorite imbedded in an unidentifiable plastic element or compound—". . . a piece of the great outside . . . dowered with outside properties. . . ."[8] The beings arrive in the form of or inside small brittle strangely coloured spheres about as big as baseballs—a spore or seed is suggested—and take off at the story's end in a more active flame-like corruscating form, as if naturally equipped with anti-gravity and an ionic drive.

The colour itself in this story—the colour of the brittle spheres, later that of the corruscations—at first seems impossible, since colour is something in the brain's coding system rather than anything inherent in outside objects. But Lovecraft says, "It was only by analogy that they called it a colour at all."[9] It is possible to think of textures, layered transparencies, and the like that would be completely novel on earth and give novel visual effects. However, the same colour turns up in the spectroscope when the unidentifiable material of the meteorite is analysed—and this is harder to understand.

As Edmund Wilson pointed out in his *New Yorker* article, this remarkably gripping story (which gave me the gloomy creeps for weeks as a kid, when it turned up as a dark intruder in *Amazing*) describes phenomena rather remarkably like the effects of atomic radiation: mutations, morphological peculiarities in the newborn or newly budded, and the deadliest radiation sickness. Also, the corruscations given off by the beings about to depart from earth are very like those given off by the strange radioactive substance in Stewart Edward White's and Samuel Hopkins Adams' gripping early science-adventure novel *The Mystery*. In both cases showers of sparks are mentioned and much is made of the resemblance to St Elmo's Fire.

Hyperspace-Travel: This may occur in "The Dunwich Horror," though that richly textured story is more an extrapolation from black magic and Arthur Machen than from science; at any rate the monsters walk "Not in the spaces we know, but *between* them"[10]—which suggests interpenetrating universes and makes us think with a shiver about the immense amount of empty space in even the solidest substance. Here an extreme form of the impossible hybrid between species is the main subject-matter: the offspring of woman and horrendous, emphatically extraterrestrial monster. Also the huge extraterrestrials (or extracosmicals!) in "The Dunwich Horror" have a fascinating morphology: they are made of gigantic tissue-ropes that interweave and slide against each other—living knots bigger than barns.

From "The Dunwich Horror" and his other later stories it can be argued that Lovecraft was a transition-writer between horror fiction and speculative fiction and that he did all the hard, thankless work transition-writers do (*cf.* the transition-writers between the stories observing all sexual taboos and the stories observing none) and that his stories suffered from the same unavoidable defects.

But "The Dreams in the Witch House" is Lovecraft's most carefully worked out story of hyperspace-travel. Here (1) a rational foundation for such travel is set up; (2) hyperspace is visualised; and (3) a trigger for such travel is devised.

(1) Our three-dimensional continuum is embedded in a four-dimensional continuum (another name for hyperspace) in such a freakishly convoluted way that it is possible to travel in seconds through hyperspace to points many light-millennia distant in normal space—and also to other continua, in some of which time does not exist, so that one does not age there.

By travelling hyperspace one can escape from any prison, enter and leave all manner of locked rooms.

An old Salem witch, Keziah Mason, and her rat-bodied, man-headed and man-handed familiar Brown Jenkin mastered hyperspace-travel as early as 1692 and used it to keep the Witch Cult alive in Arkham down to 1932, hiding out in a centuries-boarded-up attic in Arkham and in other witch-holes dotted about this cosmos and other universes. They tempt Walter Gilman, a brilliant young student of mathematics at Miskatonic University, to join the Witch Cult and finally doom himself in episodes of hyperspace-travel which he keeps trying to explain rationally as dreams.

These hyperspace trips take Gilman to points as close as the boarded-up attic just above the ceiling of his rented room in the Witch House and as distant as other planets and even "the throne of Azathoth at the centre of ultimate chaos."[11] One touch is amazingly fine: after one night visiting the planet of a star in the constellation Hydra, Gilman next day finds himself psychologically attracted to that point in Hydra as it moves under the earth, rises in the southeast about midday, and slowly mounts the sky—until the compulsion which had begun as an impulse to stare at a spot on the floor turns into an urge to leap mystically upward, a marvellously realistic linkage between man and cosmos. Certainly the boy who in his early teens hectographed *The Rhode Island Journal of Astronomy* made excellent use in his fiction of the astronomical knowledge he piled up.

(2) Lovecraft makes a bold attempt to describe what hyperspace looks like and how it strikes the other senses as Gilman travels through it with

Keziah Mason and Brown Jenkin. It looks, in brief, like the wildest of modernistic art and sounds like pandemonium; everything is "marvellously transmuted and obliquely projected." In hyperspace Keziah Mason appears as a "rather large congeries of iridescent, prolately spheroidal bubbles," while Brown Jenkin takes the form of "a very much smaller polyhedron of unknown colours and rapidly shifting surface angles."[12] There's a resourceful little rat-man for you!

Logical purists and other spoil-sports may object at this point that three-dimensional eyes can't see the fourth dimension and that it's silly to try to visualise hyperspace; all you can do is write mathematical formulae describing it. But what the deuce!—Bohr picturing the atom as a tiny solar system stimulated tens of thousands of imaginations, even if we're now told this attempt was naive. One of the finest things speculative fiction can do is try to picture "the unpicturable;" some analogies are remarkably suggestive and great notions may turn up in this way.

(3) The trigger or secret of hyperspace travel in "The Dreams in the Witch House" is advanced mathematical knowledge intuitively applied —you simple think yourself into hyperspace, hyper-travel a bit, and then . . . Hey, Presto! . . . think yourself out again. You see a direction others can't see. Gilman is first helped to see this direction by the strange angles of the walls and ceilings of his rented room; later, on a weird high-gravity planet Keziah and Brown Jenkin point two arms and a forepaw in directions which determine a vector along which Gilman moves to get back into hyperspace. True, three vectors in three-dimensional space add up to only one more vector. Still, there might be another answer—two and two make twenty-two as well as four—and at the least we have here a fine recreation of early twentieth-century reactions to the news that there is a fourth dimension: the wistful desire to be inspired to "see" that direction in three-dimensional space.

This "secret of hyperspace travel" is on first acquaintance something of a whopper—hard to swallow—yet to have used machinery would have weighted down Lovecraft's story unbearably, especially since Keziah had to be flitting in and out of hyperspace back in 1692. Yet the more one considers it, the more one finds something very neat, even elegant, about making hyperspace-travel one more form of psionic power or telekinesis: hyper-levitation! As a matter of fact, Selena, the beautiful mysterious intruder in Sloane's *To Walk the Night,* uses advanced mathematics and extrasensory perception to time-travel. In the same respect Keziah Mason is the speculative ancestress of Barbara Haggerswell in Moore's *Bring the Jubilee* and Lucy Fisher in Simak's *Way Station.* The romantically minded may think of her as Robert Graves' Triple Goddess in her hag persona.

Time Travel, generally achieved by personality-exchange between things as much as a billion years apart, is exploited richly and detailedly in "The Shadow out of Time," a work so often reprinted and discussed that anything said about it will tend to cover old ground. But once again —and also in *At the Mountains of Madness*—Lovecraft does the scientists and science-references very well: palaeontology, anthropology, psychology, biology, geology, even engineering.

In both *At the Mountains of Madness* and "The Shadow out of Time" it is clear that Lovecraft has become deeply interested in picturing in detail the careers of galactic races and the future history of mankind; that, although still holding onto the supernatural-horror pattern in his stories, he was trending more and more in the direction of creativity like Olaf Stapledon's. The extraterrestrials are the real heroes of these long stories. Their unending struggles for survival and to increase their store of knowledge, their wise, rational, enlightened, and even "humane" cultures, are Lovecraft's finest vision of mind embattled against space and time. Between the two stories he devotes at least 10,000 words to such matters, apart from wordage spent on biological descriptions, architectural visionings of their cities, and the adventures of the human protagonists in those eldritch metropolises.

By collating these two short novels, one can discover an imagined history of the earth, not altogether unlike Robert Heinlein's "future history," though on a much vaster scale and concerned mostly with the past. Lovecraft appeared to set some store by it, as he worked into it both the octopoid Cthulhu creatures and the Mi-Go of "The Whisperer in Darkness," though neither of these races figure actively in the two tales.

A little after the material of the moon was wrenched from the South Pacific and before the continents had begun to separate and drift away from their Antarctic area of origin and before there was any life on earth —in short, in Azoic times, perhaps a billion and a half years ago—the star-headed, barrel-bodied Old Ones came flying through the ether, each on his five membranous wings, after the fashion of the Mi-Go. They built cities both on land and under the sea, being vastly adaptable. They created earth life for food, allowing some to evolve unsupervised—the plants and animals we know. They also created hypnotically-controlled protoplasmic masses which were their chief machines. These shoggoths eventually evolved mental powers which made them extremely dangerous to their creators. (Here we begin to see Lovecraft's own evolving sympathy for his monsters: by and large he is for the Old Ones and against the shoggoths.)

The continents begin their long drifts. New lands rose from the Pacific in time to receive the Cthulhu spawn or cosmic octopi sifting down from infinity. There were wars between them and the Old Ones, ending in stalemate.

Next comers to earth were a race of cone-shaped beings, half-animal, half-vegetable, as were the Old Ones. They established themselves in and around the land mass which eventually became Australia.

Then about six hundred million years ago, near the beginning of the Palaeozoic Era, there arrived on earth and three other solar planets a half-polypous race we may call the Blind Beings. They had travelled through several universes and were constituted only in part of matter as we know it. They flew without wings, used winds as weapons, and built windowless basalt cities. They dominated earth for a time, preying particularly on the cone-shaped beings.

Then the minds of the Great Race migrated from transgalactic Yith into the bodies of the cone-shaped beings. They were a match for the horrifying Blind Beings and managed to drive them underground into great cavern worlds, but were unable to exterminate them. (Here again Lovecraft favours the Great Race against their adversaries; in a sense, indeed, the Great Race came to earth as saviours.)

During the Carboniferous Period, rather late in the Palaeozoic, Europe, then conjoined more closely with Africa, supported a serpent people, the Valusians.

Then in the Permian Period, about one hundred and fifty million years ago, there was a great rebellion of the shoggoths against their masters. The Old Ones won out, though their ability to fly was beginning to fail, while the shoggoths kept evolving new powers.

The Mesozoic dawned, the era of reptiles. During the Jurassic Period the Mi-Go came flying from Pluto, challenging the Old Ones and winning from them the northern hemisphere. The Mi-Go were mountain dwellers and may today account for some of the tracks attributed to the "Abominable Snowmen."

Somewhat later, the Great Race, menaced by the vast eruption of the Blind Beings, migrated mentally en masse into the bodies of the hardy coleopterous or beetle race which succeeds mankind as the intellectual earth-born lords of earth. The Blind Beings, having had their revenge, retired to their caves and gradually died out.

The glacial ages of the late Cenozoic worked great hardship on the Old Ones, who were driven from their terrestrial cities by the shoggoths, though perhaps surviving under the sea.

Then the anthropoid races began to appear, perhaps earliest among them "the furry prehuman Hyperborean worshippers of Tsathoggua."[13] The kingdom of Lomar existed in a polar area 100,000 years ago and was wiped out by the yellow Inutos.[14] In 50,000 B.C. a great-headed brown people held South Africa. In 15,000 B.C. the Cimmerians flourished. Then come modern times. By 5,000 A.D. the cruel empire of Tsan-Chan is in existence;[15] in 16,000 A.D. there are "dark conquerors," possibly African.

The human race is followed, as we have seen, by a mighty beetle civilisation which comes to hold the era-leaping minds of the Great Race.

The last intelligent denizens of earth are spiders—the first earth-born land-dwellers proving to be the last intelligent race to dominate the planet.

As the sun grows cold, Venus becomes the home of intelligent life, then Mercury. The Great Race transfers itself to the bodies of bulbous vegetable entities on that planet and later to cavern-dwelling beings there, which seem to be the last intelligent race of the solar system.

This is certainly, on the whole, a pessimistic view of the destiny of man, created by accident by superior beings, preceded in his brief dominion by vastly superior races, suffering a fate so dreadful that the narrator of "The Shadow out of Time" refuses to set it down, and superseded by the insects. It can be viewed, of course, not so much as a serious speculation by Lovecraft in any of its parts, as an attempt to create a subtly gloomy background for two horror stories. One wonders if the technological achievements of the past quarter century would have caused him to revise it much. Likely not.

One notes in it nods to his friends Robert E. Howard and Clark Ashton Smith: the mention of Cimmeria, Valusia, and Tsathoggua.

Perhaps Lovecraft would have written more about earth's imagined nonhuman races except for the limitations of his medium. The fiction of supernatural horror can only hint, unlike speculative fiction, which seeks to exhaust imagination, or as Lovecraft put it in his previously quoted letter to Smith, "give the imagination a ground for limitless expansion."

Yet Lovecraft went beyond hinting. He even speculated about the governments of the Old Ones and of the Great Race. Of the former he says, "The prevailing intellectual and aesthetic life was highly evolved, and produced a tenaciously enduring set of customs and institutions. Government was evidently complex and probably socialistic,"[16] while of the latter he remarks, "The Great Race seemed to form a single, loosely knit nation or league, with major institutions in common, though there were four definite divisions. The political and economic system of each unit was a sort of fascistic socialism, with major resources rationally distributed, and power delegated to a small governing board elected by the votes of all able to pass certain education and psychological tests. Family organisation was not overstressed, though ties among persons of common descent were recognised, and the young were generally reared by their parents. . . .

"Industry, highly mechanised, demanded but little time from each citizen; and the abundant leisure was filled with intellectual and aesthetic activities of various sorts.

"The sciences were carried to an unbelievable height of development, and art was a vital part of life. . . .

"Crime was surprisingly scant, and was dealt with through highly efficient policing. Punishments ranged from privilege deprivation and imprisonment to death or major emotion wrenching, and were never administered without a careful study of the criminal's motivation."[17]

In these rather conservative speculations, one gets a hint of the sort of utopia Lovecraft may well have favoured: an aristocracy of the mind—those with the finest controlled imaginations ranking the highest; the most strongly and actively thinking minds ruling the duller, though with some tenderness for all mentality; beings ranked by Imagination Quotient, the "dyspeptic ploughman" subordinate to the poet able to conjure up "the peerless beauty of Narath with its hundred carven gates and domes of chalcedony."[18]

Through a lifetime of thinking about the monstrous shapes he feared, from the Night-Gaunts of his childhood to the Blind Beings of his last years, Lovecraft came to love them. It is with the deepest and most real feeling that William Dyer, Miskatonic geologist, exclaims of the Antarctic Old Ones, ". . . poor Old Ones! Scientists to the last. . . . God, what intelligence and persistence! What a facing of the incredible! Radiates, vegetables, monstrosities, star-spawn—whatever they had been, they were men!"[19]

Notes

1. "Autobiography: Some Notes on a Nonentity," in *Beyond the Wall of Sleep*, p. xiv.—S.T.J.
2. *The Californian: 1934-1938*, p. 26.—S.T.J.
3. *Ibid.*—S.T.J.
4. *Collected Works*, VII, pp. 196-97.—S.T.J.
5. *Collected Works*, I, p. 221.—S.T.J.
6. Richard L. Tierney takes Leiber to task on this point: "Lovecraft was actually ignoring a major facet of science as it was known to most intelligent persons at the time he wrote his stories; namely, the Michaelson-Morley experiment which had disproved the 'cosmic aether' theory three decades earlier and which had necessitated thereby the theory of relativity. Fritz Leiber tries to pass off this matter as a relatively minor point, by pointing out that 'vast membranous wings' could have been used somewhat like sails to track through space, utilising the energy of photon-impact; but Lovecraft never mentions the idea, and to defend his use of the 'cosmic aether' is only to say that delib-

erate ignorance of the facts as known to science seems merely an attempt to establish a *misconception* as being somehow more 'aesthetic' than the *truth.''* Letter to the Editor, *Nyctalops*, I, 5 (October 1971), 51.—S.T.J.

7. The authorities mentioned are: "[Sir Edward Burnett] Tylor, [Sir John] Lubbock, [James George] Frazer, [Jean Louis Armand de] Quatrefages [de Breau], [Margaret] Murray, [Henry Fairfield] Osborn, [Sir Arthur] Keith, [Pierre Marcellin] Boule, G. Elliot Smith, and so on." *Collected Works*, I, p. 220.—S.T.J.

8. *Collected Works*, I, p. 66.—S.T.J.

9. *Ibid.*—S.T.J.

10. *Ibid.*, p. 174.—S.T.J.

11. *Collected Works*, II, p. 258.—S.T.J.

12. *Ibid.*—S.T.J.

13. "The Shadow out of Time," in *Collected Works*, I, p. 395.—S.T.J.

14. Lomar and the Inutos originated, of course, in "Polaris" (1918).—S.T.J.

15. The first mention of the empire of Tsan-Chan occurred in "Beyond the Wall of Sleep": the "soul-petrifying voice of an agency from beyond the wall of sleep" tells the narrator: "... we are all roamers of vast spaces and travellers in many ages. Next year I may be dwelling in the Egypt which you call ancient, or in the cruel empire of Tsan-Chan which is to come three thousand years hence. *Collected Works,''* III, p. 31.—S.T.J.

16. *At the Mountains of Madness*, in *Collected Works*, II, pp. 59, 60.—S.T.J.

17. "The Shadow out of Time," in *Collected Works*, I, pp. 398-99.—S.T.J.

18. "The Silver Key," in *Collected Works*, II, p. 387.—S.T.J.

19. *At the Mountains of Madness*, in *Collected Works*, II, p. 90.—S.T.J.

The Influence of *Vathek* on H. P. Lovecraft's *The Dream-Quest of Unknown Kadath*

By Peter Cannon

As Peter Penzoldt has remarked, Lovecraft read a vast amount of weird fiction in his life, and his own tales can often be traced to works of similar plot and theme by other writers, although sometimes such similarities may be superficial or coincidental. In the following source study, Peter Cannon (1951–) has noted the many parallels between Beckford's Vathek *and Lovecraft's novel-length dream fantasy.*

In "Supernatural Horror in Literature" Lovecraft treats "the celebrated *History of the Caliph Vathek* by the wealthy dilettante William Beckford" as a major work in the Gothic tradition, discussing it at some length at the beginning of Chapter 5.[1] The influence of this novel is evident in *The Dream-Quest of Unknown Kadath,* Lovecraft's extended dream fantasy, which he began writing late in 1926, a few months after the composition of "Supernatural Horror in Literature."[2] Clearly Lovecraft had *Vathek* in mind at the time he was writing *The Dream-Quest,* for in a letter to August Derleth from December of 1926 he says the tale "is written continuously like *Vathek* without any subdivision into chapters."[3] Indeed, *The Dream-Quest* is Lovecraft's only longer work not to be subdivided into chapters.

Besides the continuous form, Lovecraft seems also to have found in *Vathek* a model for the structure of *The Dream-Quest,* with its rapidly shifting scenes and exotic colouring. *The Dream-Quest* is in fact the most loosely constructed of his longer tales, appropriate to its dream-like quality, and the most "Oriental" in tone and imagery.

In terms of plot, each novel concerns a protagonist (Randolph Carter in *The Dream-Quest,* the Caliph Vathek in *Vathek*), who sets out on a dangerous and forbidden quest, a prideful journey that no ordinary mortal would dare to undertake. The motivations of the two protagonists, however, are entirely different. Greed drives Vathek to seek the great treasure in the Halls of Eblis, while an aesthetic impulse prompts Carter to try to recover the lost world of his dreams.

Many specific details in *The Dream-Quest* match up with ones in *Vathek*. The monumental "tower of Koth," which Carter and his companions the ghouls ascend through the land of the gugs, is remininscent of Vathek's sinister tower that he uses for black magical purposes and as a stronghold. Lovecraft does not say how many stairs in the tower of Koth Carter has to climb, but Carter does descend "seven hundred steps" to enter dreamland at the beginning of the novel. This may faintly echo Vathek's tower of "fifteen hundred stairs." In *Vathek* the Caliph and Norounihar descend a large staircase that leads to "the vast portal of ebony," the entrance to the Halls of Eblis, where the Giaour awaits them holding a golden key. This golden key, used by the Giaour to unlock the gate leading to the Halls of Eblis for Vathek, may well have inspired the "silver key" (in the story "The Silver Key," written earlier in 1926), which allows Carter to enter his dreamland.

The unpleasant Giaour, the East Indian in *Vathek*, appears to have been the original for the evil, not quite human merchants in *The Dream-Quest*. These merchants bear a definite physical resemblance to the Giaour. Lovecraft gives this description of them: "The mouths of the men who came from [the galley] to trade were too wide, and the way their turbans were humped up in two points above their foreheads was in especially bad taste."[4] Turbans are of course suggestive of India. The "abominably hideous" Giaour, "the man, or rather monster,"[5] has a "horrid mouth," and originally presents himself to Vathek as a merchant. Included in the extraordinary merchandise that he produces are marvellous slippers, knives, and sabres, "the whole enriched with gems that were hitherto unknown" (*Vathek*, p. 198). The merchants in *The Dream-Quest* deal in rubies. At one point the Giaour gives Vathek a draught from "a phial of a red and yellow mixture" (*Vathek*, p. 204) to cure his debilitating thirst. Later this mixture is suspected of being a poison. In *The Dream-Quest* one of the evil merchants gives Carter some wine in "a curious bottle" formed from "a single hollowed ruby" (*Dream-Quest*, p. 300), which puts him to sleep after he takes one sip. While he is a prisoner of the creatures Carter speculates on their purpose in capturing him. "So Carter inferred that the merchants of the humped turbans, hearing of his daring search for the Great Ones in their castle on Kadath, had decided to take him away and deliver him to Nyarlathotep for whatever nameless bounty might be offered for such a prize" (*Dream-Quest*, p. 301). The basic purpose of the Giaour is to deliver Vathek to his doom, though he deceives Vathek into thinking he will be rewarded. In a later episode Carter is again captured by one of the evil merchants, who takes him on the back of a shantak bird to "the remote and prehistoric monastery wherein dwells uncompanioned the High-Priest not to be described" (*Dream-Quest,* p. 351). Brought before the high-priest, "of which legend whispers such fiendish and abnormal possibilities," Carter manages to push his captor "into that gaping well which rumour holds to reach down to the hellish Vaults of Zin where gugs hunt ghasts in the dark" (*Dream-Quest,* p. 354). In an incident in *Vathek,* Vathek and his followers begin kicking the Giaour until finally he rolls down into a great chasm. "The Indian persevered in his onward direction; and, as he had been apprehended, glancing from the precipice with the rapidity of lightning, was lost in the gulf below" (*Vathek,* p. 208). A sardonic sense of humour characterises the evil merchants. During his initial capture Carter is "not chained, but three of the dark sardonic merchants stood grinning nearby" (*Dream-Quest,* p. 301). The "blacker than ebony" Giaour has a cruel, sardonic sense of humour, and on first meeting Vathek "began to laugh with a hideous noise" (*Vathek,* p. 198). The sound of the voice of the merchant that plies Carter with wine is "unbearably hateful."

The vision of Sarkomand, which the frescoes of the monastery on Leng depict, and the ruins which Carter discovers resemble in certain particulars the scene that Vathek and Norounihar view prior to gaining entrance to the Halls of Eblis. Carter sees the following in the frescoes:

> Great gardens and columned streets led from the cliffs and from each of the six sphinx-crowned gates to a vast central plaza, and in that plaza was a pair of winged colossal lions guarding the top of a subterrene staircase. Again and again were those huge winged lions shewn, their mighty flanks of diorite glistening. . . . twin titan lions guard eternally the steps that lead down from dreamland to the Great Abyss. (*Dream-Quest,* p. 352)

Carter soon afterwards comes across this titanic plaza in his travels.

> Then he realised he was still, with the phosphorescent clouds of a northern light shining sickly above him. All around were crumbling walls and broken columns, and the pavement on which he lay was pierced by straggling grass and wrenched asunder by frequent shrubs and roots. Behind him a basalt cliff rose topless and perpendicular; its dark side sculptured into repellent scenes. . . . Ahead stretched double rows of pillars, and the fragments and pedestals of pillars, that spoke of a broad and bygone street; and from the urns and basins along the way he knew it had been a great street of gardens. Far off at its end the pillars spread to mark a vast round plaza, and in that open circle there loomed gigantic under the lurid night clouds a pair of monstrous things. Huge winged lions of diorite they were, with blackness and shadow between them. Full twenty feet they reared their grotesque and unbroken heads, and snarled derisive on the ruins around them. . . . They were the changeless guardians of the Great Abyss. . . . *(Dream-Quest,* pp. 354–55)

The corresponding section in *Vathek* reads:

> A deathlike stillness reigned over the mountain and through the air; the moon dilated on a vast platform the shades of the lofty columns; the gloomy watch-towers, whose number could not be counted, where covered by no roof; and their capitals, of an architecture unknown in the records of the earth, served as an asylum for the birds of night. . . .
>
> Having thus spoken, he presented his hand to Norounihar; and ascending the steps of a vast staircase, reached the terrace, which was flagged with squares of marble, and resembled a smooth expanse of water, upon whose surface not a blade of grass ever dared to vegetate. On the right rose the watch-tower, ranged before the ruins of an immense palace, whose walls were embossed with various figures. In front stood forth the colossal forms of four creatures, composed of the leopard and the griffin, and though but of stone, inspired emotions of terror.
>
> . . . the rock yawned, and disclosed within it a staircase of polished marble, that seemed to approach the abyss. (*Vathek,* p. 269)

The above passages contain points of similarity too numerous to be mere coincidence.

Close parallels are found in the climactic scenes of the two novels. Both Vathek and Carter reach their destinations after perilous adventures, each deluded into expecting a great reward for his efforts. The castle where Carter finds himself and the Halls of Eblis where Vathek comes are both of vast proportions. ". . . it took Carter long to discern the far walls and high distant ceiling, and to realise that he was indeed not again in the boundless air outside" (*Dream-Quest,* p. 375). The caliph and his consort find "themselves in a place which, though roofed with a vaulted ceiling, was so spacious and lofty, that at first they took it for an immeasurable plain" (*Vathek,* p. 270). Carter is met by "a tall slim figure with the young face of an antique Pharaoh . . . whose proud carriage and smart features had in them the fascination of a dark god or a fallen archangel" *(Dream-Quest,* pp. 377–78). Vathek and Norounihar discover a similar figure in Eblis. "His person was that of a young man, whose noble and regular features seemed to have been tarnished by malignant vapours. . . . his flowing hair retained some resemblance to that of an angel of light" (*Vathek,* p. 271). The "Pharaoh" speaks in "mellow tones," while Eblis speaks in "a voice more mild than might be imagined." Neither of these emissaries informs his respective visitors of their dismal fates until the last moment. In the end, however, Carter manages to escape and recovers his "marvellous sunset city," while Vathek is eternally damned.

Lovecraft may have derived many details from *Vathek* (and also the *Arabian Nights* and the work of Lord Dunsany), but still *The Dream-Quest* stands as a highly original fantasy piece. Where Beckford uses a conventional *Arabian Nights* setting, Lovecraft creates in his tale a dream landscape uniquely his own, peopled as it is by friendly cats and obliging ghouls and night-gaunts among other creatures of his imagination. In *Vathek* Beckford maintains a comic distance from his central character, whom he portrays as a selfish buffoon. We the reader can have little sympathy for Vathek or care much about his fate. *Vathek* amounts finally to a vehicle for the projection of Beckford's inner fantasies, with no meaning beyond this. Lovecraft too includes light, almost comic touches in *The Dream-Quest,* but his intent remains basically serious. He clearly identifies with Carter, who serves as a Lovecraft persona, moving through the action of the story as essentially a disembodied consciousness in contrast to the sensual and physical Vathek. Lovecraft has a point to make. As Nyarlathotep, the Crawling Chaos, indicates when he says, " 'For know you, that your gold and marble city of wonder is only the sum of what you have seen and loved in youth' " (*Dream-Quest,* p. 379), the source of Carter-Lovecraft's dreamland is the prosaic world of New England. In this statement Lovecraft comments on man's capacity for wonder and his ability to find it in seemingly mundane reality.

Notes

1. See *Collected Works,* III, pp. 363–64.—S.T.J.
2. While the majority of "Supernatural Horror in Literature" was completed by the end of 1926, Lovecraft was adding portions to it right up to its initial publication in *The Recluse* in July 1927.—S.T.J.
3. H. P. Lovecraft, *Collected Works,* VI, p. 94.
4. H. P. Lovecraft, *The Dream-Quest of Unknown Kadath,* in *Collected Works,* II, p. 299. All subsequent references to this work will be indicated in parentheses following quotations.
5. William Beckford, *Vathek, an Arabian Tale,* in *Shorter Novels of the Eighteenth Century* (1786; first included in Everyman's Library 1930; rpt. London: J. M. Dent & Sons, 1967), p. 198. All subsequent references to this work will be indicated in parentheses following quotations.

Poe and Lovecraft

By Robert Bloch

A correspondent and colleague of Lovecraft's, Robert Bloch's many novels and stories have given him fame in the fields of mystery and horror fiction. But Bloch (1917–   ), a Poe scholar of some note, has authored several articles on Lovecraft, and the following outlines a resemblance between Lovecraft and Poe that has been largely ignored by critics.

Comparisons between Edgar Allan Poe and Howard Phillips Lovecraft are, I suppose, inevitable; seemingly, in recent years they are also interminable.

I shall not, therefore, repeat the usual recital of similarities to be found within their work—there will be no mention of black cats, *revenants* or Antarctic settings *per se*.

But at the same time I have no intention of making a calculated bid for attention by deliberately asserting, as some have also declared,[1] that no real resemblance exists aside from superficial employment of stock characters and themes common to virtually all stories in the *genre*.

To me, this is an untenable statement: Lovecraft, like every writer of fantasy and horror fiction subsequent to Poe, was necessarily influenced by the work of his predecessor—and to a certain extent his work needs must be derivative in some slight sense. Actually, Lovecraft's homage to Poe in his essay, "Supernatural Horror in Literature," indicates a degree of appreciation and admiration which leaves no doubt as to the profound impression made upon him by the earlier master.

But to me the most fruitful area of comparison lies within an examination of the backgrounds and personalities of the two writers themselves.

Consider the facts. Both Poe and Lovecraft were New England born. Both were, to all intents and purposes, fatherless at an early age. Both developed a lifelong affinity for poetry and the elements of a classical education. Both utilised archaisms in their writing styles, and affected personal eccentricities which in time became consciously cultivated.

Although Poe spent a part of his youth in England and travelled along the Atlantic seaboard in later life—and while Lovecraft ventured up into

Canada and down into Florida on vacations a few years prior to his death—neither man ever ventured west of the Alleghanies.[2] Lovecraft, on one occasion, did skirt to visit E. Hoffmann Price briefly in his New Orleans home, but essentially he and Poe were Easterners. Their outlook was, to a marked degree, provincial; even parochial.

Both men distrusted "foreigners" in the mass; both retained a profound admiration for the English. These attitudes are plainly evident in their work, which is in many particulars removed and remote from the main current of American life.

A reader attempting to capture some glimpse of the United States in the 1830–1850 period would gain small enlightenment from the poetry and fiction of Poe. At a time when the entire nation was engaged in a westward thrust, beginning with the peregrinations of the mountain men and ending with the great Gold Rush in the year of Poe's death, one searches in vain for a west which does not seemingly even exist in his literary compass.[3]

Byronic heroes sequestered in British and continental *locales* scarcely reflect the American attitudes or aptitudes in the era of Old Hickory, Davy Crockett, the fall of the Alamo, the Mexican War and the growing turmoil over slavery.

Nor would a reader find more typically American protagonists amongst the pedants, professors and regionally-oriented recluses of Lovecraft's tales, in which there's scarcely a hint of the manners and *mores* of the Roaring Twenties or the Great Depression which followed in the ensuing decade. Aside from a few remarks regarding the influx of immigrants and concomitant destruction of the old folkways and landmarks, plus brief mentions of the (intellectually) "wild" college set,[4] Lovecraft ignores the post WWI Jazz Age in its entirety: Coolidge, Hoover, FDR, Lindbergh, Babe Ruth, Al Capone, Valentino, Mencken and the prototypes of Babbitt have no existence in H.P.L.'s realm. It is difficult to believe that Howard Phillips Lovecraft was a literary contemporary of Ernest Hemingway.

And yet a further comparison between Lovecraft and Poe remains; one of profound importance in any consideration of their work, because it softens any charge that the two writers were totally unaware of the actual world and unrealistic in their treatment of their times.

I refer, of course, to their mutual interest in science. Both Poe and Lovecraft were acute observers of the scientific and pseudoscientific developements of their respective days, and both men utilised the latest theories and discoveries in their writing. It is only necessary to cite Poe's use of mesmerism, his employment of the balloon hoax, his detailing of data in the *Arthur Gordon Pym* novella, to prove the point.

Lovecraft, for his part, relies on scientific background material in his *Pym*-like *At the Mountains of Madness,* "The Shadow out of Time" and other efforts; notable is his immediate adoption of the newly-discovered "ninth planet" in "The Whisperer in Darkness."

Lovecraft's interest in astronomy undoubtedly led to his increasing interest in other fields of scientific endeavour, just as Poe's early experiences at West Point must have fostered his preoccupation with codes and ciphers. And both men, as professional writers, were well and widely-read in the contemporary work of their day: Poe, as a working critic, demonstrates his knowledge in his nonfictional efforts and Lovecraft, in his correspondence, proves himself no stranger to Proust, Joyce, Spengler, and Freud.

But the point is that Poe and Lovecraft deliberately chose to turn their backs on contemporary style and subject-matter and create their own individual worlds of fantasy. In this above all else they were similar.

And in this, above all else, we readers of Poe and Lovecraft are fortunate indeed. We shall never know, and never care, what Edgar Allan Poe thought of Andy Jackson's "kitchen cabinet" or how H. P. Lovecraft regarded the Teapot Dome scandal. Small loss, when both have given us glimpses of worlds peculiarly and provocatively their very own.

For the final similarity is this—Poe and Lovecraft are our two American geniuses of fantasy, comparable each to the other, but incomparably superior to all the rest who follow in their wake.

Notes

1. See August Derleth's *H.P.L.: A Memoir,* p. 88.—S.T.J.
2. In 1922, however, Lovecraft made a trip to Cleveland to visit Samuel Loveman; but he found the Ohio landscape "quite unlike—and inferior to—New-England. . . . The villages are insufferably dismal. . . . They have no ancient features, and totally lack the mellow charm and scenery which make New-England villages so delightful." (Lovecraft to Mrs F. C. Clark, 4 August 1922; in *Collected Works,* V, p. 191.) Lovecraft also had vague plans to visit Clark Ashton Smith in California, but never took decisive steps to bring this about.—S.T.J.
3. With the lone exception of *The Journal of Julius Rodman.* [Note also the poem "Eldorado," which concerned the gold rush.—S.T.J.]
4. See "The Thing on the Doorstep."—S.T.J.

H. P. Lovecraft
in Hawthornian Perspective

By Peter Cannon

It is only recently that Lovecraft's work has been regarded as a fertile subject for serious literary analysis. In the following article, Peter Cannon (1951–) has linked Lovecraft's "The Festival" with Hawthorne's "Young Goodman Brown," indicating the moral message that runs through both tales. Cannon has written an honours thesis and a master's thesis on Lovecraft, plus several shorter critical articles, and is one of the strong new forces in modern Lovecraft criticism.

Winfield Townley Scott, in his sympathetic essay "His Own Most Fantastic Creation: Howard Phillips Lovecraft," points to Lovecraft's achievement as a regionalist. He observes:

> The purpose of shocking—of frightening or horrifying—is in literature a meretricious one. Tricks for their own sake are only a sort of joke. Lovecraft's better claim is in his regionalism. Though it is a haunted regionalism, reactionary with his eighteenth-century obsession, it is nonetheless genuine; and in this Lovecraft resembles, not Poe—whom he much admired and with whom he has often been compared—but Hawthorne.[1]

Lovecraft, like Hawthorne, turned to his native New England—to its history, culture, landscape and architecture—for the realistic background that forms such an effective complement to the supernatural features in the best of his stories. Poe, in contrast, used few actual geographical locales in his tales. In his accurate depiction of his native region in his fiction, Lovecraft belongs firmly in the tradition of New England local colourists.

The Puritan past of Massachusetts inspired Lovecraft's imagination as much as it did Hawthorne's. To Robert E. Howard he wrote: "it is the night-black Massachusetts legendry which packs the really macabre 'kick.' Here is material for a really profound study in group-neuroticism; for certainly, no one can deny the existence of a profoundly morbid streak in the Puritan imagination."[2] He goes on in the letter to discuss the Mathers, the Salem witchcraft, and Puritan theology—all elements that he incorporated into his tales. A passage from Cotton Mather's

Magnalia provided the basis for "The Unnamable."[3] The paintings of
Richard Upton Pickman in "Pickman's Model," another story that
mentions Mather, evoke a particularly sinister vision of Puritan Massachusetts. "The Picture in the House" deals with repression and perversion in backwoods New England, while "The Dreams in the Witch
House" explains the Salem witchcraft in terms of Einsteinian space-time.

Lovecraft and Hawthorne, of course, differ fundamentally in their
respective uses of these common elements. Hawthorne was concerned
with exploring the moral nature of man, with guilt and sin. The Puritans,
with their gloomy psychology and rigid morality, formed an ideal group
to investigate in his fiction. Lovecraft, in affecting a cosmic viewpoint,
was indifferent to man and his moral plight. Human beings remain entirely subordinate to mood and supernatural effect in his work. Throughout his letters and essays expounding his theories of the weird tale, Lovecraft places emphasis on aesthetics for their own sake. And yet, despite
this pose of indifference, Lovecraft could not help but comment on
man's nature, on his relation to the universe, as all great writers do.

A comparison of "The Festival" with Hawthorne's "Young Goodman Brown," two tales that resemble one another roughly in plot, illustrates how Lovecraft could approach making the sort of moral statement characteristic of Hawthorne. At the opening of "The Festival" the
narrator is proceeding to the town of his ancestors, Kingsport (a
transformed Marblehead, Salem's neighbour on the Massachusetts
North Shore). Like Goodman Brown, he has been called to a Sabbath
rendezvous. Goodman Brown in Hawthorne's tale takes an opposite
direction, leaving his town, Salem, for the surrounding woods. Both, in
any event, move from civilised locales to wilder, unknown regions. In the
dream-like descriptions of the strangely deserted, seventeenth-century
town and its antique inhabitants, Lovecraft succeeds in creating, despite
his overcharged language, a sombre atmosphere of mystery and foreboding. The tone is quite reminiscent of Hawthorne. When at last the
narrator reaches the cavern beneath the meeting house and the Sabbath
celebration, which recalls "Young Goodman Brown" with its central
pillar of flame and the evidence of kinship between the narrator and the
townsfolk, he has an awful revelation. He recognises that these
creatures, the living corpses of his ancestors, represent the embodiment
of evil, and that this evil has persisted through the centuries and he as
their descendant is tainted by it. This is not so far removed from Goodman Brown's recognition of man's universal guilt, that all men belong to
a fallen brotherhood. Note that each makes a symbolic descent into the
unconscious, one going below the earth, the other into the woods, to

reach a new understanding of human nature.

This is not to say that "The Festival" is as good a work of fiction as "Young Goodman Brown," a more subtle and finely crafted story that explores man's dark side on much more profound levels. Lovecraft's protagonist merely suffers the conventional ghost-story shock at the end, while Young Goodman Brown has a complex moral reaction to his trip into the psyche. "The Festival," in fact, is one of Lovecraft's lesser tales, and is mainly notable as an attempt to capture the mood of Marblehead at the time he first glimpsed that ancient town on a winter's evening in 1922.[4] In other works, such as "The Rats in the Walls" and "The Shadow over Innsmouth," Lovecraft handles this theme of the subconscious survival of evil with more sophistication and skill.

In his discussion of Hawthorne in his long essay, "Supernatural Horror in Literature," Lovecraft criticises Hawthorne for his concern with the human condition, and thus reveals his own aesthetic bias. To be fair, Lovecraft admits that he is necessarily focusing on a narrow aspect of Hawthorne. He states:

> The heritage of American weirdness was his to a most intense degree, and he saw a dismal throng of vague spectres behind the common phenomena of life; but he was not disinterested enough to value impressions, sensations, and beauties of narration for their own sake. He must needs weave his phantasy into some quietly melancholy fabric of didactic or allegorical cast, in which his meekly resigned cynicism may display with naive moral appraisal the perfidy of a human race which he cannot cease to cherish and mourn despite his insight into its hypocrisy. Supernatural horror, then, is never a primary object with Hawthorne; though its impulses were so deeply woven into his personality that he cannot help suggesting it with the force of genius when he calls upon the unreal world to illustrate the pensive sermon he wishes to preach.[5]

On the theoretical level Lovecraft clearly implies that he values "impressions, sensations, and beauties of narration for their own sake," giving no indication that his work could possibly be interpreted in symbolic or allegorical terms.

Later in the essay Lovecraft remarks briefly on Hawthorne's notebooks. "Some of Hawthorne's notes tell of weird tales he would have written had he lived longer—an especially vivid plot being that concerning a baffling stranger who appeared now and then in public assemblies, and who was at last followed and found to come and go from a very ancient grave."[6] Lovecraft himself kept a commonplace book in which he made notes for stories, some of which appear similar to the sort that Hawthorne made. Lovecraft quotes examples in a letter.

> A very ancient colossus in a very ancient desert. Face gone. No man hath seen it.

Man climbs mountain toward some horrible goal. Cloud passes over, Man seen no more.

Man makes appointment with old enemy for final settlement. Enemy dies meanwhile. *But appointment is not broken.*

Old house and gardens—take on a singular aspect as seen at twilight by narrator.[7]

Perhaps Lovecraft was partly inspired by Hawthorne's example to keep a commonplace book.

Lovecraft displays a familiarity with Hawthorne's late unfinished romances—those unsatisfactory works whose symbolic features fail to serve any real symbolic function. He says of *The Ancestral Footstep* that "the notes for a never-written tale to be called *The Ancestral Footstep* shew what Hawthorne would have done with an intensive treatment of an old English superstition—that of an ancient and accursed line whose members left footprints of blood as they walked. . . ."[8] This abortive work could conceivably have influenced the plot of "The Rats in the Walls." It likewise concerns a protagonist who comes to England to claim an estate abandoned long ago by an ancestor who fled to America under a mysterious and evil shadow.

Understandably Lovecraft devotes two pages of his study to praising *The House of the Seven Gables,* for in this novel he found a theme in close sympathy with one of his own—the working out of a family curse over the generations. While he commends the sense of atmosphere created in the picture of family decay and of the sinister old house, Lovecraft disapproves of the happy ending. In his own works, such as *The Case of Charles Dexter Ward,* written during the period while he was preparing "Supernatural Horror in Literature," an investigation by the protagonist into his family past always results in his being overwhelmed and destroyed by the horrors he discovers there. To make a distinction, Hawthorne emphasises the effects of guilt over time in *The House of the Seven Gables,* whereas Lovecraft in his family history tales deals with the bestial in man and its hereditary transfer. Again, though, Lovecraft fails to realise that by employing these themes in his work he gives it value beyond mere horror fiction.

Hawthorne today is read mainly by students and scholars. He is too old-fashioned a writer to appeal to a popular audience. Lovecraft has readers in the millions, but is just beginning to be appreciated in academic circles. Lovecraft's work may never gain the critical acceptance that Hawthorne's has, and yet it quite clearly deserves to be examined on its own terms as serious literature.

Notes

1. Winfield Townley Scott, "His Own Most Fantastic Creation: Howard Phillips Love-craft," in *Exiles and Fabrications,* p. 52.
2. Lovecraft to Robert E. Howard, 4 October 1930; in *Collected Works,* VII, pp. 174–75.
3. Cf. Lovecraft to Bernard Austin Dwyer, June 1927; in *Collected Works,* VI, p. 139.—S.T.J.
4. Cf. Lovecraft to Rheinhart Kleiner, 11 January 1923; in *Collected Works,* V, pp. 203–05.—S.T.J.
5. "Supernatural Horror in Literature," in *Collected Works,* III, p. 381.
6. *Ibid.,* p. 382.
7. Lovecraft to Rheinhart Kleiner, 10 February 1920; in *Collected Works,* V, pp. 107–08.
8. "Supernatural Horror in Literature," in *Collected Works,* III, p. 382.

IV
PHILOSOPHICAL, PSYCHOLOGICAL, AND HISTORICAL ANALYSES

Facts in the Case of H. P. Lovecraft

By Barton L. St Armand

A leading Lovecraft scholar, Prof. Barton L. St Armand made his debut in the field by authoring the brilliant biographical and critical study, "H. P. Lovecraft: The Outsider in Legend and Myth" (M.A. thesis: Brown University, 1966). Also to his credit is the philosophical-literary essay, "H. P. Lovecraft: New England Decadent." The following article, originally presented as a lecture to the Rhode Island Historical Society in November 1969, explores Lovecraft's lengthiest fictional work, The Case of Charles Dexter Ward, *as exemplifying the "sense of place" in his work. Prof. St Armand, also a Poe scholar of some renown, has just published* The Roots of Horror in the Fiction of H. P. Lovecraft.

A rather unusual assortment of readers may have been stirred by a minor item in *The New York Times Book Review,* 17 May 1970. Included under the heading of "Revivals" in the "European Notebook" of Mark Slonim, it announced to its American audience that:

> A most striking phenomenon in France, Italy, and Spain is the number of translations (mostly very good)[1] of the American science-fiction writer H. P. Lovecraft. Not only are they widely read in Paris, Rome, and Madrid, but Lovecraft is also hailed by the leading critics as superior to Poe. The Spanish essayist José Luis Garcia recently included Lovecraft in a list of 10 best writers of the world,[2] and the sophisticated French periodical *L'Herne* dedicated a special large issue to the greatest American master of supernatural literature.

While most readers probably turned the page in continued puzzlement and uninterest, never having heard of H. P. Lovecraft in the first place, and at any rate doubting such effusive foreign "discoveries" as inherently suspect, that "unusual assortment" I have mentioned would have found this brief notice exciting news, a tremendously meaningful "straw in the wind." This saving remnant might be broken down further into three general groups composed of, first, a number of sophisticated and well-established creative writers and critics; second, a naive and even slightly fanatical cadre of science-fiction collectors and "fans," mostly high school or college students; and, third, those deeply interested in Rhode Island history, especially its traditional genealogical, political, and literary dimensions.

To answer "Who was H. P. Lovecraft?" is a great deal more easy than to explain why he should receive such belated and enthusiastic recognition in Europe, or how the three groups cluster together in common response to his growing critical reputation. So I shall first attempt to answer for those who still lie beyond the pale of dedicated "lovecraftimania"—to coin a word matching in its significant absurdity the heading "Lovecraftiana," which is used to describe not only the materials deposited in the John Hay Library of Brown University but also those startlingly expensive items stamped by his hand which are now to be found in several rare book catalogs. Yet the biography only reveals that this "greatest American master of supernatural fiction" led an intellectually fascinating and factually boring life.

Howard Phillips Lovecraft was born on 20 August 1890, at his grandfather's big Angell Street house in Providence. In this house Howard grew up, surrounded by adoring adults, after his father was confined to Butler Hospital and died of syphilis when his son was only eight.[3] Although Lovecraft was something of a child prodigy—writing stories and poetry and conducting scientific experiments long before this tragic event—his over-protective mother discouraged him from seeking companionship with children his own age and continually told him that he had a "repulsive" and "hideous" face. Young Howard proceeded to build his own dream-world, peopling it with mythological creatures and beings from the past, while to outside appearances he cultivated the pose of the eighteenth-century sceptic, a bored spectator who found human life and the universe dull, mechanical, and ultimately meaningless. Writing later about his sceptical view of man and his world, which seemed almost to be inborn, Lovecraft said:

My first positive utterance of a sceptical nature probably appeared before my fifth birthday, when I was told what I really knew before, that "Santa Claus" is a myth. This admission caused me to ask why "God" is not equally a myth. Not long afterwards I was placed in the "infant class" at the Sunday School of the venerable First Baptist Church . . . and there resigned all vestiges of Christian belief. The absurdity of the myths I was called upon to accept, and the sombre greyness of the whole faith as compared to the Eastern magnificence of Mohametanism, made me definitely an agnostic, and caused me to become so pestiferous a questioner that I was permitted to discontinue attendance. . . . No doubt I was regarded as a corrupter of the simple faith of the other "infants."[4]

Certainly it seems that any "infantile" behaviour which Lovecraft may ever have exhibited in his youth was more that of the *enfant terrible* variety. What little was left of the family fortune disappeared with the passing of Lovecraft's grandfather, Whipple Phillips, in 1904, and Lovecraft and his mother were forced to move to less respectable lodgings. Howard tried attending Hope High School but suffered a nervous collapse, while his mother entered a slow "decline" which terminated in her own confinement to Butler in 1919 and her subsequent death in 1921. Thereafter Lovecraft lived with two remaining aunts and managed to widen his interests by participating in the Amateur Press movement, an association of young writers who exchanged their work in the form of privately printed newspapers. Through this outlet for his creative energies he met Sonia Greene—a beautiful widow seven years his senior— and married her in 1924, hoping to make a new start in life. Yet their honeymoon was spent typing the manuscript of a weird story, the first typescript of which Howard had left in the Providence train station.[5] Bad luck dogged him throughout his so-called "New York Exile" as financial matters went from bad to worse.

Finally hinting that the uncongenial "Babylon" of Brooklyn would force him to either madness or suicide, Lovecraft departed for Providence in 1926, suggesting to his wife that they carry on their marriage by correspondence. Again installing himself with his aunts, Howard settled down to a life of shabby-genteel contentment, subsisting on what little money he could make by ghost-writing for others and selling his own horror stories to pulp periodicals such as *Weird Tales.* He also continued to cultivate a pose as an eighteenth-century English gentleman, an upholder of Nordic superiority, and a bemused spectator of the world's foibles and follies. Adding young aspiring authors to the circle of literary friends he had made in New York, he kept up this routine of desultory reading and writing until his death on 15 March 1937. All of Lovecraft's residences, save for his grandfather's house at 454 Angell Street, are still standing, and include a flat at 598 Angell and an apartment at 10 Barnes Street (where his ghost was recently seen by a student resident).[6] His last home, an eighteenth-century style eyrie, has been moved to 65 Prospect Street, where it looks singularly unsinister, but it stood in its own day at 66 College Street, right in back of the John Hay Library, though the monolithic and slightly skewed Brown University Art Building, which now occupies the site, seems straight out of one of his stories of "Non-Euclidean" and "Cyclopean" architecture, providing a strangely appropriate monument.

In spite of the glaring fact that Lovecraft seldom published anything save in pulp magazines of the late 1920s and early 1930s, heyday of *Weird Tales* and *Amazing Stories,* he still remains Providence's only native writer of note besides Sarah Helen Whitman. And on a state level, if we discount Edwin O'Connor and S. J. Perelman, he emerges perhaps as Rhode Island's most distinguished native writer of fiction, though following in his own way, as I shall hope to demonstrate, a local colour tradition once made famous by the almost forgotten "Shepherd Tom" Hazard of the *Jonny Cake Papers.* Now, however, Lovecraft is being read not only by specialists in local or literary history but also at both top and bottom of literary circles in general. We could set the distinguished American critic, Edmund Wilson, who titled his essay on Lovecraft "Tales of the Marvellous and the Ridiculous," against Señor Garcia, and his ranking of Lovecraft with Shakespeare and Cervantes, but this again would not solve the problem. Why is Lovecraft being read at all in the 1970s?

This brings us back to two groups of Lovecraft readers. We have not yet considered the "high-brows" and the "low-brows," who evince an interest in his work which is decidedly nonhistorical in nature. The low-brow contingent used to be composed mostly of teenaged enthusiasts with an abiding interest in any pulp form from horror-pornography to science-fiction. These were, like Lovecraft himself, "outsiders" of the crumbling society of the 1930s, who sought in pulp literature an escape from the more frighteningly immediate realities of mid-Depression America.

The escape was accomplished through the generation of a *frisson nouveau,* a visceral chill or thrill created by confrontation with some monstrous evil, whether from outer space or the bite of a werewolf or some other equally esoteric origin. Origins hardly mattered, for as Franklin Roosevelt told the nation, in words which could also stand as a formula for this kind of fiction and this kind of audience, "The only thing we have to fear is fear itself." Yet Lovecraft has survived the demise of the pulps and is now apparently experiencing some kind of world-wide "revival" in an age of admittedly general affluence and relative security. Here, I think, the theory of *frisson nouveau* still holds true.

For Lovecraft's real value as a creative artist is similar to that of the Edgar Allan Poe he so much admired and so often imitated. Lovecraft sets loose the boundaries of the imagination and allows for the exploration of other worlds, which may or may not be specifically "Lovecraftian" worlds. Those young writers who formed what was called the "Lovecraft Cult" after his premature death in 1937 took over the mythos and atmospheric effects which Lovecraft had perfected, but they failed miserably because they seldom went beyond the uncanny dimensions and expansive fantasies which Lovecraft himself had only begun to explore. It is as an opener of doors that Lovecraft remains significant, though he may sometimes open doors of a truly fearsome and morbid nature.

Thus such a distinguished film critic as Vincent Canby can devote an entire review to a movie made from a Lovecraft story and damn the unimaginative film while praising the imaginative Lovecraft, further urging readers to take him and his stories seriously.[7] And thus James Schevill can justify his recent popular stage success, "Lovecraft's Follies," which "takes off," in part, from a number of the master's dreams and visions, by declaring that "Lovecraft was the first anti-hero of modern times, one of the fathers you might say of all the anti's we're experiencing today—from anti-politics to anti-matter," and that "Lovecraft, with his surreal vision of the future and his black visions of nether gods which man continually sets loose on the earth, seemed to me a good kind of guide for this journey," a journey into the ambiguities of modern technocracy and the internal chaos of the modern self.

Canby, Schevill, and Kurt Vonnegut, too, who admits to a liking of Lovecraft as a consummate prose artist and stylistic perfectionist, are all responding to the same thing that the so-called "counter-culture" of the young respond to in Lovecraft. For, in his tales and sketches, Lovecraft not only shadows forth the diminished nature of twentieth-century man in an immense and alien universe, but he also restores something which has been lost to the spiritual nature of that confused being. As the great Swiss psychologist and philosopher C. G. Jung writes of this modern consciousness:

> As scientific understanding has grown, so our world has become dehumanised. Man feels himself isolated in the cosmos, because he is no longer involved in nature and has lost his emotional unconscious identity with natural phenomena. These have slowly lost their symbolic implications. Thunder is no longer the voice of an angry god, nor is lightning his avenging missile. No river contains a spirit, no tree is the life principle of a man, no snake is the embodiment of wisdom, no mountain cave the home of a great daemon. No voices now speak to man from stones, plants, and animals, nor does he speak to them believing they can hear. His contact with nature has gone, and with it has gone the profound emotional energy that this symbolic connexion supplied.[8]

Although H. P. Lovecraft's view of an intimate contact with nature is a dark one, still in his own way he does restore much of that "profound emotional energy" which Jung describes as being lost in our modern world. Lovecraft re-creates that dialogue of cosmic voices, as the characters in his stories are seized, in spite of themselves and their innate scientific scepticism, by forces which compel horrified obedience and primitive response. His appeal and his concern are with primal roots of human feeling—fear, disgust, wonder, awe—and with an epic backdrop of the fantastic and the dreadful which we find in ancient folk-chronicles such as *Beowulf,* which become in turn the source for a popular modern myth-cycle as mannered as that of Lovecraft, namely J. R. R. Tolkien's *Lord of the Rings.*

As the modern world and modern literature moved more and more into the ego, the completely solipsistic world of stream-of-consciousness, Lovecraft and others like him moved further and further away from that world into the dark, immense, and unknown regions which exist beyond, behind, or below the ego. And when Lovecraft explored consciousness itself, he did not stop at the delineation of merely personal motives and sensations; he went far beneath them into the archetypes and the images which helped to shape, as well as to define, their substance. His two great themes both involve the Triumph of the Shadow. In one class of his stories, this triumph is the dominance of Jung's interior "shadow" of the collective unconscious, coming from deep inside the human self to overwhelm its conscious, "civilised," or "daylight" realm in a dark eclipse of atavism and violent instinct (as in the famous short tale, "The Rats in the Walls"). Other stories, which tend more toward science-fiction than to psychological thrillers, detail the incursion of forces outside and beyond the self, raising the plight of the individual to a cosmic level, and subsequently questioning both man's place in the universe and his conception of his own destiny (as in the significant novella, "The Shadow out of Time"). Even these approaches, however, can be referred back to the tradition of the so-called "Gothic Novel," of which Lovecraft was so consciously a part, and especially one of its main spokesmen, Mrs Ann Radcliffe, who differentiated between the terms "terror" and "horror" by demonstrating that while terror "expanded" the soul to intimations of the sublime (Lovecraft's science-fiction), horror "contracted" the soul to a freezing-point of near-annihilation (Lovecraft's psychological chillers).[9] At a time when such words as "outer-space" and "soul" have become current and when there is paradoxically a growing interest in witchcraft, ritual, magic, the daemonic, and all forms of the occult, a "Lovecraft revival" should not be a totally unexpected phenomenon.

Now I should like to return to that neglected third group—those interested in the use of Rhode Island history and in the uses of history in general—and consider Lovecraft as a serious writer possessed of a remarkable talent. Specifically, this talent has to do with the transmutation of those native materials he used so extensively and intensively in fiction. In particular, I shall concentrate on Lovecraft's short novel *The Case of Charles Dexter Ward* (1927–28)[10] because both Lovecraft and the novel's locale have been attacked recently as having a mutually deleterious effect one upon the other, and that is an impression I should like to correct.

One of those twentieth-century critics to take Lovecraft seriously is Colin Wilson, a young English philosopher and creative writer who, in the introduction to his own Lovecraftian novel, *The Mind Parasites,* writes of how he first discovered him. The discovery was made in a lonely English cottage—a setting appropriate for reading of weird tales and the onslaught of Gothic horrors—just as many American servicemen first discovered both the power and relevance of Lovecraft and Poe in cheap paperback editions issued by the armed forces. Understandably, Gothic horror and flapping evils are more real on a lonely English moor or in a foxhole in *No Man's Land,* but it is the follow-up to Wilson's discovery which becomes even more interesting when seen in retrospect:

> My book [*The Strength to Dream*], containing a chapter on Lovecraft, appeared in England in 1961, and I thought I had done with Lovecraft. But later that year, I found myself in Providence, lecturing at Brown University. There I met the Blake scholar, Foster Damon, who looks and sounds like Mark Twain, and he showed me the house where Poe had lived and told me of legends that still survived. But here, in this town of clapboard houses, with its streets ankle-deep in leaves, my imagination was haunted by another writer— Lovecraft. I found that his stories now returned to mind a dozen times a day. I went and looked at the house in which Lovecraft had lived; I spent hours in the university library reading Lovecraft's letters in manuscript, and a thesis that somebody had written on his life and work. Here I read for the first time *The Case of Charles Dexter Ward* and "The Shadow over Innsmouth." And I had to admit that there was something about Lovecraft that makes him very hard to dismiss. In many ways, I found him more impressive than Poe. Poe's imagination was simply obsessed by death. In some ways, his most typical story is "The Premature Burial," which is the kind of nightmare that might occur to any of us. Basically, Poe is a gentle romantic, a lover of beautiful, pale women and ancient Gothic mansions set among wooded hills. Lovecraft is not so concerned with death as with terror. Poe is pre-Dracula: Lovecraft is very much post-Dracula. Poe's world is the world we all live in, seen through eyes that were always aware of "the skull beneath the skin." Lovecraft's world is a creation of his own, as unique and nightmarish as the world of Hieronymous Bosch or Fuseli.[11]

I would not agree with Wilson's estimate of Poe—whose poem "The Conqueror Worm," for example, far from proves that he is merely a "gentle romantic"—but even more would I quarrel with his reconstitution of Lovecraft which continues throughout the same essay. For Wilson's unpardonable sin, as I see it, is to separate Lovecraft from that very Providence atmosphere which indeed brought the author and his works back so strongly into Wilson's mind. Thus in the same piece we find Wilson saying that Lovecraft's main problem was that "He was born into a dreary provincial city—attractive enough in its own way, but as painfully narrow and dull as the Norway in which Henrik Ibsen grew up." Or that, "What I am suggesting is that the emphasis upon the gruesome and violent was, to a large extent, Lovecraft's way of keeping himself mentally healthy in the dull, stifling atmosphere of Providence." Or, once again that he "was a frustrated product of a rainy provincial town."

It is my contention that Lovecraft would never have been Lovecraft without Providence—its history, its atmosphere, its legends, its peculiar and individual character—and that, genius that he was, it is not so much escape from but improvement on the rich native materials that lay in his own back yard that helps to make his tales so intriguing and so striking. Perhaps what I am really saying is that Lovecraft, like his Southern contemporary William Faulkner, is a great local colour writer, who sometimes goes beyond the conventions of mere local colour quaintness or picturesqueness in order to get at terrifying ambiguities having to do with the scope and status of human nature itself.

The city of Providence and the state of Rhode Island thus become for Lovecraft a kind of *prima materia*—a basic, irreducible substance— which he transmutes through the alchemy of his art into a rarefied and golden product. There was an almost symbiotic relationship between the author and his environment, and here Wilson's categorisation of Lovecraft as a romantic would seem to be truly valuable, though there were actually two Lovecrafts—one classic and one romantic, one an eighteenth-century mind and one a nineteenth-century Gothic sensibility. The eighteenth-century side of his personality manifested itself in Lovecraft's admiration for colonial times, his sardonic scepticism, his view of himself as a detached spectator of the world and its problems, and his intense interest in science and technology. This attitude could sometimes become both escapist and defensive, although it also led Lovecraft to become, like his eighteenth-century counterpart Horace Walpole, one of the great letter writers of the century. At times he could sputter in a letter to a friend that "I thank the powers of the cosmos that I am a Rhode Island Englishman of the old tradition! Even if my culture-stream be a thinned and effete one, it is at least something as distinguished from nothing at all!" Indeed, he once turned down a high-paying job in Chicago during one of the most desperate periods of his life, simply because Chicago did not have any eighteenth-century buildings.[12]

The other dimension of his character, the romantic, balanced off the wit, urbanity, rationality, and cosmopolitan nature of the classic side which comes through the letters. Lovecraft was like a man poised between the end of the eighteenth and the beginning of the nineteenth century, and his choice of a Gothic form of writing reflects that literature which had developed at precisely this point in history. Thus Lovecraft chooses the mode of the "Gothic Novel," reminiscent of such thrilling and supernatural best-sellers of the 1790s and 1800s as *The Castle of Otranto, The Monk, The Mysteries of Udolpho,* and *Frankenstein.* His romantic dimension was embodied in that side of his personality which delighted in the weird, the ethereal, the remote, the shadowy, and the terrifying—a thrill for the sake of a thrill—though we have already noted that Lovecraft's science-fiction tales go beyond this toward Ann Radcliffe's shadowy "sublime." Closely connected with this predilection is what Wilson calls Lovecraft's "provinciality" and what I would call his sense of place—his love of the particular and peculiar atmosphere of a very definite and circumscribed locality, just as Wordsworth and the Lake Poets made the Lake District of England famous for its individual aura of beauty and picturesqueness. Lovecraft focuses on Providence and its outskirts so much so that, like many romantics, he develops an almost mystical attachment to the place he has chosen to celebrate in art. In a revealing letter to his aunts during his so-called "New York Exile" in the middle 1920s, when an anomalous marriage and the threat of out-and-out poverty had depressed his spirits, Lovecraft exclaimed that:

> To all intents and purposes I am more naturally isolated from mankind than Nathaniel Hawthorne himself, who dwelt alone in the midst of crowds, and whom Salem knew only after he had died. Therefore, it may be taken as axiomatic that the people of a place matter absolutely nothing to me except as components of the general landscape and scenery. . . . My life lies not among people but among scenes—my local affections are not personal, but topographical and architectural. . . . I am always an outsider—to all scenes and all people—but outsiders have their sentimental preferences in visual environment. I will be dogmatic only to the extent of saying that it is *New England* I *must* have—in some form or other. Providence is part of me—I *am* Providence. . . . Providence would always be at the back of my head as a goal to be worked toward—an ultimate Paradise to be regain'd at last.[13]

It would be difficult to find in literature a more complete identification of author and subject than this.

Lovecraft did at last regain his lost paradise, while at the same time he incorporated it into the substance of his tales and sketches. More specifically he made it the hub of a long fictional effort which has a particular relevance for those with an interest in any kind of historical endeavour. For his *The Case of Charles Dexter Ward* is a fable about the problems of history itself and also a warning about the dangers of historical research. It concerns itself with a young antiquarian, Ward himself, who delves into the ancient history of his own past and finds there something so potent and so evil that at last it overwhelms and destroys him, thus embodying a typical Lovecraft theme. Yet it is not Ward but the city of Providence, with all of its history and tradition, which is really the main character of the book, as "Egdon Heath" is in Hardy's *Return of the Native.* However, since *The Case of Charles Dexter Ward* is also the story of a sick mind, Providence appears in two aspects during the course of the narrative—it is both an Eden before the Fall of Man, and an Eden after the Fall of Man. And Lovecraft redoes Genesis by maintaining that Paradise is lost not through eating an apple but through reading an historical document, though the import of both Genesis and *The Case of Charles Dexter Ward* remain the same—dangerous love of knowledge, obsession with knowing itself. Before Ward finds out too much, Providence is to him a lyrical and romantic garden, a place of gorgeous, fantastic architecture and rainbow skies. Thus Lovecraft writes of the young Charles, who still trails Wordsworthian clouds of glory—

> Sometimes, as he grew taller and more adventurous, young Ward would venture down into the maelstrom of tottering houses, broken transoms, tumbling steps, twisted balustrades, swarthy faces, and nameless odours, winding from South Main to South Water, searching out the docks where the bay and sound steamers still touched, and returning northward at this lower level past the steep-roofed 1816 warehouses and the broad square at the Great Bridge, where the 1773 Market House still stands firm on its ancient arches. In that square he would pause to drink in the bewildering beauty of the old town as it rises on the eastward bluff, decked with its two Georgian spires and crowned by the vast new Christian Science dome as London is crowned by St. Paul's. He liked mostly to reach this point in the late afternoon, when the slanting sunlight touches the Market House and the ancient hill roofs and belfries with gold, and throws magic around the dreaming wharves where Providence Indiamen used to ride at anchor. After a long look he would grow almost dizzy with a poet's love for the sight, and then he would scale the slope homeward in the dusk past the old white church and up the narrow precipitous ways where yellow gleams would begin to peep out in small-paned windows and through fanlights set high over double flights of steps with curious wrought-iron railings.[14]

Now, anyone who has lived in Providence has probably seen exactly this sight and felt precisely this way—as late afternoon sunlight bathed College Hill in its glow—and what is interesting about Lovecraft's approach here, I think, is actually how realistic a writer he is, realistic in the sense of faithful reporting of detail and minute attention to physical fact. Just because Lovecraft writes weird stories does not imply that the structure of those stories is similarly vague, awesome, or cumbersome, like some Frankenstein horror out of a bad film. A good deal of *Charles Dex-*

ter Ward is made up of just this same sort of painstaking, factual description, obviously based upon Lovecraft's own direct and personal contact with the city he so loved. He warned his young weird-tale-writing friends that—

> To make a fictional marvel wear the momentary aspect of exciting fact, we must give it the most elaborate possible approach—building it up insidiously and gradually out of apparently realistic material, realistically handled. The time is past when adults can accept marvellous conditions for granted. Every energy must be bent toward the weaving of a frame of mind which shall make the story's departure from nature seem credible—and in the weaving of this mood the utmost *subtlety* and verisimilitude are required. In every detail except the chosen marvel, the story should be accurately true to nature. The keynote should be that of scientific exposition—since that is the normal way of presenting a "fact" new to experience, and should not change as the story slides off from the possible to the impossible.[15]

Unfortunately Lovecraft often violated his own rule about being too realistic about the chosen marvel, the horrific monster who finally flaps his way in at the end. Here he also violates Mrs Radcliffe's stricture against damaging the sublime at the expense of the particular, for as she warns, "They must be men of very cold imaginations with whom certainty is more terrible than surmise." Monsters are so realistically detailed in certain Lovecraft stories that we tend to be disappointed; since Lovecraft has a constitutional aversion to seafood ("Fish of any kind . . . nauseates me beyond control," he wrote to a friend) these monsters often seem like plates of giant fried clams or creamed codfish blown up to unnatural size and endowed with predatory intent.[16] But in *Charles Dexter Ward* Lovecraft's realism and his tight structure are at their height, and he even adds to the effect by introducing a good many documents and pseudodocuments as well. Thus we get extracts from ancient diaries and papers stored in The Rhode Island Historical Society and modern items from the *Providence Journal,* such as the one included under the headline "Nocturnal Diggers Surprised in North Burial Ground."

"It was this morning discovered by Robert Hart, night watchman of the North Burial Ground," Lovecraft fabricates,

> that ghouls were again at work in the ancient portion of the cemetery. The grave of Ezra Weeden, who was born in 1740 and died in 1824 according to his uprooted and savagely splintered slate headstone, was found excavated with a spade stolen from an adjacent tool shed. Whatever the contents may have been after more than a century of burial, all was gone except a few slivers of decayed wood. There were no wheel tracks but police have measured a single set of footprints which they found in the vicinity, and which indicate the boots of a man of refinement. . . . Members of the Weeden family, notified of the

happening, expressed their astonishment and regret; and were wholly unable to think of any enemy who would care to violate the grave of their ancestor. Hazard Weeden of 598 Angell Street recalls a family legend according to which Ezra Weeden was involved in some very peculiar circumstances, not dishonourable to himself, shortly before the Revolution; but of any modern feud or mystery he is frankly ignorant. Inspector Cunningham has been assigned to the case, and hopes to uncover some valuable clues in the near future (166).

But what has led up to such ghastly incidents as these, joined to other strange and sinister phenomena, such as an outbreak of vampirism "around two distinct localities; the residential hill and the North End, near the Ward home at Olney Court, and the suburban districts across the Cranston line near Pawtuxet"? It can be traced simply to obsession with antiquarianism, genealogy, and historical research. Charles Dexter Ward, in exploring twigs and branches of his family tree, has come upon an ominous ancestor, Joseph Curwen, who fled to Providence soon after the witchcraft trials began in Salem. Curwen, he discovers after much delving and probing, was a wizard and alchemist,[17] aligned with certain dark powers who wish to return to earth, which they originally inhabited. Curwen has learned the secret of immortality, but his dastardly plans and the cult he has been in league with are stopped right before the Revolutionary War by those same Rhode Islanders who banded together to burn the *Gaspee* and who finally defied tyrannical King George outright. Here Lovecraft performs a fascinating trick with the rich residue of local legend and tradition—the threat of Curwen and his unholy alliance with the devil becomes, according to Lovecraft's retelling, the first spark of the American Revolution, and Rhode Island in a real sense is thus not only the first colony to declare its independence from Great Britain, but also the first (and only one, for that matter) to declare its independence from the powers of evil and black magic.

Such personages of note as the first president of Brown University— James Manning—Dr Bowen, Esek Hopkins, John Carter, Captain Mathewson, Captain Whipple, and all four of the Brown brothers, meet at such spots as Sabin Tavern or the "great room of Thurston's Tavern at the Sign of the Golden Lion on Weybosset Point across the bridge" in order to formulate plans for a raid against Curwen, who has retired to his farmhouse just off the Pawtuxet Road. Once again, all this is handled with minute and documentary fidelity, as Lovecraft gleans his facts both from local history books and from legend in order to flesh out his fantasy as well as ground it in the solid substance of history itself. Thus we learn, for example, that James Manning was noted for possessing the largest periwig in the colonies, an historical fact, and that the girl whom Curwen manages to wed in a marriage of convenience, Eliza Tillinghast, worked in 1757 at the age of nine a sampler which "may still be found in the rooms of The Rhode Island Historical Society." Gradually Lovecraft leads us along as if we were reading history or newspaper to the final flapping horror, and the hoax is complete.

But *The Case of Charles Dexter Ward* is not simply a hoax, or merely an intricate and ingenious retelling of Rhode Island history. It is a curious fable about uses of human knowledge and bounds of historical research for—as Ward searches out his own family history and comes up with the daemonic figure of Joseph Curwen—he is an Everyman who also searches throughout the whole genealogical background of the family of man, an antiquarian who finds in the past of human beings only horror, atavism, bestiality, and perversion. The simple moral of *The Case of Charles Dexter Ward* is that it is dangerous to know too much, especially about one's own ancestors. Lovecraft expresses this best in the beginning paragraph of another tale, "The Call of Cthulhu," where he writes:

> The most merciful thing in the world, I think, is the inability of the human mind to correlate all its contents. We live on a placid island of ignorance in the midst of black seas of infinity, and it is not meant that we should voyage far. The sciences, each straining in its own direction, have hitherto harmed us little; but some day the piecing together of dissociated knowledge will open up such terrifying vistas of reality, and of our frightful position therein, that we shall either go mad from the revelation or flee from the deadly light into the peace and safety of a new dark age.[18]

Charles Dexter Ward does indeed go mad, he does indeed sink into those black seas of infinity, but the instrument of his destruction is not science, but rather historical and genealogical research, and the infinity is not the infinity of outer space or the universe, but that infinity of the past —that sublime terror which Lovecraft in another short novel would call "The Shadow out of Time." But what is even more horrible in the case of Charles Dexter Ward is that he is literally possessed by the past, which in the form of his ancestor Curwen reanimates itself in his body, usurps his mind, and plunges him fully into an alien and evil world. The process is slow and insidious, but Ward's accumulation of historical knowledge at first poisons his mind and then begins to warp his personality completely, as his eyes turn into the eyes of another man and his brain turns into the brain of an ancestor who died, or was supposed to have died, a hundred years before. It is this unholy knowledge of the past which accomplishes Ward's fall from grace and state of Eden-like romanticism and happiness. And as Ward grows more and more possessed, similarly does his Providence environment grow more and more sinister. Compare, for example, Ward's impression of almost that same downtown scene, quoted before, with the following one, which occurs after Ward is already deep in those fabulous historical researches that have at last led him to explore libraries of certain unsavoury counts whose home base is Transylvania. "Old Providence," Ward exclaims at his first sight of home:

> It was this place and the mysterious forces of its long, continuous history which had brought him into being, and which had drawn him back toward marvels and secrets whose boundaries no prophet might fix. Here lay the arcana, wondrous or dreadful as the case might be, for which all his years of travel and application had been preparing him. A taxicab whirled him through Post Office Square with its glimpse of the river, the Market House, and the head of the bay, and up the steep curved slope of Waterman Street to Prospect, where the vast gleaming dome and sunset-flushed Ionic columns of the Christian Science Church beckoned northward. Then eight squares past the fine old brick estates his childish eyes had known, and the quaint brick sidewalks so often trodden by his youthful feet. And at last the little white overtaken farmhouse on the right, on the left the classic Adam porch and stately bayed facade of the great brick house where he was born. It was twilight, and Charles Dexter Ward had come home (155-56).

But he has also come home to a twilight of horror. Possessed completely by his ancestor Curwen, Ward begins to conjure up again all the evil and mischief supposedly eradicated by that party of colonial Rhode Island gentlemen who surprised the alchemist-wizard at work and annihilated him. Here, newspaper reports of bodies being stolen from North Burial Ground and the vampire scare in Cranston play their part, although Lovecraft once again bases a good deal of his fantasy on hard and concrete fact, for Sidney S. Rider, Rhode Island historian and antiquarian, actually does report a real case of vampirism which occurred about the time of the outbreak of the American Revolution.[19] Lovecraft's Curwen, returned in the person of Charles Dexter Ward, snatches bodies not to feast upon their blood but to feed upon their minds—as an alchemist, he has discovered the secret of reanimating their physical brains by reconstituting what is left of their "animal salts." As Lovecraft writes of Curwen and those who are in league with him:

> What these horrible creatures—and Charles Ward as well—were doing or trying to do seemed fairly clear from their letters and from every bit of light both old and new which had filtered in upon the case. They were robbing the tombs of all the ages, including those of the world's wisest and greatest men, in the hope of recovering from bygone ashes some vestige of the consciousness and lore which had once animated and informed them (187).

Once again, it is an unholy and obscene quest or even thirst for knowledge which remains Lovecraft's eldest primal sin. And for him there is only one salvation possible from the stain of this sin—one must descend

into the depths of evil in order to combat it, one must risk madness oneself in order to conquer madness. Thus most Lovecraft stories, like most
Poe tales, end with a descent into the maelstrom, a plunge into the pit
which is also an exploration of the subconscious part of the human mind,
what Freud called the Id and what Jung called the Collective Unconscious. It is only through this harrowing descent that the world can be
saved from the evil which Curwen and others like him would unleash
upon it. What is always found by those who descend into the Lovecraft
maelstrom—usually cellar or cave—are bones and some unnamable,
dark thing—bones of the past, bones which indicate man's own descent
from Darwin's apes and anthropoids, and the Beast himself, the raging
animal nature of man, always ready to spring forth from the jungle.[20] In
The Case of Charles Dexter Ward a courageous and conscientious doctor
of psychiatry, Marinus Willett, accomplishes this descent and learns the
secret of the cave at peril of losing his own reason altogether, which
Lovecraft allegorises as the doctor's flashlight, giving some illumination
to the foetid darkness. Here Lovecraft would seem to leave the "real"
world altogether, but notice in the following description of a portion of
Willett's journey how minute and detailed he is about this essentially
psychological horror:

> But Marinus Bicknell Willett was sorry that he looked again; for surgeon and
> veteran of the dissecting-room though he was, he has not been the same since.
> It is hard to explain just how a single sight of a tangible object with measurable
> dimensions could so shake and change a man; and we may only say that there
> is about certain outlines and entities a power of symbolism and suggestion
> which acts frightfully on a sensitive thinker's perspective and whispers terrible
> hints of obscure cosmic relationships and unnamable realities behind the pro-
> tective illusions of common vision. In that second look Willett saw such an
> outline or entity, for during the next few instants he was undoubtedly as stark
> mad as any inmate of Dr. Waite's private hospital. He dropped the electric
> torch from a hand drained of muscular power or nervous coördination, nor
> heeded the sound of crunching teeth which told of its fate at the bottom of the
> pit. He screamed and screamed and screamed in a voice whose falsetto panic
> no acquaintance of his would ever have recognised; and though he could not
> rise to his feet he crawled and rolled desperately away over the damp pavement
> where dozens of Tartarean walls poured forth their exhausted whining and
> yelping to answer his own insane cries. He tore his hands on the rough, loose
> stones, and many times bruised his head against the frequent pillars, but still
> he kept on. Then at last he slowly came to himself in the utter blackness and
> stench, and stopped his ears against the droning wail into which the burst of
> yelping had subsided. He was drenched with perspiration and without means
> of producing a light; stricken and unnerved in the abysmal blackness and hor-
> ror, and crushed with a memory he never could efface. Beneath him dozens of
> those things still lived, and from one of the shafts the cover was removed. He
> knew that what he had seen could never climb up the slippery walls, yet shud-
> dered at the thought that some obscure foothold might exist (195–96).

This scene takes place in the cellar of the cottage which Ward has bought near Rhodes-on-the-Pawtuxet, but in Lovecraft there are always cellars beneath cellars beneath cellars and depths below depths. Here ultimate horror is not described, only the reactions of Dr Willett who confronts it. And though his mind is nearly destroyed, Dr Willett escapes with the secret which will finally save Providence and the world from the evil designs of Curwen and his quest for unholy knowledge and power. The secret itself is a magic formula that can reverse the alchemical process Curwen has set in motion, but it is not the formula alone which allows the good doctor to rid the world of the fruit of Charles Dexter Ward's antiquarian research. The formula has to be supplemented by translation of a strange note in an unfamiliar language, which finally reveals that Ward and Curwen inhabit the same body, a body which must be destroyed. Yet means of deciphering this note, found to be written in "pointed Saxon minuscules of the eighth or ninth century A.D." is discovered at last in the John Hay Library of Brown University. For, if according to Christian tradition man is both lost and saved in a garden— the Garden of Eden and the Garden of Gethsemane—then according to Lovecraft's mythology man is both lost and saved in a library. Locked away in the John Hay special collections can be found volumes like the "dreaded *Necronomicon* of the mad Arab, Abdul Alhazred," the reading of which can drive men mad.[21] But it is also the library which preserves not simply knowledge, but wisdom, which is the right use of knowledge, that wisdom of knowing when to stop which Charles Dexter Ward abandoned in searching back through his own genealogy and ancestry. The library only collects knowledge, it does not coordinate it, and so it remains the brake on human emotion and obsession, that small placid island of peace in the middle of those black seas of infinity. Thus the immediate effect of the library on Dr Willett and on Charles Dexter Ward's father is to calm them and assure them of ultimate, rational success. As Lovecraft writes:

> Willett and Mr. Ward were mute and baffled. They had met the unknown, and found that they lacked emotions to respond to it as they vaguely believed they ought. With Willett, especially, the capacity for receiving fresh impressions of awe was well-nigh exhausted; and both men sat still and helpless till the closing of the library forced them to leave (207).

So *The Case of Charles Dexter Ward* comes to its natural, and perhaps even optimistic, end. Curwen is stopped and destroyed, though Ward himself must also pay the price of physical destruction in order to save his soul from eternal possession by the forces of darkness. And so Providence and the world return to normal, never knowing the fate they escaped or the evil that hovered about them on cosmic and malodorous wings. Yet I think, still in opposition to Colin Wilson, Lovecraft could never have conjured up the power of evil in the first place if he had not based the greater part of his narrative on the physical reality of Providence itself—its atmosphere, its lore, its picturesqueness, its history—that richness and fulness which Lovecraft only made more rich and more full. The relation of the author to his chosen place was symbiotic, if not mystical, with more in it perhaps than is dreamt of in our philosophies. Can the line between fact and fiction, reality and vision actually break down, Lovecraft was asking, and can that breakdown involve cosmically sinister consequences, sublime "terror" as well as psychological "horror"? I have quoted one of the pseudodocuments which Lovecraft includes in *The Case of Charles Dexter Ward,* about the grave robbing of a colonial tomb in North Burial Ground. Now as a curious supplement to that, I offer the following from the *Providence Journal,* 26 June 1968—"Coffin, Man's Body Stolen from Cemetery in Cranston"—

> A coffin and a man's body have been stolen from an historical cemetery in Cranston, and an almost completely decomposed body in a coffin was found yesterday . . . behind Esek Hopkins Junior High School in Providence.
> Police are uncertain if the body and coffin, found about 4 behind the school, are the same body and coffin taken from a tomb in Historical Cemetery 19 near 460 Scituate Avenue, Cranston.
> The coffin with the body in it was found on the embankment facing the passing traffic on Route 146. Police said the front half of the top of the coffin was broken open, exposing the remains.
> Cranston police said one of seven bodies was stolen sometime in the last two days from a large stone vault in the cemetery. The vault was entered through a heavy steel door, which was left ajar. . . .
> The name N. S. Prior is chiselled over the door of the vault. Cranston city hall records say the tomb is registered to Nicholas S. Prior, a soldier in the Revolutionary War.
> City Clerk Astrid D. Leidman said records indicate that he died in March, 1787. . . .
> Police said that a copy of the Providence Journal, dated Aug. 26, 1945, was found inside the coffin. Dr Edwin Vieira, state medical examiner, claimed the body. It was taken to the state morgue at Howard.

That, to be sure, is a rather morbid item, but even more it is a very "Lovecraftian" item. If anyone, after reading this, would wish to investigate it more fully, look up all the facts, dig more deeply into its history and peculiarity, they are certainly free to do so, but I am tempted to leave it where I found it—in a grisly little envelope marked "Bodies Found" in the newspaper "morgue" of the *Providence Journal.* It simply seems to be a natural part of the Providence that Lovecraft knew.

But just as the mythic and mystic Providence of *The Case of Charles Dexter Ward* never really did know the total significance of the conjurations and black magic which was happening all around it, neither, strangely enough, does the real Providence seem to know, even today, the man who identified himself so completely with its uniqueness and its traditions. When he died in 1937, Lovecraft's passing went virtually unnoticed in the city where he had been born forty-seven years before—a city which he often compared lovingly to himself—"Providence," he wrote, "of the old brick sidewalks and the Georgian spires and the curving lanes of the hill, and the slat winds from over mouldering wharves where strange cargo ships of old have swung at anchor." He had added that he was "more naturally isolated from mankind than Nathaniel Hawthorne himself, who dwelt alone in the midst of crowds, and whom Salem knew only after his death." It would have amazed Howard Phillips Lovecraft to think that some day he himself would be part of the legends of Providence, yet in its long and important history he remains alone in literary distinction—an outsider still, in his accomplishments and in his fame.

Notes

1. Actually, according to Prof. Dirk W. Mosig, many of the Lovecraft translations are very poor, notably the Sugar edition of *Opere Complete* and the French translations by Jacques Papy. The best translation is perhaps a German one by the poet H. C. Artmann.—S.T.J.
2. No one has been able to track down this remark by Garci (not Garcia). Slonim himself, when questioned, could provide no reference.—S.T.J.
3. Lovecraft's father died of paresis, according to the death certificate. Dr Keller ("Shadows over Lovecraft") tried to argue that Lovecraft himself may have been syphilitic, but this was disproven by Dr Kenneth Sterling (cf. his rebuttal to Keller's "Shadows over Lovecraft").—S.T.J.
4. "A Confession of Unfaith," in *To Quebec and the Stars,* pp. 87-88.—S.T.J.
5. "Imprisoned with the Pharaohs," ghost-written for Harry Houdini.—S.T.J.
6. Cf. Ann Banks, "Lovecraftimania at Brown," *Brown Alumni Monthly,* LXXII, 5 (February 1972), 23.—S.T.J.
7. Cf. Vincent Canby, "Dreadful Doings in Dunwich," *The New York Times,* 12 July 1970, Sec. II, pp. 1, 21.—S.T.J.
8. C. G. Jung, "Approaching the Unconscious," *Man and His Symbols* (New York, 1964), 95.
9. Lovecraft defended his "cosmic interest" and taste for the sublime in the following terms, which once again smack of the eighteenth century and Burke's essays "On Taste" and *On the Sublime and the Beautiful,* just as Lovecraft's idea of the imagination was much closer to pre-Romantic or proto-Romantic conception of "fancy" than to Coleridge's transcendental idea of imagination as "a repetition in the finite mind of the eternal act of creation in the infinite I AM." Lovecraft writes:

> "I could not write about 'ordinary people' because I am not the least interested in them. Without interest there can be no art. Man's relations to man do not captivate my fancy. It is man's relations to the cosmos—to the unknown—which alone

arouses in me the spark of creative imagination. The humanocentric pose is impossible to me, for I cannot acquire the primitive myopia which magnifies the earth and ignores the background. Pleasure to me is wonder—the unexplored, the unexpected, the thing that is hidden and the changeless thing that lurks behind superficial mutability. To trace the remote in the immediate; the eternal in the ephemeral; the past in the present; the infinite in the finite; these are to me the springs of delight and beauty. Like the late Mr. Wilde, 'I live in terror of not being misunderstood.' "

"The Defence Remains Open!", *In Defence of Dagon,* part of Lovecraft's correspondence with "Transatlantic Circulator," an informal group of epistolary critics; April 1921; MS., John Hay Library, Brown University. [Also in *Leaves,* II (1938), 117–19 (as "In Defense of Dagon").—S.T.J.]

10. The novel was written entirely in 1927.—S.T.J.
11. Colin Wilson, "Preface" to *The Mind Parasites.*
12. There is some inaccuracy here. The job offered was the editorship of the then struggling *Weird Tales,* and what Lovecraft feared was that the magazine would fold (it was then $40,000 in debt), leaving Lovecraft stranded in the unaesthetic Chicago.—S.T.J.
13. Letter to Mrs F. C. Clark, MS., John Hay Library, Brown University.
14. H. P. Lovecraft, *The Case of Charles Dexter Ward,* in *Collected Works,* II, p. 108. Hereafter all references to the novel will appear parenthetically in the text.
15. Lovecraft, quoted by August Derleth in *H.P.L.: A Memoir,* p. 80.
16. Dorothy Walter has significant remarks on this aspect when she says that Lovecraft "relied too often on references to things distasteful to himself that he assumed would produce similar feelings of aversion or fear or disgust in others, . . . [e.g.] fishy odours, . . . the strangeness of the foreigner; the unpleasantness of things squirmy and slimy; and chiefly of all, the sensation of cold" (*Lovecraft and Benefit Street*).—S.T.J.
17. Lovecraft takes the pains to tell us that "his birth was known to be good, since the Curwens or Corwins of Salem needed no introduction in New England." "Curwen," "Carwin," or "Corwin" is indeed an old Salem name, a "Jonathan Corwin" being listed as a judge in the Salem witchcraft trials along with Nathaniel Hawthorne's ancestor, John Hathorne. The name however may also owe something to the first American author of "Gothic" tales, Charles Brockden Brown, whose ambiguous villain in the romance *Wieland* is named "Carwin." Lovecraft had previously borrowed the name of another Brown character, Arthur Mervyn, and changed it slightly to provide a title for his early tale, "Arthur Jermyn." Lovecraft continued to use authentic local names in his work, and his protagonist in "Rats in the Walls," a Mr Delapore, owes his cognomen to Sarah Helen Whitman's genealogical researches, in which she believed she had traced both her maiden name (Power) and her fiancé Edgar Allan Poe's name back to a common celtic source (Poer or Delapoer). The fact that Curwen is an alchemist reflects Lovecraft's early interest in the origins of scientific method (another early story was entitled "The Alchemist") as well as his affinity to, and knowledge of, Hawthorne's works, for the theme of an alchemical "elixir of life" can be found both in Hawthorne's short tale "The Birthmark" and the late, unfinished *Dolliver Romance,* while Lovecraft's mythic New England City "Arkham" is an uneasy combination of old Salem and old Providence.
18. *Collected Works,* I, p. 130. Is Lovecraft actually against "knowing too much"? Cf. Prof. Mosig's H. P. Lovecraft: Myth-Maker" (p. 105).—S.T.J.
19. J. Earl Clauson, "Vampirism in Rhode Island," *These Plantations* (Providence, 1937), 67–69.
20. Theme of two surviving pieces of Lovecraft juvenilia, "Beast in the Cave" and "White Ape," both dealing with cases of atavism and reversion to type. [Yet "White Ape" is nothing more than Lovecraft's "Facts concerning the Late Arthur Jermyn and His Family," the title having been changed by the editor of *Weird Tales* when it first appeared there. It is hardly juvenilia, written sometime in 1920—S.T.J.]

21. It is never mentioned that a copy of the *Necronomicon* is in the John Hay Library; but there is certainly one at the neighbouring Miskatonic University Library in Arkham.—S.T.J.

"The White Ship":
A Psychological Odyssey

By Dirk W. Mosig

Among the most neglected aspects of Lovecraft's fictional oeuvre
*are his so-called "Dunsanian fantasies," early tales inspired by the work
of the Irish fantaisiste Lord Dunsany. Yet, in spite of possible stylistic
derivation, virtually all of these tales reflect some definite facet of Lovecraft's philosophical and aesthetic thought. Professor Dirk W. Mosig
(1943–) has chosen to examine "The White Ship" and to indicate the
many interpretations provided by this openly allegorical tale.*

H. P. Lovecraft's 'Dunsanian" tales are often hastily dismissed as
mere imitations, and the Providence scribe is primarily remembered for
his straight horror masterpieces and his "Cthulhu Mythos" narratives.
Nevertheless, this widespread attitude neglects the fact that H. P. L. was
writing in the so-called "Dunsanian" vein before having heard of Lord
Dunsany or having read any of his dream-like tales.

"Polaris" was written a whole year prior to his encounter with Lord
Dunsany and his works, and clearly shows that Lovecraft's mind, at the
time, was running in a parallel channel to Dunsany's. It is quite possible
that, had Lovecraft never come across Lord Dunsany, he would still have
written most of his "Dunsanian" tales.

Among Lovecraft's dream fantasies, one of the most provoking is
"The White Ship," written in 1919, only a year after "Polaris." At the
time, H.P.L. was aware of Lord Dunsany, and parts of the story are
reminiscent of the latter's City of Never. But while the tale shows similarity to Dunsany's "Wonderful Window" and "The Dream of King
Karna-Vootra," it is impossible to determine how much of "The White
Ship" is original, and how much sheer imitation. In any case, there is little doubt that the message, the inner meaning, is truly Lovecraftian.

This excellent piece is perhaps the most openly allegorical in the whole
Lovecraft *opus*. Basil Elton, the "keeper of the light," is in communion
with the never silent ocean, the traditional symbol of the Unconscious.
"Sometimes at night the deep waters of the sea [grew] clear and phosphorescent, [and granted him] glimpses of the ways beneath." These

were glimpses of "the ways that were and the ways that might be [and] the ways that are." Like Jung's Collective Unconscious, the ocean is "more ancient than the mountains," and is full of the "memories and dreams of Time."[1]

That Lovecraft had in mind an allegorical psychological meaning for the ocean in this tale is not as farfetched as it sounds. A few months before "The White Ship" was written, his poem "Aletheia Phrikodes" appeared in *The Vagrant,* containing these enlightening lines:

> Things vague, unseen, unfashion'd, and unnam'd
> Jostled each other in the seething void
> That gap'd, chaotic, downward to a sea
> Of speechless horror, foul with writhing *thoughts* (my italics)[2]

It is out of this psychic ocean that the fabled White Ship appears, the archetype of the emergence of the Self. Upon its deck is a robed, bearded man, or "Wise Old Man" archetype, who beckons Elton (the ego) to embark on the odyssey to self-realisation.

"Very brightly did the moon shine on the night [he] answered the call," and he boarded the vessel after walking "on a bridge of moonbeams." The Ship sailed, "golden with the glow of that full, mellow moon." According to C. G. Jung, the moon symbolises the "Mother Archetype," and its appearance in dreams often indicates the presence of a mother "complex." The mother complex, characteristic of an individual whose personality is dominated by his mother, consists of ideas, feelings, and memories clustering around the nuclear element provided by man's racial experiences with mothers throughout the ages. Such a complex is not necessarily "bad," and often leads to a greater capacity for friendship and kindness toward others, a feeling for history, and a conservative attachment to the values of the past. . . . (!)

The mystic vessel sails past the land of Zar, where dwell dreams and thoughts of beauty now forgotten. In this sphere, so reminiscent of Jung's Personal Unconscious, Elton recognises many things he had once seen "through the mists beyond the horizon and in the phosphorescent depth of the ocean." But he does not set foot on the land of Zar, "for it is told that he who treads [there] may nevermore return to his native shore." Material repressed into the Personal Unconscious is not likely to return to its "native shore" in the realm of consciousness. . . .

Next, the White Ship passes by Thalarion, "the City of a Thousand Wonders, wherein reside all those mysteries that man has striven in vain to fathom," the deepest region of the Collective Unconscious, which can never be made conscious. It is "populated by daemons and things," the archetypes derived from man's primordial past. Archetypes are innate axial systems, gaining power and consistency from actual experiences in each individual's lifetime. They resemble skeletons which acquire mobility only when covered by the flesh and muscle of experience. Sure enough, the streets of Thalarion are "white with unburied bones. . . ."

The psychic vessel sails past the walls of this archetypal city, and follows "a southward-flying bird, whose glossy plumage matched the sky out of which it appeared." What is this mysterious bird? Does it represent the faith in man's destiny, the guide that will lead to the final goal of perfect Selfhood? Or is it only the deceiving symbol of an unattainable illusion?

When the White Ship comes to what appears to be "a pleasant coast gay with blossoms of every hue . . . bursts of song . . . [and] faint laughter so delicious," the keeper of the light of consciousness becomes eager to reach it. But this is Xura, "the Land of Pleasures Unattained," the upper region of the Collective Unconscious, where dwell irrational emotions and atavistic instincts. . . . The wind blowing over the idyllic shore is promptly filled with "the lethal, charnel odour of plague-stricken towns and uncovered cemeteries," and the White Ship sails "madly away from that damnable coast," following the enigmatic "bird of heaven."

The boat finally reaches what appears to be its destination, Sona-Nyl, "the Land of Fancy." Here neither time nor space nor suffering nor death are found: the ego has reached a state of harmony with the forces of the unconscious, a state of practical self-realisation, actualising all of his latent potential for the appreciation of beauty. He is also in harmony with the universe, having achieved a near-perfect balance between his inner world and the external world of objective reality. But although this state of psychic integration, of intellectual and emotional wholeness, appears to last for "aeons," it is not enough. . . .

For against the full moon, the beckoning "celestial bird" reappears, and Elton feels "the first stirrings of unrest," yearning to depart for mystical Cathuria. Cathuria is the "Land of Hope . . . which no man hath ever seen," and where reside "the perfect ideals of all we know." This Platonic land, the mythical heaven for which men have hoped since time immemorial, unable to accept the reality of their ephemeral existence, is also the hypothetical end-state of complete self-realisation. (Complete psychic integration, the total equalisation and fusion of all systems in the human psyche into the Self, implies total entropy, and this cannot occur during the life of the individual. Without a gradient, the flow of energy comes to a standstill—a condition possible only in death. . . .) But Lovecraft, the rationalist, could not interpret that final stage in the same way as Jung, the mystic.

Small wonder, then, that when the White Ship sails for Cathuria, "the abode of the gods," against the best advice of the wise bearded man, it encounters only disaster. Upon approaching the mist-shrouded basalt pillars of the West, which "reach even to the heavens," the voyager beholds "not the Land of Cathuria, but a swift-rushing resistless sea," which carries him, helpless, to "a monstrous cataract, wherein the oceans of the world drop down to abysmal nothingness." Cathuria is an illusion, an unattainable dream, for which Elton has foolishly rejected "the beautiful Land of Sona-Nyl." And "over the brink of the torrent," the celestial bird flaps "its mocking blue wings."

Then, Darkness comes. Only cold awareness of bleak reality remains among the shambles of shattered dreams. . . . In the darkness, a vessel crashes on the "cruel rocks," and when dawn comes, the corpse of a strange blue bird is found upon the rocks. And the ocean told its secrets no more. . . .

Lovecraft, the materialistic philosopher, clearly rejected the kind of mystical and metaphysical elements which Jung would propose in his analytical theory years later. Cathuria, the mythical goal of spiritual perfection (ultimate Selfhood), does not exist. The "bird of heaven" leads not to the place of ultimate beauty, but only to "abysmal nothingness." It is better to live in a state of limited inner and outer harmony than to undertake the wasteful pursuit of a mystical realm beyond the immediate and tangible well-being of a well-adjusted personality. Striving for the "Land of Hope" is not only wasteful, but positively unhealthy, since it may lead to the personality breakdown of obsessive neurosis. This was Freud's position, and it seems to have been the view of the thinker from Providence.

The above interpretation of "The White Ship" as the allegorical rejection of psychological mysticism by Lovecraft's positivistic intellect is, of course, highly speculative and debatable. No claim is made for its validity and, as usual, other interpretations are possible.

An alternative eludication would be to consider "The White Ship" as a statement on the evolution of human hopes and dreams as a function of age. Elton is growing older, and in his loneliness he finds solace not only in his childhood memories, but also in his illusions and hopes for a future with "no suffering nor death" and, beyond this, the ultimate "city of the gods." Later Lovecraft exploited this theme—the futility of human dreams and hopes—in another masterly fantasy. "The Quest of Iranon," which elicits an unparalleled and unforgettable mood of sadness and melancholy in the receptive reader. "Iranon," written in 1921, in the same year as the vastly different yet thematically related "The Outsider," is probably one of the finest efforts of H.P.L. in the "Dunsanian" vein, despite Lovecraft's severe criticism of this piece during his later years.

Another possibility is that the "Land of Hope" stands for the scientific utopia of the future. Man hopes to find in Science the panacea for all evils and the path to a perfect, glorious future. Instead, the revelations of science bring him face to face with the intolerable abyss of reality, where all his dreams are shattered, and he discovers the truth about his own meaninglessness and insignificance in a purposeless, mechanistic universe. . . . This idea was fully developed in Lovecraft's later tales, such as the famous "Call of Cthulhu."

Or perhaps the White Ship itself is the vessel of Science, leading to Sona-Nyl, the Land of Fancy, and of physical, material, and intellectual well-being, which man rejects for the superstition of Cathuria, "which no man hath seen." But the rejection of mechanistic science leads only to emptiness, and not to the mythical land of metaphysical glory. The White Ship is shattered, and the ocean of truth reveals its secrets no more. . . .

Arguments for these and other possible explanations could doubtlessly be advanced. Nevertheless, in the case of "The White Ship," a psychological interpretation appears to be, by far, the most adequate, in view of the explicit references to obvious psychological elements throughout the tale.

It is likely that the Providence dreamer had more to say in his memorable fantasy tales than a superficial reading would suggest. Only the careful study of the diverse elements in his fictional and poetic works, within the context provided by factual biographical data and his serious philosophical essays and letters, can lead to a better understanding of the work of this unique and neglected literary genius.

Notes

1. For all references to "The White Ship," see Collected Works, III, pp. 41–46.—S.T.J.
2. "Aletheia Phrikodes" is the central section of "The Poe-et's Nightmare"; cf. Collected Poems, pp. 44–50.—S.T.J.

Lovecraft and the
Cosmic Quality in Fiction

By Richard L. Tierney

Poet, novelist, short-story writer, and critic, Richard L. Tierney holds an important place in modern Lovecraft scholarship. His "The Derleth Mythos" was one of the first essays to point out the fallacies in August Derleth's criticism and pastiches of Lovecraft, while the following essay explores what may be the single most important aspect of Lovecraft's work—the cosmic quality, which largely gives Lovecraft his unique place in world literature. Tierney's recent novel, The Winds of Zarr, *has been called one of the finest fictional works in the Lovecraftian tradition.*

One very neglected aspect of H. P. Lovecraft—neglected, perhaps, because of its elusive nature—is his thought on what might be called the "cosmic" quality in fiction.

For Lovecraft, this cosmic quality was not primarily an intellectual position nor a philosophical outlook, but rather, a feeling or mood that could be evoked in rare people by even rarer passages in literature. It could also be evoked in these same people—and perhaps even more powerfully—by a direct, almost mystical apprehension of the universe as revealed by the implications of the modern sciences, especially astronomy.

Most of us learn at a fairly early age that the earth is round, and that it circles the sun. A few of us may even learn that the sun is only one of countless billions in an apparently limitless universe. Then, having no practical use for such knowledge, we soon go back to living our mundane lives as if we were on a flat, stationary earth at the centre of things. Lovecraft, however, was one of those rare people who can never forget that they are inhabitants of the universe rather than merely "the world."

This does not, of course, mean that H.P.L. was unaware of the details of the world he lived in. He was very much aware of them, as his letters abundantly testify—perhaps more aware than most people. Above all, he was without question more aware than the average person of the *inter-relatedness* of all things, even the tiniest, in the cosmic whole. This is quite apparent, for instance, in the lines from his sonnet "Continuity":

> A faint, veiled sign of continuities
> That outward eyes can never quite descry;[1]

This is the region of awareness where the spirit of science and the spirit of mysticism are seen to be ultimately one and the same—a region almost impossible to describe to those who have not voyaged there.

That Lovecraft equated the cosmic outlook with mysticism is evident in his letter of 7 November 1930 to Clark Ashton Smith, in which he states: "A favourable environment would probably do no more than increase the size of the cosmic minority—for even among the naive & ignorant the mystic inclination is not widespread."[2] In an earlier letter to Smith, dated 17 October 1930, he calls the cosmically receptive a "sensitive minority" and goes on to say: "Racially, moreover, it is almost exclusively Nordic."[3] In this H.P.L. was mistaken, if we take him literally, for every race has produced its "sensitive minority" of the mystically inclined who sense a "something" beyond the veil which is almost impossible to communicate to others. The Japanese, for instance, call that "something" by the name *yugen*. In essence, it is the spirit of Zen—the direct experience of the universe which can only be lived but never grasped conceptually.

That Lovecraft saw the cosmic feeling as being "almost exclusively Nordic" is probably due to the fact that the writers in whom he sensed it most strongly were working in the same northern European tradition as himself. That tradition is the one we call Gothic. Its early conventional stage-settings, designed to evoke moods of mystery, horror and dark wonderment—often with supernatural overtones—included crumbling castles, shadowy forests, graveyards, raging storms at midnight and, usually, a monstrous family secret or curse. Later, when these devices were wearing thin, they began to be replaced by some of the more awesome revelations of modern science, particularly the black, limitless depths of space in which all manner of mysteries and terrors might conceivably lurk. In this replacement, Lovecraft himself was to play an important part—as Fritz Leiber has so well pointed out in his admirable article "A Literary Copernicus."

In the letter to Smith last quoted above, Lovecraft identifies some of the "surprisingly small quota" of writers he believes possess cosmic feeling: ". . . We can easily see the cosmic quality in Poe, Maturin, Dunsany, de la Mare, & Blackwood. . . ."[4] Poe was the earliest fiction writer to possess this trait to an extremely high degree—though, as has been pointed out by William Scott Home,[5] we see it most strongly in his non-fiction essay "Eureka."

Lovecraft continues: "I profoundly suspect the cosmicism of Bierce, James, & even Machen."[6] Elsewhere, however, he writes:[7] "Of living creators of cosmic fear raised to its most artistic pitch, few if any can hope to equal the versatile Arthur Machen. . . ."[8] Although H.P.L. considered "The White People" to be Machen's best tale, it was probably in "The Great God Pan" that he sensed the Welsh writer's cosmicism most strongly. In that story, Machen speaks of "The unutterable, the unthinkable gulf that yawns profound between two worlds, the world of matter and the world of spirit," and of the awful consequences of crossing it. This seems to have been the germ of inspiration for Lovecraft's own tale "The Dunwich Horror," in which monstrous beings bridge the gap between their alien dimension and our own.[9]

Lovecraft goes on to tell Smith: "Among the individuals of my acquaintance it [the cosmic quality] is rarer than hen's teeth. You have it yourself to a supreme degree, & so have [Donald] Wandrei & Bernard Dwyer; but I'm hanged if I can carry the list any farther." Evidently H.P.L. meant *writers* he knew, for a little further he states: "One fellow —named [Ira A.] Cole—whom I used to correspond with had it as keenly as anybody on the globe, but unfortunately he took to 'hearing voices' & finally 'got religion'. . . ."[10]

Those who have read Clark Ashton Smith's cosmos-spanning blank verse epic "The Hashish-Eater," or Donald Wandrei's end-of-the-universe prose-poem "The Red Brain," can hardly doubt Lovecraft's judgement where these two authors are concerned. As for Ira A. Cole, a long, recently-discovered poem of his titled "Atlantis"[11] does indeed suggest a mystical flare—though not, in my opinion, of a sort to compare with the inimitable Klarkash-Ton.[12]

No doubt there will always be contention as to which author has the cosmic quality and which has not. The difficulty is only partly due to the fact that, as H.P.L. pointed out to Smith, those who have it are "rarer than hen's teeth." A greater difficulty is that those who cannot sense it can often not be convinced that it exists at all. In a way cosmic awareness presents the same problem as colour vision: either one has it or one doesn't—and if one has it, how does one explain it to the colour blind?

Perhaps the problem can be simplified for analysis by dividing fiction into the following three categories:

(1) *Human centred.* This contains not only all mainstream fiction but most science-fiction and fantasy as well. Its premise is that humans, *as they are now,* are the focus of interest and that their problems and goals are somehow *important.* Probably all fiction up to the middle of the nineteenth century falls into this category, and certainly all commercial literature up to the present moment. Few stories would sell were they not

based on the premise that human endeavour of some sort is somehow meaningful. Human emotion is necessary to carry the reader along through identification; this is true even if the protagonist is a being of the remote future or the denizen of another planet or galaxy.

(2) *Human evolution centred.* This category concerns humanity as it may be in some future time, evolved to a new stage—not different from us in a merely social sense (customs, dress, laws, etc.) but qualitatively. Nietzsche was perhaps the first to emphasise this outlook strongly, and some of the best examples of it in modern literature are Olaf Stapledon, Arthur C. Clarke, Don A. Stuart[13] and A. E. Van Vogt. H. G. Wells, too, suggested it strongly in some of his novels of the future. Perhaps the most outstanding recent author in this vein is Colin Wilson, whose novels *The Mind Parasites* and *The Philosopher's Stone* powerfully evoke the feeling that Man may be on the brink of a more meaningful stage of evolution beyond our present comprehension. For the central contention of this branch of literature is that Man as he exists now is profoundly unsatisfactory—but that a new act is coming in the play.

(3) *Cosmos centred.* This, the subject of the present analysis, might better be called "uncentred," perhaps, for it attempts to ease the reader away from his preconceived notions entirely and leave him with the awed feeling that he really knows nothing about the cosmos at all—but is *about to know.* Its limitation is that it can never really describe, only suggest.

In addition to the authors Lovecraft mentioned as having the cosmic outlook, he must undoubtedly have sensed it in William Hope Hodgson, especially in *The House on the Borderland* and *The Night Land.* He would also have detected it in H. G. Wells, perhaps most strongly in parts of *The Time Machine* and *The War of the Worlds,* as well as in the short story "The Star." And had he lived longer, he would surely have granted its presence in Olaf Stapledon's epic of universal evolution, *Star Maker,* which appeared in 1937.

Finally, Lovecraft did not fail to recognise his own possession of the cosmic trait. In the above-quoted letter to Smith he states: "As for me, I think I have the actual cosmic feeling very strongly. . . . My most poignant emotional experiences . . . concern the lure of unplumbed space, the terror of the encroaching outer void, & the struggle of the ego to transcend the known & established order of time, space, matter, force, geometry, & natural law in general."[14] This is illustrated beyond doubt in "The Silver Key," perhaps the most poetically beautiful story Lovecraft ever wrote.

Notes

1. From Sonnet XXXVI of *Fungi from Yuggoth,* ll. 5–6.—S.T.J.
2. *Collected Works,* VII, p. 215.—S.T.J.
3. *Ibid.,* p. 196.—S.T.J.
4. *Ibid.*—S.T.J.
5. *H.P.L. Supplement No. 3,* ed. Meade Frierson, 1972.
6. *Collected Works,* VII, p. 196.—S.T.J.
7. "Supernatural Horror in Literature," in *Collected Works,* III, p. 399.
8. This statement appears to be rhetoric, for Lovecraft flatly contradicts it by saying in a letter to Bernard Austin Dwyer, [1932], "[The] imagination [of Machen] is not cosmic" (*Collected Works,* VIII, p. 4).—S.T.J.
9. Actually, the plots of the two tales are remarkably similar: both concern the life of an anomalous child who is, as Lovecraft states, the offspring of "no mortal father"—on the one hand Pan, on the other Yog-Sothoth. Lovecraft mentions Machen himself in the story, and it is likely that the lush descriptions of the countryside around Dunwich in Lovecraft's tale were also inspired by Machen, whose descriptions of nature are always filled with hints of the sinister. Then, too, the death of Lovecraft's character Wilbur Whateley and Machen's depiction of the death of Helen Vaughan are somewhat similar, though Lovecraft's is the more elaborate.—S.T.J.
10. *Collected Works,* VII, p. 196.—S.T.J.
11. Meade Frierson, ed., *HPL,* pp. 19–21.
12. H.P.L. often addressed Clark Ashton Smith with this jocular nickname.
13. Pseudonym of John W. Campbell.—S.T.J.
14. *Collected Works,* VII, p. 197.—S.T.J.

Dystopia as Utopia:
Howard Phillips Lovecraft
and the Unknown Content
of American Horror Literature

By Paul Buhle

The growing importance of Lovecraft's work can be signalled by the increasing efforts to place his oeuvre *and thought in historical perspective. Although Matthew H. Onderdonk made some slight headway in this department, the most revolutionary and significant contribution has been done in the following article by Paul Buhle (1944–). Buhle, former editor of* Radical America, *received his doctorate from the University of Wisconsin, and is editor of* Cultural Correspondence, *"a strategic journal of popular culture," and associate editor of* Radical History Review *and* Minnesota Review, *in the Spring 1976 issue of which the following article appeared. Buhle has contributed to such periodicals as* Nation, Harper's Bookletter, Monthly Review, *and others, and is co-editor of* A Concise History of Woman Suffrage *(University of Illinois Press, 1978).*

Man imagines himself free from fear when there is no longer anything unknown. . . . Enlightenment is mythic fear turned radical. The pure immanence of positivism, its ultimate product, is no more than a so-to-speak universal taboo. Nothing at all may remain outside, because the mere idea of outsideness is the very source of fear.

Max Horkheimer and Theodore Adorno,
Dialectic of the Enlightenment

Emotions and feelings that the philosophers of the machine had neglected or despised, were now reasserting themselves above all, the trunk of the past, which had been cut down, was now sending up numerous suckers, suckers infested with grubs and covered by fungus almost before they had left the ground. In their baser manifestations, these new forces would curb socialism; in their most humane aspects, they would add to its mechanical futurism a certain element it had always lacked.

Lewis Mumford, *The Condition of Man*

Someday the piecing together of dissociated knowledge will open up such terrifying vistas of reality, and of our frightful position therein, that we shall either go mad from the revelation or flee from the deadly light into the peace and safety of a new dark age.

H. P. Lovecraft, *The Call of Cthulhu*

Every schoolchild reads Poe, but our national credo of "Progress" has for centuries denied the darker views of life. Radicals (and by no means only radicals) feel surrounded by a horrific nightmare, but most Left creations have, at least until recent decades, sought to cheer the spirit with our own version of Progress or to confine misery and mystery to the realistic portraits of today's world. In the end it is much the same: we want to *banish* Horror from the field of emotions, to strip life of all that is perilous to touch and consider. The literary critics have largely shared these taboos, glancing uneasily over their shoulders now and again at the voluminous literature of "Blackness." Constance Rourke's *American Humor* and Harry Levin's *The Power of Blackness* are virtually alone in showing the sense of horror to be organic to the American tradition. The late dean of American criticism, Edmund Wilson, spoke for many when he brushed aside violent humour and pulp horror as vulgar and uninteresting. Left critics like V. L. Parrington and Granville Hicks likewise read out the horrorists in favour of the uplifting function of the "progressive," realistic novel.

One can understand and even sympathise with this radical myopia. The seemingly assured arrival of Socialism in the days before the First World War, the threat of Fascism and Nazism in the 1920's to 1940's, the infinite horrors of imperialism and the charred and broken lives resulting from the multitudinous forms of class oppression at home— these allowed scant ground for consideration of the irrational save as a weapon in the hands of the enemies of humankind. But the times have given cause for other visions. Since the Second World War, we have more clearly begun to see America as a Civilisation and not merely a conglomerate of opposing classes and groups. The events of the 1960's, the mixture of drugs, music, and heightened sexual imagery in renewed Utopian dreams indicate that "nonrationalism" or supra-rationalism is not the exclusive property of the Right but ground that must be politically contested. Most of all, perhaps, the dawning of popular awareness of the rest of world-historic experience—from the anthropological and journalistic stories of nonindustrial societies gone or about to be destroyed, to the tales of Third World anti-Imperialist triumphs—have shown how limited and fragmented our view of the human essence has been. Among the analysts of American literature, perhaps Leslie Fiedler's post-1930's-radical conception of "American Love and Death" is the closest precursor to a wider perspective. He set a new standard for American literary criticism by showing the omnipresent death pageantry to be the result of erotic failure, the sexual alienation of *Homo Americanus*. But Fiedler's conclusions missed the heart of the problem at every vital point. Of course the themes of morbidity have "something to do" with a lack of sexual attainment in the major characters and even perhaps in the authors. But what? Freudianism is no more satisfactory in itself than the mechanical Marxism that describes Horror as the simple product of Imperial decadence and perversity. American madness cannot be explained in its own terms, but rather must be understood in the whole of American (and universal) history.

Fundamentally, horror calls into question those self-beliefs of Western Civilisation, which reach their highest and most mystifying point in the United States. Horror is that Romanticism, in André Breton's words, which denies the classically "good" and "undeniably wishes naught but evil," because only Evil seems to express the violent, sudden unshackling of the bonds with which Christian moral law, affirmative culture, and the increasingly empty faith in Progress have saddled the society. Horror discloses the secret of the Enlightenment, that what is claimed to be Freedom is in practise largely avaricious individualism, that Science and social knowledge have been implemented to extinguish age-old relationships of humanity and nature, and that the growing restiveness of the entire population in advanced society is to be controlled by the legal, theological, and psychiatric arms of the State rather than serving as the opportunity for masses to confront their anguish and expectations.

Horror speaks first in America to the terror of asociality. The project of New World conquest contained both a Utopian search for geographic infinitude and a characteristic European modernising desire to escape the contradictions of class society by establishing the ultimate self-made class society, based upon Protestantism stripped of its mediaeval mental relics. The colonial American on the edge of the forest can aspire to the individual liberty of self and property unknown in the Old World save to the very rich—but at the same time, he lacks many of the social ties, the remnants of ancient customs, to give unified meaning to the apparently chaotic universe around him. The more he partakes of secular existence that economic-social opportunity affords, the less he is certain of the mysteries outside his material grasp, of the shadows and wonders that torment him. For this prototype of the ultimate Westerner, these mysteries are his Last Frontier, the one that refuses successively the trapper, the homesteader, the pilots of railroads, tractors, automobiles, and even spaceships: an apparently uncontrollable chaos of the physical universe and the universe of the mind, a magical realm open to "poetic" intervention alone, be it actual poetry, dance, cosmic speculation or the close observation of all details of life including those neglected by bourgeois social science and literary realism. Seen from the conqueror's viewpoint, this chaos is intolerable, horrifying beyond words—all his hubris, his puerile dreams and expectations, his empires of thought and deed crumble to dust before it. Asociality is the mirror to all this, for it is the consequence of all activities undertaken for any purpose other than the purposes of humanity. Age-old antagonisms that permanently disturb Europe drive into a frenzy the New World Man who has resolved somehow to escape them.

It is not for nothing that the "primitive" tribesman fears the introduction of history: once irrevocable time is granted, all the cyclical certainties of Nature fall away and something of the spirit is lost. Modern (i.e., American) fear is the opposite. Our *historic* confidence is called into question, our assumed destiny evidently exposed like all other social and biological systems to the process of decline, decay, and replacement. Our foreboding is that Marx was right, and the end of this social world we know means the dawning of an age almost unimaginable and somehow linked to that older existence so long ago left behind.

In asociality and in history, Horror is the natural concomitant to the Socialist critiques of Capitalism. Horror foreshadows and fulfils the Marxian prediction of Socialism or Barbarism by placing in true perspective the breakdown of the West, the rampant and apparently meaningless violence between its subject-citizens, the random terror and mass starvation, organised murder and brutal suppression—in short, the World News Roundup. To the extent that Socialism remains a mere option to realise the Western project—a collective harnassing of all the nonhuman forces and species to the demands of industrialisation and urbanisation —Horror remains to claim the territory of the imagination for Dystopia. But already Horror itself has pointed to other alternatives. In wrestling with the multitude of social and psychological contradictions, Horror reveals its immanent content, the hidden Utopianism of its negative Romanticism. Only as Socialism suffers new jolts and is forced to accommodate forces outside its tradition can it encompass, realise, and transcend Horror, resolving the outermost points of fear and desire into social participation.

Howard Phillips Lovecraft was the most articulate spokesman of the new pulp fantaisistes, architect of a cosmic horror which combined American literary accomplishments with twentieth-century scientific uncertainty in the universe, and a belief as old as oral story-telling in the power of the mind to reveal the splendid potentials of existence. Regretfully, we have not even a *Eureka* to use as a key to his writings, so that his philosophical position must be inferred from tales, correspondence, and criticism. As Barton St Armand has best seen, Lovecraft had in mind the same, grand modern tragedy as Poe; like Poe, his horror themes were mere literary devices, powerful enough to create a whole generation of horror writers but not powerful enough to sustain his own epic mission.[1] Yet for all these weaknesses, and a disability in treating sexual themes even deeper than Poe's morbidity, Lovecraft compensated his readers with a rare power of vision emerging almost unmediated from his dreams. This oneiroscopic imagery, he hinted at his most lucid moments, perhaps self-conscious only among a minority, was nonetheless the latent possession of all human minds.

Lovecraft was in the first instance a direct descendant of the local colour of Mary Wilkins Freeman and other New England artists. Such traditions gave him a sense of self extending back centuries, with a defined aesthetic of village life and beauty that American Renaissance writers would easily have recognised. Indeed, his descriptions of regional architecture, particularly of his home town of Providence, Rhode Island, are among his most carefully developed prose. Like Hawthorne and Freeman, he also found there the locus of horror, for as he wrote in an early tale: "The true epicure of the terrible, to whom a new thrill of unutterable ghastliness is the chief end and justification of existence, esteems most of all the ancient, lonely farmhouses of backwoods New England; for there the dark elements of strength, solitude, grotesqueness, and ignorance combine to form the perfection of the hideous" ("The Picture in the House").[2] And not only the backwoods, with their fables of incest and degeneration; Lovecraft saw the horrors of the New England centres of commerce as well. His ghouls travel through those tunnels actually found in Providence extending from mansions to the sea, for the secret transfer of slaves; he relocates Devil Worship in the opulent "Kingsport" (apparently Marblehead, Massachusetts), product of a corruption of the spirit always close to the Puritan hubris and perhaps the penalty for fostering capitalism (see "The Festival").

Lovecraft was the profound child of Poe, and one of the most serious scholars of that writer in a time when, in the High Culture of America, his reputation had gone into a decline.[3] Lovecraft's fictional god of horror was not the vengeful and moral Jehovah but his own invention, "Nyarlathotep," the "Crawling Chaos" felt "through this revolting graveyard of a universe [in] the muffled, maddening beating of drums, and . . . the monotonous whine of blasphemous flutes from inconceivable, unlighted chambers beyond Time."[4] This gave a definite cosmic character to Poe's unification of the terrible and the beautiful, and was akin not so much to Poe's simple morbidity (like "The Pit and the Pendulum") as to his more "philosophical" horrors like the "House of Usher," "Masque of the Red Death," and his poems "Silence, a Fable" and "Shadow, a

Parable."[5] The Southern links to Lovecraft's own Rhode Island are also significant; its historic "Plantations" and its analogous decadence, more attuned to death than to life, its vivid architecture and cultural traditions a counterpoint to its wrecked and decaying class of Anglo-Saxon rulers.

Lovecraft built upon Poe's sepulchral foundation, adding the work of modern terror writers Arthur Machen and Lord Dunsany to give him more modern techniques and spirit.[6] But like his fellow fantaisistes of the 1920's, he was also deeply affected by a scientific influence, or rather the impress of the great iconoclast of science, Charles Fort. In *The Book of the Damned* (1919), Fort had compiled phenomena beyond scientific explanation, the excluded elements of life that he described as "corpses, skeletons, mummies, twitching, tottering . . . damned alive . . . arm and arm with the spirit of anarchy . . . pale stenches and gaunt superstitions and mere shadows and lively malices."[7] This was a literary or imaginative interpretation of the indeterminacy of modern scientific discovery: unexplained disappearances (of Ambrose Bierce, among others), black rains, unnatural appearances of astral phenomena—for these Fort supplied his own poetic suggestions, like the secret movement of some great compensating force overruling man's blunders, moving through the Negative (as Poe had suggested) toward some unforseeable reconciliation of forces. An immediate best-seller, *The Book of the Damned* influenced writers like George Allan England and allowed fantaisistes like Lovecraft to encompass modern psychology (as another quest into the unknown) while escaping its contemporary, reductionist interpretations of the unmysterious and unpoetic character of human existence.[8] The change of professions of one of Lovecraft's protagonists, from economics to psychology,[9] mirrors the larger literary mood of the period. But Lovecraft's hero finds not "answers" but new uncertainties which link the mental unknown to unfathomable cosmic forces, his mental "distortion" perceived by the outside world as madness, allowing his perception of a Reality beyond day-to-day existence ("The Shadow out of Time"). Thus Lovecraft restated Poe's message at a higher level by adding the literary implications of scientific relativity, and proclaimed "the essentially intellectual wonder of one who looks out upon the whirling, grotesque, and unfathomable reaches which engulf the entire world."[10] Of all the wonders, *Time* was the greatest. As his friends suggested, Lovecraft felt himself out of place in an apparently wonderless age, his protagonist and alter ego forming "chimerical notions about living in one age and casting one's mind all over eternity for knowledge of past and future ages" ("The Shadow out of Time").[11] The summation of these influences was an incorporation and simultaneous transcendance of the Romantic mood or (in the spirit of Hegel who viewed Romanticism as "self-transcending") its continuation by other means. Lovecraft was a life-long student of Romantic influences like the *Arabian Nights,* and of the great purveyors of Romantic themes as were Coleridge and De Quincey. He reached even further than they into the power of the Dream, since so many of his own tales were inspired by the horrific visions he had had since early childhood. He argued that "no first rate story can ever be written without the author's actually experiencing the moods and visions concerned in a sort of oneiroscopic way,"[12] while one of his early protagonists muses:

> I have often wondered if the majority of mankind ever pause to reflect upon the occasionally titanic significance of dreams, and of the obscure world to which they belong. Whilst the greater number of our nocturnal visions are perhaps no more than faint and fantastic reflections of our waking experiences—Freud to the contrary with his puerile symbolism—there are still a certain remainder whose immundane and ethereal character permits of no ordinary interpretation, and whose vaguely exciting and disquieting effect suggests possible minute glimpses into a sphere of mental existence no less important than physical life, yet separated from that life by an all but impassable barrier. ("Beyond the Wall of Sleep")[13]

Yet in the major literature of the nineteenth century, the Romantic had fallen victim to Lovecraft's *bête noir,* the "mannered" writing of Dickensian sentimentality and the didactic masters of Realism. The mainstreams of both Romanticism and Realism dealt with the objective world —Romanticism through emotion, Realism through reason—and thereby obviated the imagination capable of grouping "strange relations and associations among the objects of visible and invisible nature."[14] Mystery in the twentieth century had largely become pure mysticism—as in the poetry of T. S. Eliot which Lovecraft abjured as dead-ended—and Realism had become the reduction of the world to what his friend Clark Ashton Smith called the "Five senses and three dimensions [that] hardly scratch the hither surface of infinitude," only embellished with meaningless adventure.[15] Science had cut off even the nineteenth-century imaginative fiction of marvellous machines, transforming the emerging Science-Fiction (as Lovecraft saw two generations early) into what are essentially Space Westerns. What remained was an incorporation of the real and the fantastic, whereby imagination reached beyond the limits of truth. This was not a simple return to the supernatural of preindustrial cultures; it was rather, as Lovecraft scholar Matthew Onderdonk has written, the uplifting of these myths to the "supernormal," allowing the power of Romanticism to play upon subjective perception in new, more forceful and significant ways than ever before.[16] Because modern humanity so completely placed its faith in Science and Progress, its shadowy fears

"Out of Space, Out of Time" materialised as things at once all-powerful and irrational, mindless or mad.

Lovecraft's true strength, then, lay in his ability to give the modern sense of indeterminacy a weird and poetic interpretation. What Man feared was not correctly speaking the "Unknown." Lovecraft's own most terrifying dreams were of being on the verge of rediscovering something terrible and arcane, what he once referred to as "the strange spires and steep roofs, vaguely suggesting some lost horizon which was once familiar to me."[17] It was the "unknown outside, clawing at the rim of the known," the more threatening because in another sense it was known already, that was the peak of spectral horror.[18] The hideous beings under the surface of human civilisation's superficial conquest of Nature and of its own nature were ever poised to wipe out Man. But even worse than their standing threat was their very existence, and this *presence* drove their discoverers to insanity. Lovecraft says of one of his heroes that his studies of science and philosophy were an error since these "offer two equally tragic alternatives to the man of feeling and action; despair if he fail in his quest, and terrors unutterable and unimaginable if he succeed" ("From Beyond").[19] To uncover the Monsters was to co-exist with them always.

Generally in metaphor, but sometimes with a rare directness Lovecraft revealed the social content of this dread. At the close of his most famous early tale, "Dagon," a sailor pursued by monsters of "unhealthy antiquity" dreams fantastically of "a day when they may rise above the billows to drag down in their reeking talons the remnants of puny, war-exhausted mankind—of a day when the land shall sink, and the dark ocean floor shall ascend amidst universal pandemonium."[20] Lovecraft looked forward to a time he also feared, when "people will gape at the legends which their old women and medicine men will weave about the ruins of concrete bridges, subways and building foundations."[21] At an historic moment when European intellectuals recognised and even embraced decay, while Americans rarely deigned to admit its presence in their own culture, Lovecraft lived and wrote from a sense of pastness in the fragments of the America he loved. His New England's promise had been eradicated after the Civil War by the invasion of heightened industrialism, the destruction of much of the old architecture, the immigration of new groups, and the adoption of European sophistications by the reigning intellectuals. The rest of America seemed likewise stricken, with only less tradition to resist the "commercial and industrial determinism" that he so despised.

The fear of race suicide was never far from the surface of Lovecraft's conceptions. He was an avowed racist for nearly all his life, not only suspecting but dreading all non-Yankees.[22] He may as well have been writing his own sojourn in New York (the only lengthy absence from Providence in his life) when a narrator of one of his stories reflects:

> My coming to New York was a mistake; for whereas I had looked for poignant wonder and inspiration in the teeming labyrinths of ancient streets . . . I had found instead only a sense of horror and oppression. . . . Garish daylight shewed only squalor and alienage and the noxious elephantiasis of climbing, spreading stones where the moon had hinted of loveliness and elder magic; and the throngs of people that seethed through the flume-like streets were squat, swarthy strangers with hardened faces and narrow eyes, shrewd strangers without dreams, without kinship to the old scenes about them, who could never mean aught to a blue-eyed man of the old folk. . . . ("He")[23]

But to shrug off Lovecraft's racism as an atavism is inadequate; for horror was also fascination. He composed one of his most delicious tales (and his only one that dealt with women as a satanic force), "The Horror at Red Hook," from his life near that section of Brooklyn and his friends' description of it.[24] Another of his protagonists stares from his own College Hill in Providence down at the Federal Hill dwellings of Eastern and Southern European immigrants, lost in fascination about their apparently mysterious habits. Jews, Blacks, Poles, Syrians, the further removed from the Old New Englander the better—in many of his stories these were the means whereby horrible and marvellous Old Gods would return and give the existing civilisation the destruction it had earned ("The Haunter of the Dark"). Like Spengler, who greatly influenced him for a time, Lovecraft saw the collapse of the Western way of life unflinchingly; unlike Spengler, he took a pleasure uncertain even in himself over that collapse and the rages of excess that the calamity would unloose.[25]

But Lovecraft was no proto-Nazi. He disavowed any kind of government as an inherent evil. Well-meaning people (including many of his friends) were Socialists, he granted, but he thought of himself as a "pessimist and a pagan," unable to believe in the possibility of political solution. He cynically warned that the suppression of true culture for the masses was a time-bomb for the existing society:

> Granted, the machine-victim has leisure. What is he going to do with it? . . . We shall hear of all sorts of futile reforms and reformers—standardised culture-outlines, synthetic sports & spectacles, professional play leaders & study guides & kindred examples of machine-made uplife & brotherly spirit. . . . Meanwhile the tension of boredom and unsatisfied imagination will increase.[26]

Capitalism was more repulsive and dangerous than the labour movement, but no new vision for civilisation appeared anywhere: what could be done? Late in his life, the realities of Nazism and scientific discussions of race shocked him out of his racist myths; like Pound, he realised too late that his misconceptions had rendered him a fool. He still could not avow a Statist Communism. In the last months of his life he confessed himself a Norman Thomas follower, adhering to the inevitability of Socialism. As a critic fairly wrote, Lovecraft "adored the past, but he believed in a socialised future that, in its own way, might flower again where his own antecedents, he knew, had withered in blood and in wealth."[27]

Vastly more important than any death-bed converions to Socialism was, however, Lovecraft's recognition of a revolutionary *cultural* position inherent in his writing. In his last letter, he registered his reservations about the Surrealists as too given over to subconscious impressions without the guidance of the disciplined imagination, but reaffirmed that if his own fictional heroes who had painted monsters had been real persons, they "would have been represented in a recent exhibition [of fantastic art, at the Museum of Modern Art in 1937] by several blasphemous and abhorrent canvasses."[28] This proposed alliance with revolutionary art is a key to his legacy, alongside the occasional hint we find in his writings that the protagonists can desert humankind and become one with the accursed. Thus in "The Shadow over Innsmouth," the hero comes across a town besmirched with dread, and uncovers a nest of creatures who live beneath the adjoining water and await the day when human civilisation will be overthrown. He escapes with his life, but later learns that he, too, is hereditarily one of the monsters, becoming more and more like them, and then he makes his decision:

> That morning the mirror definitely told me I had acquired *the Innsmouth look*.
> So far I have not shot myself as my uncle Douglas did. I bought an automatic and almost took the step, but certain dreams deterred me. The tense extremes of horror are lessening, and I feel queerly drawn toward the unknown sea-deeps instead of fearing them. I hear and do strange things in sleep, and awake with a kind of exaltation instead of terror. . . . Stupendous and unheard-of splendours await me below, and I shall seek them soon. *Iä-R'lyeh! Cthulhu fhtagn! Iä! Iä!* No, I shall not shoot myself—I cannot be made to shoot myself!
> I shall plan my cousin's escape from that Canton madhouse, and together we shall go to marvel-shadowed Innsmouth. We shall swim out to that brooding reef in the sea and dive down through black abysses to Cyclopean and many-columned Y'ha-nthlei, and in that lair of the Deep Ones we shall dwell amidst wonder and glory for ever.[29]

The imagination could, in this wildest dream of Lovecraft (as the contemporaneous visions of the Surrealists), allow humanity to shatter the barrier between the waking and the dreaming worlds—a twentieth-century version, perhaps, of the young Marx's notion of the "species be-ing." Extrapolating Lovecraft's implications from his limited narrative forms, one can suggest a perception that the human recognition of forces outside the Western heritage would provoke a shock of (self-) awareness: the result would be either madness or the course toward a new existence. Would Lovecraft himself, or the political champion of dreams, André Breton, have been unwilling to acknowledge a connexion between the Surrealist Manifesto of 1924, where Breton mentioned that Surrealism first occurred to him when he saw a *phrase* "knocking at the window": the faint image of a "man walking cut half way up by a window"; and the conclusion to Lovecraft's early "Dagon" (1921): "God, *that hand!* The window! The window!"[30]

In the pages of *Weird Tales,* Lovecraft was joined by several other writers whose work (like Lovecraft's) is only now being rediscovered. Clark Ashton Smith, a flamboyant rebel who predicted that the "whole fabric of Western civilisation is due for a grand debacle" and signed his letters, "Yours for the Red Apocalypse," can be termed the link between the radical catastrophists of the previous generation and the spiritual revolt of the 1960's.[31] It remains little known that Ignatius Donnelly, along with Madame Blavatsky's followers strongly active in British and American radical circles at the end of the nineteenth century, played a major role in reviving the mythology of Atlantis. However ridden with mysticism, this was a critical recognition—as Lewis Mumford has shown —of a primitive reality, the first city in civilisation. The City was the symbolic connexion of primitive peoples with a cosmic order, essentially a place to observe the heavens; simultaneously, the City was also the home of the first effective tyranny, the ruler using his godlike powers to exact sacrifices of concentrated energy. Thus, for Mumford, the original class struggle ensued, between an urban "proletariat" bearing its collective rural customs and aspirations with new sophistication, the tyrant possessing the first military "machine."[32] Hence the Fall of Atlantis, as Donnelly and others suggested, was the end of a cycle of wonder and mystery. Fallen in reality, Atlantis receded into fable and was revived in literature as the Dark Dream, which Smith elucidated as the wonderfully picturesque but dying world. On the other hand, Smith's writing was often drug-oriented (like the Utopian fragment, transparently titled "In Cocaigne"), pointing toward the abolition of Time.[33] Even more than Lovecraft, Smith was limited by his stylised, purplish prose, yet the sentiment of rebellion was ever-present. The last surviving member of Lovecraft's early circle of fellow authors, Frank Belknap Long, likewise stressed the primeval fear of humanity being supplanted by another species, and his protagonist reflected in an Einstein-inspired fashion, "Your biologist scoffs at time. He has the key but refuses to use it."[34] Through the transcendence of Time, humanity finds the ecstasy and horror that remain in the shadows of waking life.

In purely literary terms, the contributions of Lovecraft and his friends evoke the critical approach of a Lucács, who would seek to make the author's struggles the truest and most eloquent tale of all. For their time, the task was impossible to accomplish: to explain to an America in the midst of an industrial expansion and locked in the forms of nationalism —democratic and undemocratic—the illusory character of the entire project for the ultimate goal of human wisdom and happiness. And like their predecessor Poe, these writers were none too clear-minded about the cultural or political alternatives for society. Like the last of many an old radical impulse, their conceptions caused them to turn their backs on the present and future, able to express their vision only for a burning moment in the space of a tale, in a fragmentary line of a poem. A philological study, following Vico, might suggest that their use of words (as they believed themselves) had at its best moments the character of a universal myth, more on the order of ancient, oral poetry than of modern literary Realism and Experimentalism.

After them, horror lost the last shreds of utopia, and the miraculous implications of their writing become in the hands of later horror authors a deadening naturalism. There is horror aplenty in the 1930's Left avant-garde (as in Nelson Algren's "Proletarian Literature"), and after Hiroshima horror begins to assert its hegemony over American High Culture, aestheticised by such prestige writers as Joyce Carol Oates in the 1960's and 1970's. In this prose, the themes of newspapers and television are essentially reiterated—the precariousness of life, the present decay and approaching disaster, the meaninglessness of Free Will. Yet in the early days of modern Social Realism, in the 1910's and again in the 1930's, this writing was intended to offer a revolutionary critique of society. Even today, a tale-teller and poet like Charles Bukowski can find moments of insurrectionary insights among the broken and defeated characters of urban life. In the astonishing prose of Nathanael West, or LeRoi Jones-Amiri Baraka, the gaping void opens as the disaster that Western Man has prepared for himself: to be frozen into a Hollywood movie frame or have his neck slit on a dark evening in Newark, either way to crumble into nothing.

Not even the best of this horror, however, had seized upon the crucial perceptions of the Lovecraft circle about Time. One of Lovecraft's doomed heroes admits that "only History" saves him from madness;[35] here Lovecraft is toying with the self-delusion of Western man reduced to his last straw of self-confidence in everything that seems to make him whole and human. Levi-Strauss has written in *Tristes Tropiques,* "As he moves forward within his environment, Man takes with him all the positions he has occupied in the past, and all those that he will occupy in the future. . . . Some of these worlds may be apprehended in actions, others exist because we have them in our thoughts." This could be called a statement of fantasy or horror as well as one of Anthropology. As the Surrealist poet and critic, Octavio Paz, further points out, ironically no force more than Marxism has so wholly summed up the Western faith that Man humanises the cosmos and "dissolves being into meaning."[36] Self-confident "objectivity" has had the historic effect of reducing even the most revolutionary interpretations of the Subject to the possible awareness of the Here and Now, in the mistaken belief that only that which we can see really exists, has existed or will exist. If Lovecraft, like the Surrealists, continually reminded humanity of its fragility and slightness in the scale of the Universe, it was not to diminish human striving but to reopen the vents to the imagination increasingly closed since the rise of formal society, the State, and private property. Through his racist fears, moreover, he identified what Breton among others saw more directly in Aimé Cesaire's *Return to My Native Land:* how much of the old, latent potential for human experience remained in the hidden pockets of the world; and how the unleashing of these forces beyond and behind (Western) history would be the destruction of a mental universe as well as of an economic and social system, the opening to another way of life.[37] Lovecraft had prepared the way for his audience to reconcile itself to some larger notion of human essence by showing, through his horrific metaphor, the dreams of every human, the sense that Being remains outside every meaning society can give it—and perhaps outside every formal structure of the future as well, in some measure spanning the entire species experience.

Anthropologist-novelist-revolutionary Robert Briffault had attempted as early as the 1930's to express the epochal revolutionary possibilities ahead: "It is not a new economic system or a social order which is being forged and which menaces traditional civilisation. It is a new humanity."[38] The very disillusionment after World War II, and, more recently, the collapse of American prestige in Southeast Asia, gave that emerging humanity fresh oxygen to breathe, adding to its literary stock the vast experience of a popular culture revolt in the "Underground"— (for all its retrograde qualities and the susceptibility of its demands to absorption by the commodity market) poetry, graphic design, imaginative journalism, spelling an end to official censorship and artistic self-restriction in the form, content, and style of popular literature—and leaving a permanent reminder of the *will* of millions to overcome the existing order.

Notes

1. Barton St Armand, *H. P. Lovecraft: The Outsider in Legend and Myth* (unpublished Master's Thesis, Brown University, 1966).
2. *Collected Works,* III, p. 121.—S.T.J.
3. Thomas Ollive Mabbott, a Poe scholar, certifies that "H. P. Lovecraft must always be remembered as a Poe student of the highest rank." "Lovecraft as a Student of Poe," *Fresco,* VIII, 3 (Spring 1958), 37.
4. "Nyarlathotep" (prose poem), in *Writings in The United Amateur,* p. 129.—S.T.J.
5. Significantly, Lovecraft considered all four of these "philosophical" horror tales as among Poe's finest (cf. "Supernatural Horror in Literature," in *Collected Works,* III, p. 378), while finding the horrors of "The Pit and the Pendulum" "too patently *physical,* and of merely human origin" (Lovecraft to Wilfred B. Talman, 24 August 1926; in *Collected Works,* VI, p. 69).—S.T.J.
6. That Dunsany is a "terror" writer may be somewhat debatable; but his influence on Lovecraft is patent. It is likely that this influence was manifested not only in the blatant manner of Lovecraft's "Dunsanian" fantasies, not only in Lovecraft's inventing his own pantheon of "gods" as part of his myth-cycle, but also in spurring Lovecraft's developement of the dream-narrative or of the inclusion of dream elements into his tales, a technique which noticeably increased in Lovecraft's work after his reading of Dunsany.—S.T.J.
7. Charles Fort, *The Book of the Damned* (New York, 1941), p. 16.
8. In reference to this and also to the Horkheimer-Adorno passage quoted by Buhle in the beginning of this essay, we can indicate that Lovecraft felt that once a phenomenon is explained it ceases to be within the realm of the horror story: ". . . the crux of a *weird* tale is something which *could not possibly happen.* If any unexpected advance of physics, chemistry, or biology were to indicate the *possibility* of any phenomena related by the weird tale, that particular set of phenomena would cease to be *weird* in the ultimate sense because it would become surrounded by a different set of emotions" (Lovecraft to August Derleth, 20 November 1931; in *Collected Works,* VII, p. 434).—S.T.J.
9. Nathaniel Wingate Peaslee, narrator of "The Shadow out of Time."—S.T.J.
10. H. P. Lovecraft to Frank Belknap Long, 3 May 1922; in *Collected Works,* V, p. 173.—S.T.J.
11. In *Collected Works,* I, p. 377.—S.T.J.
12. H. P. Lovecraft to Clark Ashton Smith, 7 November 1930; in *Collected Works,* VII, p. 213.
13. In *Collected Works,* III, p. 23.—S.T.J.
14. "In Defence of Dagon," *Leaves,* 2 (1938), 117 (original text January 1921).
15. Smith to Lovecraft, n.d., H. P. Lovecraft Collection, John Hay Library, Brown University.
16. Matthew H. Onderdonk, "The Lord of R'lyeh."
17. *Collected Works,* VII, p. 215.
18. H. P. Lovecraft to Wilfred Blanch Talman, April 1926; in *Collected Works,* VI, p. 41.
19. In *Collected Works,* III, pp. 66-67.—S.T.J.
20. *Ibid.,* p. 8.—S.T.J.
21. H. P. Lovecraft to James Ferdinand Morton, 30 October 1929; in *Collected Works,* VII, p. 43.—S.T.J.
22. This is fantastically off the mark; see the Introductory Notes (p. 14). There is no

evidence to show that Lovecraft "dreaded" any foreign races.—S.T.J.

23. In *Collected Works,* III, pp. 230-31.—S.T.J.

24. Actually, the "satanic force" of women is infinitely stronger in "The Thing on the Doorstep" (1933), where Asenath Waite (herself the avatar of "old Ephraim Waite") displaces the psyche of her husband, Edward Pickman Derby. "The Dreams in the Witch House" (1932), with the cosmic witch Keziah Mason, also indicates the malignant powers of certain unusual members of the female sex.—S.T.J.

25. Did Lovecraft really enjoy, even masochistically, the prospect of the ultimate destruction of Western civilisation? There is no reason why he should have, since he firstly preferred civilisation to barbarism (cf. the Lovecraft-Robert E. Howard correspondence), and secondly since he felt that the West had produced, for all its follies (like Christianity, which it uncritically accepted from the East), some of the finest aesthetic fruits the world had ever known (Greek paganism and philosophy; scientific advance; Latin and English literature; Georgian architecture, etc.). And would he have been so perturbed about the invasion of foreigners into the West—into his own culture—if he had no interest in its preservation? If Lovecraft saw the decline of the West as inevitable at all (and there is reason even to doubt this, for note this remark: "No civilisation has lasted for ever, and perhaps our own is perishing of natural old age. If so, the end cannot well be deferred. On the other hand, we may be merely passing from youth to maturity—a period of more realistic and sophisticated life may lie ahead of us, filled with cynical resignation and dreams of languorous beauty rather than with the fire and faith of early life" ["The Defence Remains Open!", ms., John Hay Library]), then he saw it only in the sense that all cultures, through the process of history, decline and vanish.—S.T.J.

26. Lovecraft to [Woodburn] Harris, 25 February-1 March 1929; in *Collected Works,* VI, pp. 308-09.

27. W. T. Scott, "His Own Most Fantastic Creation," in *Exiles and Fabrications,* p. 72.

28. Lovecraft to James F. Morton, March [?] 1937; in *Collected Works,* IX, p. 436.

29. In *Collected Works,* I, pp. 368-69.—S.T.J.

30. *Collected Works,* III, p. 8. "Dagon" was written in 1917.—S.T.J.

31. See Smith to Robert Barlow, 16 May 1937, and 10 May 1938 (Lovecraft Collection). Like a number of the younger figures around Lovecraft in his last years, Barlow was an openly pro-Communist revolutionary.

32. Lewis Mumford, "Utopia, the City and the Machine," in Frank E. Manuel, ed., *Utopias and Utopian Thought* (Boston, 1966). A description of Donnelly's popular work on Atlantis is contained in Martin Ridge, *Ignatius Donnelly: Portrait of a Politician* (Chicago, 1962); the multifold radical connexions of American Theosophy have remained almost unexplored, save by Mari Jo Buhle, *Feminism and Socialism in America, 1820-1920* (unpublished dissertation, University of Wisconsin, 1974).

33. See the collection of his Atlantis tales, *Poseidonis,* ed. Lin Carter (New York, 1973), including "In Cocaigne," p. 116.

34. Frank Belknap Long, *The Dark Beasts* (New York, 1964); and see *The Hounds of Tindalos* (Sauk City, Wis., 1944), as well as Long's poetry, which parallels the work of Lovecraft and Smith.

35. Cf. "The Lurking Fear," in *Collected Works,* III, p. 177.—S.T.J.

36. Octavio Paz, *Claude Levi-Strauss: An Introduction* (Ithaca, N.Y., 1970), p. 135.

37. See in particular the reflections of C. L. R. James on Cesaire in *Black Jacobins* (New York, 1963), pp. 400-01.

38. Robert Briffault, *Breakdown: The Collapse of Traditional Civilisation* (New York, 1932), p. 203.

V

LOVECRAFT'S POETRY

A Parenthesis on Lovecraft as Poet

By Winfield Townley Scott

The first major critic to devote attention to Lovecraft's poetry was Winfield Townley Scott (1910–1968); and the following article, though written in 1945, has remained an important critical study. A major American poet himself, Scott devoted much attention to Lovecraft's life, producing, among others, the major if controversial biographical article, "His Own Most Fantastic Creation" (1944). As literary editor for The Providence Journal, Scott tried earnestly to make Lovecraft recognised by the general public, authoring many essays and reviews.

No commentator on Lovecraft has made more than a passing notice of his verse. The United Amateur Press Association, which channelled so much of his writing, was not strong on literary criticism, and in magazines of the horror story, verse had only an incidental place.[1] In Lovecraft's complete work his verse remains secondary; it has less distinction than his best stories and it is presumably less interesting than his letters. Yet the evidence is that, particularly in his youth, Lovecraft's most concentrated attention was upon the writing of poetry; that at one time or another he thought of himself as primarily a poet—as his mother referred to him in her recorded conversations with the psychiatrist at Butler Hospital. There are two good reasons for making at least a brief survey of his verse. One is that all the work of any writer as curious as Lovecraft merits consideration. The other is that a few of his poems are in themselves rather good.

What we have to go on are the approximately fifty well-filled pages of "Selected Poems" as published in the second omnibus Lovecraft volume, *Beyond the Wall of Sleep.*[2] They appear to be an adequate exhibition of Lovecraft as poet, good, bad, and indifferent.

The bulk of the poems fall into one or the other of two manners of verse brought to perfection in Lovecraft's beloved eighteenth-century England. One is the neat, or as Keats called it, "the rocking-horse" couplet. This is emulated by Lovecraft in "Old Christmas" and "New-England Fallen," and possibly carried on to Sir Walter's Scott's narrative manner in "Psychopompos." The other is the more dulcet, bucolic or elegiac tone, usually in quatrains, as mastered by Thomas Gray and James Thomson. "Providence," "On a Grecian Colonnade in a Park," "Sunset," and "On a New-England Village Seen by Moonlight" are Lovecraft poems in this manner. The first stanza of "Sunset" illustrates the literary influence flawlessly:

> The cloudless day is richer at its close;
> A golden glory settles on the lea;
> Soft, stealing shadows hint of cool repose
> To mellowing landscape, and to calming sea.[3]

All these poems, indeed most of Lovecraft's, are "early poems;" that is, they were written before his thirtieth birthday—most of them probably between 1912 and 1920.[4] They are quite dull, even at times unreadable. Their inspiration is literary and they never escape from or overcome the derivative tone. Their eighteenth-century mannerisms refuse transposition into the twentieth century. They are completely out of touch with Lovecraft's actual time as no vital poetry can ever be. And they are further damaged by the strong racial and social snobbery of Lovecraft's earlier years; what they say is frequently as restricted and eccentric as the manner in which it is said. In short, the quaintness and old-worldness, which in his horror stories became an attractive otherworldliness, remain wholly inefficient in his poetry.[5]

This same criticism can be made of another group of his poems where the dominant influence is Poe. Some of these are "Astrophobos," "Despair," and "Nemesis;" and probably others, in mood and feeling if not so slavishly in metre. One sample, from "Nemesis," will do:

> Through the ghoul-guarded gateways of slumber,
> Past the wan-mooned abysses of night,
> I have lived o'er my lives without number,
> I have sounded all things with my sight;
> And I struggle and shriek ere the daybreak, being
> driven to madness with fright.[6]

Lovecraft never got beyond schoolboy imitation in this sort of thing.

One wonders what, if anything, Lovecraft made of the American poetry of his own era; and particularly because from 1912—when he was coming to maturity and writing much of his own verse—our poetry itself had come to a great new resurgence of individuality and vitality. His letters might show. The few I happen to have seen revealed an admiration for the poetry of Robert Hillyer, a very able traditionalist, but quick disdain and misunderstanding of T. S. Eliot, with whose principles of aristocracy, royalism, and classicism Lovecraft actually had much in common. I have no idea whether he was familiar with the poetry of Hart Crane, whom he knew slightly.[7] Yet of course one can safety guess on the evidence of Lovecraft's general character and on that of his verse that his sympathies, wrapped in his eighteenth-century escape, remained profoundly apathetic to the "new" poetry of his time. Not only did Walt Whitman live and die in vain as far as Lovecraft was concerned, so even did John Keats and all the Romantics (save as decayed as Poe). Lovecraft had a fatal misconception of poetry as a living art. In his work he was anti-realistic and therefore anti-poetic.

Oddly enough, Lovecraft got away from this. Perhaps not oddly; for after all in his last decade and despite his eccentric life Lovecraft showed a much firmer sense of reality, a warmer sense of humour and of friendship. Emotionally he was more adult. A poem called "A Year Off," dated 1925, hints the first flicker of freshness in his verse. It is light, humorous, deftly done, an extravaganza of far travel which concludes with J. K. Huysmans' touch that the thoroughgoing and imaginative anticipation is probably better than the actuality. But in its course it has verbal fun with its ideas: "To dally with the Dalai Lama" is a particularly fortunate moment.[8]

Then, far more impressively, came the prolific spate of poetry between December 1929 and early January 1930. In three or four weeks Lovecraft wrote "Brick Row" and "The Messenger" and—these possibly within a week—the thirty-six sonnets, *Fungi from Yuggoth.*[9] In general their style is simple and direct, the earlier poetic derivations sloughed off. The horror of his best stories is at last used with effective understatement in verse. "They took me slumming" is, for instance, a phrase from one of the *Fungi* sonnets that would have dynamited the artificialities of his earlier poems; and almost everywhere the language is equally alive, and the horror is all the sharper for being quiet-spoken.

Perhaps as wholly satisfactory as any poem he ever wrote is the separate sonnet, "The Messenger," which Lovecraft did as answer to Bertrand K. Hart's joyous threat to "send a monstrous visitor" to Lovecraft's doorstep at 3 A.M.:

> The Thing, he said, would come that night at three
> From the old churchyard on the hill below;
> But crouching by an oak fire's wholesome glow,
> I tried to tell myself it could not be.

> Surely, I mused, it was a pleasantry
> Devised by one who did not truly know
> The Elder Sign, bequeathed from long ago,
> That sets the fumbling forms of darkness free.
>
> He had not meant it—no—but still I lit
> Another lamp as starry Leo climbed
> Out of the Seekonk, and a steeple chimed
> *Three*—and the firelight faded, bit by bit.
> Then at the door that cautious rattling came—
> And the mad truth devoured me like a flame![10]

The chilling warning of that firelight fading bit by bit and then the "cautious" rattling—these two lines are worth more than all the pages of eighteenth-century rubbish he wrote as poetry. And several of the sonnets in the *Fungi* sequence are about as keenly controlled.

Had there been, in place of the eighteenth century and Poe, another and newer influence? I am inclined to think, with nothing to go on but internal evidence, that Lovecraft had been reading Edwin Arlington Robinson. In his "A Year Off" the phrase "shame the sages" certainly echoes Robinson's line, "Bereft enough to shame a sage," in "The Poor Relation." And the phrasing, the tone, the general approach of the *Fungi* sonnets are repeatedly Robinsonian.

To go at the problem in reverse of influence and chronology, let us look first at these Lovecraft lines from several sonnets:

> No one had seen me take the thing—but still
> A blank laugh echoed in my whirling head. . . .
>
> But evil with some portent beyond speech. . . .
>
> Farmer Seth Atwood was past eight when
> He tried to sink that deep well by his door. . . .
> We laughed, and hoped he'd soon be sane again.
>
> Out of what crypt they crawl, I cannot tell. . . .
>
> John Whateley lived about a mile from town. . . .
>
> I cannot tell why some things hold for me
> A sense of unplumbed marvels to befall. . . .[11]

And there are more, but those will do.

Compare with these the technique of such famous Robinson sonnets, as "Reuben Bright":

> Because he was a butcher and thereby
> Did earn an honest living, and did right. . . .

as "Haunted House":

> There were no trackless footsteps on the floor
> Above us, and there were no sounds elsewhere. . . .

as "The Dead Village":

> And over the forgotten place there clings
> The strange and unrememberable light
> That is in dreams. . . .

or—among others—"Alma Mater":

> Out of what scum and up from what abyss
> Had they arrived—these rags of memory? . . .

The interested reader must collate the *Fungi* sonnets and those of Robinson to feel the full force of the case. I mean only to indicate the evidence. One additional part of it may be Robinson's suddenly increased fame in the late 1920's and the gathering into a separate book of his *Sonnets, 1889–1927* in 1928, just a year before Lovecraft wrote *Fungi from Yuggoth*. The resemblances strike me as unmistakable, and the fact that Lovecraft had hitherto written verse only under influences indicates that yet another took over in his last and best verse.[12]

His best remains restricted. Unlike Robinson's, it touched no depths of human significance. Its terror, unlike *The Ancient Mariner*'s, had no meaning beyond itself, beyond mere nightmare. To scare is a slim purpose in poetry. But when Lovecraft at last brought his undoubted talent for horror themes into unaffected verse he made his poetry an interesting if minor portion of his total work.

Notes

1. It is ironic, therefore, that the earliest article on Lovecraft's poetry appeared in *The United Amateur* of March 1919: Rheinhart Kleiner's brief "A Note on Howard P. Lovecraft's Verse" (cf. *Writings in The United Amateur*, p. 108).—S.T.J.
2. This article was written before the publication of Lovecraft's *Collected Poems*, which, though being anything but complete, did include a greater number of poems than did *Beyond the Wall of Sleep*.—S.T.J.
3. *Writings in The United Amateur*, p. 92.—S.T.J.
4. Lovecraft, of course, began writing poetry as early as 1897, but he destroyed many of these very early poems. Lovecraft did not begin publishing poetry until 1912, with "Providence in 2000 A.D.".—S.T.J.
5. As early as 1921, John Ravenor Bullen, himself a minor poet and colleague of Lovecraft's, took an opposing view to this opinion. He remarked: "May I point out that poets of each period have forged their lines in the temper and accent of their age, whereas Mr Lovecraft purposely 'plates over' his poetical works with 'the impene-

trable rococo' of his predecessors' days, thereby running great risks. But it may be that his discerning eyes perceive that many modern methods are mongrel and ephemeral. His devotion to Queen Anne style may make his compositions seem artificial, rhetorical descriptions to contemporary critics, but the ever-growing charm of eloquence (to which assonance, alliteration, onomatopoeic sound and rhythm, and tone colour contribute their entrancing effect) displayed in the poem under analysis, proclaims Mr Lovecraft a genuine poet, and 'Old Christmas' an example of poetical architecture well-equipped to stand the test of time" (part of the "Transatlantic Circulator" papers, Lovecraft Collection, John Hay Library, Brown University). Certainly this view accords more closely with Lovecraft's own poetic theories.—S.T.J.

6. *Collected Poems,* p. 83.—S.T.J.
7. Lovecraft called Crane "a man of great scholarship, intelligence, & aesthetic taste, who can argue as interestingly & profoundly as anyone I have seen. . . . *The Bridge* really is a thing of astonishing merit." Lovecraft to Mrs F. C. Clark, 24-25 May 1930; in *Collected Works,* VII, pp. 151-52.—S.T.J.
8. *Collected Poems,* pp. 32-34.—S.T.J.
9. "The Ancient Track" was also written in mid-December; cf. Lovecraft to Elizabeth Toldridge, [19?-] 20 December 1929; John Hay Library. "Recapture," sonnet XXXIV of the *Fungi,* had been written in early November.—S.T.J.
10. *Collected Poems,* p. 91.—S.T.J.
11. From, respectively, the sonnets, "Pursuit" (II), "The Port" (VIII), "The Well" (XI), "Night-Gaunts" (XX), "The Familiars" (XXVI), and "Expectancy" (XXVIII) from the *Fungi; Collected Poems,* pp. 109, 115, 117, 122, 127, 129.—S.T.J.
12. Unfortunately, there is no external evidence that Lovecraft ever read Robinson: he mentions him in no correspondence seen by the editor. One wonders, then, if Clark Ashton Smith's vigorous poetry helped Lovecraft to escape from the eighteenth-century influence in his later poetry, just as Lovecraft's fiction seems to have been a patent influence on Smith's stories of the 1930's. Donald Wandrei's *Sonnets of the Midnight Hours*—written in 1927 and read by Lovecraft late that year (cf. *Collected Works,* VI, p. 186)—may have been the immediate trigger for the *Fungi from Yuggoth,* as their arrangement is quite similar to that used in Lovecraft's own sonnet-cycle.—S.T.J.

A Lovecraftian Nightmare

By R. Boerem

For decades, Winfield Townley Scott's article on Lovecraft's poetry remained the only important critical study of that body of his work, and only recently has Lovecraft's verse been felt worthy of in-depth analysis. R. Boerem, distinguished critic and bibliographer, has, in "A Lovecraftian Nightmare," examined the poem, "The Poe-et's Nightmare," as symbolic of Lovecraft's cosmic thought.

Lovecraft's eighteenth-century interests are demonstrated as much in "The Poe-et's Nightmare" as in anything he wrote. His use of blank verse is traditional, and his polished lines of heroic couplets reflect his reading of Dryden, Pope, Swift, and other satirists who were admired during the Augustan period. Dryden's "Mac Flecknoe" ("From dusty shops neglected authors come, Martyrs of pies .. .") is particularly interesting for comparison in subject and tone; Pope's satire on poets was influenced by it, and Lovecraft had probably read it as well. Whatever his direct influences, Lovecraft applies his couplets to a *genre* in which his models had excelled and, in so doing, constructs lines of concise wit rather than the mere rhymed prose of such narrative pieces as "Psychopompos."

"The Poe-et's Nightmare" is composed of two distinct parts differentiated by both subject and style: the blank verse narration of the nightmare and the couplet description of the poet, together making "A Fable" about the nature of Truth. The contrast between the two parts of the poem tends to heighten the effect of each, the comedy of the would-be poet making the tone of the nightmare all the more awesome, and the seriousness of the horrible truth rendering the poet all the more foolish. But if the nightmare represents a shocking revelation, its threat is restrained by being set in the context of a "real" world which allows the humorous criticism of an absurd, unwritten Poe-et.

As the title of the poem would indicate, its protagonist is not simply a poet, but a *Poe-et,* connoting Poe's romantic influences. His name, "Lucullus Languish," confirms this—"Lucullus" after the Roman general known for his practise of gastronomy, and "Languish" relating to the romantic image of the suffering poet as well as recalling Lydia

Languish, the heroine of Sheridan's *The Rivals*. Lucullus, like Lydia, is a romantic of simple-minded display. They are both needlessly dramatic, stiltedly impractical, and absurdly foolish. Lydia plays at being the romantic languishing lover; Lucullus acts the role of the languishing poet. Both succeed only in causing trouble and disappointment for themselves.

Lucullus Languish's opposed identities—his actual existence as a grocer's clerk and his assumption of the romantic role—are continually played upon in the poem as conflicting desires toward food and poetry. It becomes evident that, whatever Lucullus' aspirations, his fondness for eating makes him more a gormand than an artist. Perhaps he is a "student of the skies," but he is also a "connoisseur of rarebits and mince pies" (ll. 1–2).[1] Perhaps he does search for poetic inspiration, but he does so by overeating ice-cream and cake. His resolution to "chant a poet's lay" is easily broken by the "imperious call" of the supper hour (ll. 36, 43). Though Lucullus yearns for art, he fulfills himself with food. His true interests are far more in sympathy with his trade than he is willing to admit.

Because Lucullus' desires for expression are superficial, his poetic activity is a series of futile romantic gestures. The odes and dirges which he drops about the shop are forms of passionate expression, yet they do not "strike the chord within his heart" (l. 9). His searching the sky at night gives him a cold rather than a poem. He is charmed with his discovery of Poe (the allusions in ll. 23–24 are to "The Raven" and "Ulalume") but this only inflates his enthusiasm without bettering his art. He names a favoured grove "Tempe," a sacred place, but it is nevertheless a stunted copse and its "limpid lakes" remain mud puddles (ll. 27–31).

His poetic and gastric activities have one characteristic in common, however. The Latin motto of this first part of the poem, "Luxus tumultus semper causa est" (Mental disturbance is always caused by excess), suggests that it may have been the excess of both Lucullus' romanticism and his eating that led to his nightmare. He sought to excite inspiration with "overdoses" of ice-cream and cake (l. 12), and it is just after such an orgy of consumption that his fancies are exercised in the experience of the nightmare which was meant as a warning to "those who dine not wisely, but too well" (l. 58). His excesses have evoked the Poem he dreamed of as well as, ironically, an admonition he never expected.

Lucullus had "vow'd with gloom to woo" his muse, and he is "swath'd in gloom" in his bloated sleep (ll. 22, 64). In his romantic affectation, he has cultivated a passion for gloom, bringing it with him to his grove (l. 35). When his nightmare brings his fancies to life and transforms his poses into reality, the first changes evidence a realisation of his gloom. The "crystal deeps" (l. 18) he searched before are, in his dream, a "soundless heav'n" filled with "daemoniac clouds" (ll. 73–74). The stunted thicket in a vacant lot (ll. 26–27) becomes an "insomnious grove/Whose black recesses never saw the sun" (ll. 77–78), associated not with a "wooded plain" (l. 29) but a moor (l. 76). The mud puddles of his grove become a pool "that none dares sound; a tarn of murky face" (l. 81). Lucullus' assumed character would now be played in earnest.

As his nightmare continues, he senses foul beings around him, though he neither sees nor hears them (ll. 108–18). Then, with a flash of lightning (cf. *Fungi from Yuggoth,* VI, 13–14),[2] the area around him glows, revealing what seem to be daemonic beings, groping trees, "moving forms, and things not spoken of" (ll. 118–35). A fire-mist blots out his view, followed by "the hot, unfinished stuff of nascent worlds" (l. 142) and, in the matter of newborn worlds, the poet is reborn "free from the flesh" (l. 148) which had been restraining him, free from his gorging to pursue his Poe-etic hopes.

In his aethereal state, the poet sees the mist clear to "a feeble fleck/Of silver light" which is what "mortals call the boundless universe" (ll. 142–44). Surrounding this, "each as a tiny star,/Shone more creations, vaster than our own" (ll. 155–56). The universe is hardly of great significance, being a fleck surrounded by larger flecks, these together forming "but an atom in infinity" (l. 170). In "the surge of boundless being," the earth is less than unimportant.

With his new-found consciousness, the poet begins to survey the endless vision before him and to "know all things" (l. 182). What he discovers is an endless course of existence which complements his knowledge of the insignificance of the human realm, physically, with the knowledge that, temporally, it has even less importance. Earth is a "speck, born but a second, which must die/In one brief second more" (ll. 198–99).

Once he realises the microscopic insignificance of "that fragile earth;/That crude experiment; that cosmic sport" (ll. 199–200), he can only reflect bitterly on the "proud, aspiring race of mites" who, through ignorance, "vaunt themselves/As the chief works of Nature" (ll. 202–08). The inhabitants of the thinnest film on the smallest, most fleeting speck of dust believe themselves the purpose of nature! In this context, it is not difficult to understand how this "moral vermin" (cf. *Gulliver's Travels,* II, 6), this "morbid matter by itself call'd man" (ll. 202, 219), would be only one of many minor "fest'ring ailments of infinity" (l. 218).

But this vision is too horrible for Lucullus to bear. Sickened, he turns away, mocked by his aethereal guide for searching after truth only to find it repulsive. The poet is reminded that he had originally sought to:

> . . . meditate
> On things forbidden, and to pierce the veil
> Of seeming good and seeming beauteousness
> That covers o'er the tragedy of Truth. (ll. 232–35)

But he learns that such good and beauty, however unreal, serve to palliate the Terrible Truth, helping mankind to "forget his sorry lot . . . [by] raising Hope where Truth would crush it down" (ll. 236–37).

Then is given a sight yet beyond what he had experienced before: "a rift of purer sheen, a sight supernal,/Broader than all the void conceived by man" (ll. 246–47). Here even his guide becomes awed, but the touch of celestial rhythm provokes a soulful horror in Lucullus. Though urged to find the unutterable Truth, his soul flees in terror.

Lucullus, of course, awakes to vow "no more to feed on cake, or pie, or Poe" (l. 276), that is, that he will no longer overindulge himself either in eating or in romantic quests for Truth. His point of view changed, his gloom lifts, and he becomes contented and successful as a grocer's clerk. The poem ends with a warning to all those who seek the "spark celestial" to restrain themselves from being "overzealous for high fancies" lest they, too, experience the "unutterable thing."

By itself, the couplet part of the poem would be a light satire, but the sombre narration of the dream lends a gravity to the composition. Blank verse is traditionally the medium for "high" or prophetic statements, and Lovecraft's Latin captions identify the focus of the vision's meaning. The *Aletheia Phrikodes,* the Monstrous Truth, is that "*Omnia risus et omnia pulvis et omnia nihil*" ("All is laughter, all is dust, all is nothing"). Whatever forces are involved in the universe, the vision makes quite clear that Good and Beauty are concepts used by humanity to hide its own insignificance. He who probes beyond these values risks the loss of the peace of mind they provide. The face of Truth is monstrous and is not seen with impunity: Lucullus' soul flees in madness.

The philosophic stance of "The Poe-et's Nightmare" can be readily found in Lovecraft's other writings. In his letters he expresses a disgust of romanticism;[3] the probability of mankind's meaninglessness is asserted in other letters,[4] though he finds poetry and other such cultivations palliatives for the knowledge of this meaninglessness.[5]

J. Vernon Shea[6] quotes a letter in which Lovecraft states that he found the greatest merit in weird stories "which bring in sharp reminders of the vast unplumbed recesses of space that loom perpetually around our insignificant dust-grain," as does "The Poe-et's Nightmare." In his fiction, a parallel could be drawn between many of Lovecraft's searchers and Lucullus. Basil Elton in "The White Ship" reaches the land of Fancy but, unsatisfied, destroys his chance for happiness by searching for the land of Hope. "Arthur Jermyn" destroys himself after discovering the truth about his family. "The Outsider" discovers a type of hopelessness, and other searchers—in such stories as "The Call of Cthulhu" and "The Shadow over Innsmouth"—are destroyed by their desire for enlightenment.

"The Poe-et's Nightmare," then, is a Lovecraftian nightmare which, in its philosophical expression of a central Lovecraftian theme, stands as an emblem to Lovecraft's poetry and fiction.

Notes

1. For all references to "The Poe-et's Nightmare," see *Collected Poems,* pp. 42–51. —S.T.J.
2. From "The Lamp":
   > "It blazed—great God! . . . But the vast shapes we saw
   > In that mad flash have seared our lives with awe."

   Fungi from Yuggoth, in *Collected Poems,* p. 113.—S.T.J.
3. Boerem refers to a letter to Clark Ashton Smith (17 October 1930) in which Lovecraft states: "The *one* form of literary appeal which I consider *absolutely unsound, charlatanic, & valueless*—frivolous, insincere, irrelevant, & meaningless—is that mode of handling human events & values & motivations known as *romanticism.* . . . Here is sheer puerility—the concoctions of false glamours & enthusiasms & events out of an addled & distorted background which has no relation to anything in the genuine thoughts, feelings, & experiences of evolved & adult mankind." (*Collected Works,* VII, p. 195.)—S.T.J.
4. Cf. letters to Rheinhart Kleiner, 14 September 1919 (*Collected Works,* V, pp. 86ff.); to Zealia Brown Reed (Bishop), 13 February 1928 (*Collected Works,* VI, pp. 227ff.); and to Frank Belknap Long, 27 February 1931 (*Collected Works,* VII, pp. 311–12).
5. Cf. letter to the Kleicomolo, October 1916; in *Collected Works,* V, pp. 26–27.
7. "H. P. Lovecraft: The House and the Shadows," p. 87.

The Continuity of the
Fungi from Yuggoth

By R. Boerem

Perhaps the most important of Lovecraft's ventures into poetry is the sonnet series, Fungi from Yuggoth. *Written largely in about a week (27 December 1929 to 4 January 1930), this cycle of thirty-six sonnets represents a radical departure from Lovecraft's earlier Georgian verse, and presents a firm, vigorous, and almost modern poetic style. In spite of its fame, however, few commentators have been successful in interpreting the message of the series as a whole. In the following article, R. Boerem puts forth the intriguing theory that the cycle may not be merely a collection of random vignettes but a unified whole.*

The *Fungi from Yuggoth* is a description of a dream journey past the material limitations of conscious man. The description is given in a sequence of sonnets, seven of which are of the English form, the majority of the rest being modelled after the Italian. Lovecraft has kept the Italian division of the sonnet into the octet and sextet, and it is to be noted that, with only five exceptions, he writes a complete sentence of thought within the ending couplet and each of the quatrains, the point being that he has adopted a very restricted form in which to write his descriptions. The reader who dislikes the content of these verses will at least have to admit to their skill.

Some sets of verse are written in such a way that the reader may choose at random among them, but the *Fungi from Yuggoth* is, as has been stated, a sonnet sequence with certain order that must be read from beginning to end to reveal its full effect. The order of the sequence is vague in some places and some of the sonnets seem out of place but, generally, there is a certain pattern which shifts the reader's concentration away from the earthly plane and back again to a contemplative ending.

For convenience of discussion, the poem may be divided into seven "parts," each of which is more or less centred on a particular theme or interest. The first part, sonnets one to three, is an introduction.[1] The narrator has discovered "the book that told the hidden way/Across the void" (III, 5-6), the key to "those vague visions/ . . . that brood/Dim in the gulfs beyond this earth's precisions" (III, 9-11). As in Lovecraft's Randolph Carter stories, the "key" to these visions of infinitude is associated with dreaming, escaping from one's present through memories of the past and eventually through ancestral memories of circumstances, perhaps, beyond time itself.

The second part (IV-VI) is a dream-like transition from the immediacy of the dreamer's own presence to a series of comparatively objective dream scenes. The narrator, in the fourth sonnet, sees himself in the dream world but he has left his material body and is deprived of it. He has, in other words, fully entered the dream and cannot escape from it. A daemon, traditionally a higher, guiding being (cf. Lovecraft's "The Poet's Nightmare," ll. 166ff.), promises the narrator (V) a return to his "home" in the darkness of the night, or a return, perhaps, to his true ancestral origin. The "sunset's gate" (V, 9) they pass is the entrance, of course, into night, the environment of dreams. They enter an ancient cave (VI) and light a lamp which, following the common metaphor of light as knowledge, shows them images, knowledge, leaving them both in awe.

The third part (VII-XII) may be seen as a listing of mental images, provoked by the flash of light, which illustrate the effect of the unearthly upon the familiar features of the narrator's daytime world. Zaman's Hill (also mentioned in "The Ancient Track") becomes the scene of disappearances. Innsmouth is unnaturally dark. The courtyard in the city is inhabited by the dying and the dead, the doomed worshippers of alien devils. Atwood's well holds an unknown terror; the horror by Briggs' Hill path is revealed.

The next part (XIII-XXI) presents the ancestral earth alluded to in the first. Hesperia (XIII) is literally the "land to the west" and thus the land of sunset at the beginning of darkness. Beyond, "past the starry voids" (IV, 12), lies Yuggoth. Antarktos (with connotations of Antarctica) is one of those ancient lands, the secret of which was revealed through the window (XVI) and described (XVII-XVIII). Other sounds and creatures are shown to come from other parts of the ancient earth, from "sunken valleys on the sea's dead floor" (XIX, 14), or from the north ("They come in legions on the north wind's swell" [XX, 5]). But the earth is finally destroyed and what was created by chance is disintegrated by chaos: "Then, crushing what he chanced to mould in play,/The idiot Chaos blew earth's dust away" (XXI, 13-14).

The next six sonnets (XXII-XXVII) roughly centre on the void outside time and matter (XXII, 3) where Azathoth mindlessly creates cosmic laws from chance. The dream descriptions of the other world (XXIII, XXIV, XXV, XXVII) are related except, perhaps, sonnet XXVI which fits somewhat to the theme if one considers the "two crouching things" (XXVI, 13) to be from the chaos. But if this glance at the void is unclear, it is as fittingly so, perhaps, as any such glance at the void would be. But, at any rate, it quickly ends, for the next part leads the narrator (and the reader) back to wakefulness.

In the sixth part (XXVIII–XXXIII) the narrator muses on his sense of the marvellous (XXVIII, XXX) and its worth. There are nostalgic descriptions of scenes which evoke the narrator's imagination (XXIX, XXXIII), and the relation of the act and the result of probing behind the material of the present into the dark past (XXI, XXXII); the dreamer's present, daylight, life is again emphasised. These verses act, as does the second part, as a transition, this time a transition from dream to wakefulness.

The last three sonnets (XXXIV, XXXV, XXXVI) end the poem with the dreamer's "recapture" (XXXIV)[2] by wakefulness and realisation that a "primal star and year/Had sucked [him] back from man's dreamtransient sphere" (XXXIV, 13–14), i.e., that he had been drawn back to reality by the "year" (time) and the "star" (matter). The poem ends with a statement that the narrator had learned from his dream journey of the "faint, veiled sign of continuities" (XXXVI, 5) and can now sense his proximity to "the fixt mass whose sides the ages are" (XXXVI, 14).

The *Fungi from Yuggoth* describes the detail of a dream journey which in turn, reflects upon reality to give it a new appeal. If it is true that the true home of man's spirit is in the unknown (V, 1, 14), then it must also be a support to the wakeful material life that the unknown exists: "its lure alone makes life worth living" (XXVIII, 13). The continuities of the ancient world are "less a dream than this we know" (XXXVI, 12), and, though part of the unknown to those living in present reality, these continuities may be approached through the dreaming of the imagination because man possesses a subconscious memory of earth's past.

This has hardly been an attempt to explicate the poem. Those familiar with Lovecraft's writings and the Cthulhu mythos will find even more in its description. A full investigation of the poem's imagery (e.g. the "sunset" image) and its relation to the Mythos needs yet to be undertaken, as does a more complete explication. It is hoped, however, that the *Fungi from Yuggoth* is here shown to have a decipherable meaning even for a reader unfamiliar with Lovecraft, and that it is, not just a collection, but a unified sequence of sonnets to be read as an entirety.

Notes

1. For all references to the Fungi from Yuggoth, see Collected Poems, pp. 109–34. —S.T.J.

2. It is interesting to note that "Recapture" was apparently written over a month before the rest of the sonnets (cf. letter to James F. Morton, 6 December 1929; in Collected Works, VII, p. 90), and only inserted into the series (the other thirty-five of which were written consecutively) later by Lovecraft, apparently on a suggestion by R. H. Barlow (cf. the T.Mss. of the Fungi from Yuggoth in the Lovecraft Collection, John Hay Library, Brown University).—S.T.J.

EPILOGUE:

To Howard Phillips Lovecraft

By Clark Ashton Smith

Lover of hills and fields and towns antique,
How hast thou wandered hence
On ways not found before,
Beyond the dawnward spires of Providence?
Hast thou gone forth to seek
Some older bourn than these—
Some Arkham of the prime and central wizardries?
Or, with familiar felidae,
Dost now some new and secret wood explore,
A little past the senses' farther wall—
Where spring and sunset charm the eternal path
From Earth to ether in dimensions nemoral?
Or has the Silver Key
Opened perchance for thee
Wonders and dreams and worlds ulterior?
Hast thou gone home to Ulthar or to Pnath?
Has the high king who reigns in dim Kadath
Called back his courtly, sage ambassador?
Or darkling Cthulhu sent
The Sign which makes thee now a councilor
Within that foundered fortress of the deep
Where the Old Ones stir in sleep,
Till mighty tremblors shake their slumbering continent?
Lo! in this little interim of days,
How far thy feet are sped
Upon the fabulous and mooted ways
Where walk the mythic dead!
For us the grief, for us the mystery. . . .
And yet thou art not gone

Nor given wholly unto dream and dust:
For, even upon
This lonely western hill of Averoigne
Thy flesh had never visited,
I meet some wise and sentient wraith of thee,
Some undeparting presence, gracious and august.
More luminous for thee the vernal grass,
More magically dark the Druid stone
And in the mind thou art for ever shown
As in a magic glass;
And from the spirit's page thy runes can never pass.

APPENDIX I

The Collected Works
of H. P. Lovecraft[1]

I. *The Dunwich Horror and Others.*

The Best Supernatural Stories of H. P. Lovecraft. Selected and with an Introduction by August Derleth. 1963, 1966, 1971, 1973. xx, 431 pp. Contents: ix–xx:
"H. P. Lovecraft and His Work," by August Derleth; 10–18: "In the Vault;"
19–32: "Pickman's Model;" 33–52: "The Rats in the Walls;" 53–59: "The Outsider;" 60–88: "The Colour out of Space;" 89–97: "The Music of Erich Zann;"
98–120: "The Haunter of the Dark;" 121–29: "The Picture in the House;"
130–59: "The Call of Cthulhu;" 160–202: "The Dunwich Horror;" 203–11:
"Cool Air;" 212–77: "The Whisperer in Darkness;" 278–80: "The Terrible Old
Man;" 281–307: "The Thing on the Doorstep;" 308–69: "The Shadow over
Innsmouth;" 370–431: "The Shadow out of Time."

II. *At the Mountains of Madness and Other Novels.*

Selected and with an Introduction by August Derleth. 1964, 1968, 1971, 1975.
xi, 432 pp. Contents: ix–xi: "H. P. Lovecraft's Novels," by August Derleth;
1–100: *At the Mountains of Madness*; 101–221: *The Case of Charles Dexter
Ward*; 222–47: "The Shunned House;" 248–83: "The Dreams in the Witch
House;" 284–89: "The Statement of Randolph Carter;" 290–385: *The Dream-
Quest of Unknown Kadath*; 386–97: "The Silver Key;" 398–432: "Through the
Gates of the Silver Key" (with E. Hoffmann Price).

III. *Dagon and Other Macabre Tales.*

Selected and with an Introduction by August Derleth. 1965, 1969, 1971, 1975.
ix, 413 pp. Contents: vii–ix: "Introduction," by August Derleth; 3–8: "Dagon;"
9–18: "The Tomb;" 19–22: "Polaris;" 23–33: "Beyond the Wall of Sleep;"
34–40: "The Doom that Came to Sarnath;" 41–46: "The White Ship;" 47–55:
"Facts concerning the Late Arthur Jermyn and His Family" (as "Arthur
Jermyn"); 56–59: "The Cats of Ulthar;" 60–65: "Celephais;" 66–72: "From
Beyond;" 73–85: "The Temple;" 86–90: "The Tree;" 91–98: "The Moon-Bog;"
99–110: "The Nameless City;" 111–15: "The Other Gods;" 116–22: "The Quest
of Iranon;" 123–51: "Herbert West—Reanimator;" 152–59: "The Hound;"
160–66: "Hypnos;" 167–86: "The Lurking Fear;" 187–95: "The Festival;"

196-203: "The Unnamable;" 204-29: "Imprisoned with the Pharaohs;" 230-39: "He;" 240-59: "The Horror at Red Hook;" 260-68: "The Strange High House in the Mist;" 269-96: "In the Walls of Eryx" (with Kenneth Sterling); 297-301: "The Evil Clergyman;" 302-08: "The Beast in the Cave;" 308-16: "The Alchemist;" 316-22: "Poetry and the Gods" (with Anna Helen Crofts); 322-27: "The Street;" 327-34: "The Transition of Juan Romero;" 335-36: "Azathoth;" 336-39: "The Descendant;" 340-42: "The Book;" 342-44: "The Thing in the Moonlight;" 347-413: "Supernatural Horror in Literature."

IV.   *The Horror in the Museum and Other Revisions.*

1970, 1976. ix, 383 pp. Contents: vii-ix: "Lovecraft's 'Revisions,' " by August Derleth: 3-9: "The Crawling Chaos," by H. P. Lovecraft and Elizabeth Berkeley [i.e. Winifred V. Jackson]: 10-15: "The Green Meadow," by H. P. Lovecraft and Elizabeth Berkeley [i.e. Winifred V. Jackson]; 16-21: "The Horror at Martin's Beach" (as "The Invisible Monster"), by Sonia Greene [Davis]; 22-26: "Four O'Clock," by Sonia Greene [Davis]; 27-41: "The Man of Stone," by Hazel Heald; 42-64: "Winged Death," by Hazel Heald; 65-74: "The Loved Dead," by C. M. Eddy, Jr; 75-86: "Deaf, Dumb and Blind," by C. M. Eddy, Jr; 86-94: "The Ghost-Eater," by C. M. Eddy, Jr; 95-103: " 'Till A' the Seas,' " by Robert H. Barlow; 104-39: "The Horror in the Museum," by Hazel Heald; 131-55: "Out of the Eons," by Hazel Heald; 156-75: "The Diary of Alonzo Typer," by William Lumley; 176-88: "The Horror in the Burying Ground," by Hazel Heald; 189-233: "The Last Test," by Adolphe de Castro; 234-51: "The Electric Executioner," by Adolphe de Castro; 252-67: "The Curse of Yig," by Zealia Bishop; 268-304: "Medusa's Coil," by Zealia Bishop; 305-72: "The Mound," by Zealia Bishop; 373-83: "Two Black Bottles," by Wilfred Blanch Talman.

V.   *Selected Letters I: 1911-1924.*

Edited by August Derleth and Donald Wandrei. 1965, 1975. xxix, 362 pp. Contents: xxi-xxix: "Preface," by August Derleth and Donald Wandrei; 3-362: Letters (Nos. 1-178).

VI.   *Selected Letters II: 1925-1929.*

Edited by August Derleth and Donald Wandrei. 1968, 1975. xxiv, 359 pp. Contents: xxi-xxiv: "Preface," by August Derleth and Donald Wandrei; 3-359: Letters (Nos. 179-359).

VII.   *Selected Letters III: 1929-1931:*

Edited by August Derleth and Donald Wandrei. 1971. xxiii, 451 pp. Contents: xxi-xxiii: "Preface," by August Derleth and Donald Wandrei; 3-451: Letters (nos. 360-516).

VIII.   *Selected Letters IV: 1932–1934.*

Edited by August Derleth and James Turner. 1976. xxxii, 424 pp. Contents: xx-ix–xxxii: "Preface," by James Turner; 3–424: Letters (Nos. 517–710).

IX.   *Selected Letters V: 1934–1937.*

Edited by August Derleth and James Turner. 1976. xxxvii, 436 pp. Contents: xxxiii–xxxvii: "Preface," by James Turner; 3–436: Letters (Nos. 711–930).

Note

1. All volumes are published by Arkham House, Sauk City, Wis.

APPENDIX II

Supplementary Readings

I. Works by Lovecraft

The *Collected Works* (1963–76; 9 vols.; see Appendix I) contain a great majority of the fiction, the essay "Supernatural Horror in Literature," the important revisions, and a hefty though at times capricious sampling of the letters. Fiction not included are the prose poems (available in paper in *The Doom That Came to Sarnath,* ed. Lin Carter, and in part in *Writings in The United Amateur: 1915–1925,* ed. Marc A. Michaud; they are also in *Beyond the Wall of Sleep* and were printed as four separate and beautifully printed collector's editions by Roy A. Squires [1969–70], but these sources are rather difficult to obtain), and the very early juvenilia (included in part in *The Shuttered Room and Other Pieces*). Other minor fictional works are also excluded. The textual quality of these volumes is very poor: words, phrases, and whole paragraphs are often omitted. The compilation of a new corrected edition of Lovecraft's work is, however, underway.

As for Lovecraft's essays, the miscellaneous collections such as *Marginalia, Something about Cats and Other Pieces, The Shuttered Room and Other Pieces,* and *The Dark Brotherhood and Other Pieces* are the primary sources, though much valuable and obscure material is also included in *The Lovecraft Collectors Library,* ed. George T. Wetzel, *To Quebec and the Stars,* ed. L. Sprague de Camp, and *Uncollected Prose and Poetry,* ed. S. T. Joshi and Marc A. Michaud. For amateur journalistic works by Lovecraft, the major sources are *The Conservative: Complete, Writings in The United Amateur,* and *The Californian: 1934–1938,* all ed. Marc A. Michaud; though Volume 5 of the *Lovecraft Collectors Library* is not to be overlooked.

Both *Collected Poems* and *A Winter Wish,* ed. Tom Collins, are crucial inasmuch as there is little overlapping in the contents of the two volumes. The latter, however, is a textual nightmare, and can only be read with an errata list. In these collections is the bulk of Lovecraft's verse, though a sizeable portion still remains unreprinted or unpublished.

Volumes V–IX of the *Collected Works* are the primary sources for letters, although the letters here are in almost every instance highly abridged. Also to be sought is *Lovecraft at Last,* by H. P. Lovecraft and Willis Conover, a compendium of the correspondence of the two associates, whose value derives not only from the wealth of light it sheds on Lovecraft's final months but from its beautiful production—binding, type, illustrations, facsimiles, etc. All in all it is physically one of the most exquisite books in modern publishing. An immense amount of Lovecraft's correspondence remains unpublished; some of it is in the

John Hay Library of Brown University, and there is some in the New York Public Library and the State Historical Society of Wisconsin; but a large bulk is in the hands of private collectors.

A word on foreign translations: most are, despite Marc Slonim's assertion to the contrary, extremely poor; among the worst being the French translations of Jacques Papy and the Italian translations of Alda Carrer, Giovanni De Luca, *et al.* Some of the better ones are the German translation by the poet H. C. Artmann in the volume, *Cthulhu: Geistergeschichten* (1968), and the Italian translations by Roberta Rambelli, *Nelle Spire di Medusa* and *Sfida dall'infinito* (1976). Bernard da Costa's *Epouvante et Surnaturel en Littérature* (1971) is not to be despised, nor are the translations by Jacques Parsons in the special Lovecraft issue of *L'Herne*, 12 (1969). Many other fair to good editions in Spanish, Portuguese, Dutch, German, French, Japanese, Swedish, Norwegian, Danish, and other languages exist.

II. *Works About Lovecraft*

A. Biographical

An immense amount of work has been written about Lovecraft's life; the majority of this is memoirs, and the inadequacy of the two formal biographies— Derleth's *H.P.L.: A Memoir* and de Camp's *Lovecraft: A Biography*—has been noted in the Introductory Notes. The first piece of formal biography, Winfield Townley Scott's "His Own Most Fantastic Creation: Howard Phillips Lovecraft" (1944), is an interesting and often perspicacious short work, but is marred by prejudice, harshness, and idiosyncrasy. Arthur Koki's master's thesis, "H. P. Lovecraft: An Introduction to His Life and Writings" (in spite of the title there is little literary criticism here), repeats some of the information contained in J. W. Thomas' "H. P. Lovecraft: A Self-Portrait," but is thankfully purged of most of its biased judgements, and may perhaps be at present the best sustained biographical account; although if the researches of R. Alain Everts and Kenneth W. Faig—the two foremost Lovecraft biographers—were ever set down (as have been in part in the latter's unpublished *Lovecraftian Voyages*), the result would surely be the most accurate recounting by far of Lovecraft's life.

Of the memoirs, some of the finest of the longer ones are W. Paul Cook's *In Memoriam: Howard Phillips Lovecraft,* from which many classic stories about Lovecraft have arisen, and Frank Belknap Long's recent *Howard Phillips Lovecraft: Dreamer on the Nightside.*

For Lovecraft's very early years, the primary source is Kenneth Faig's "Howard Phillips Lovecraft: The Early Years;" also valuable are R. Alain Everts' "The Lovecraft Family in America" and David H. Keller's "Lovecraft's Astronomical Notebook." W. T. Scott's biography is also useful.

Much has been written of Lovecraft's involvement with amateur journalism, especially in such memoirs as Alfred Galpin's "Memories of a Friendship," Rheinhart Kleiner's "A Memoir of Lovecraft," Samuel Loveman's "Howard Phillips Lovecraft," H. Warner Munn's "HPL," E. A. Edkins' "Idiosyncrasies of H.P.L.," James F. Morton's "A Few Memories," and Edward H. Cole's "Ave Atque Vale!". Of some use are Derleth's "Addenda to *H.P.L.: A Memoir*" (cf. Part II: "Lovecraft's *Conservative*"), Helen V. Wesson's "The

Phenomenon of HPL,'' and Sam Moskowitz's ''H. P. Lovecraft and the Munsey Magazines.'' For data on this period outside of amateur journalism, see Muriel Eddy's *The Gentleman from Angell Street* and C. M. Eddy's ''Walks with H. P. Lovecraft.''

The J. W. Thomas and Koki theses, both quoting many letters by Lovecraft, are crucial in picturing Lovecraft's marriage to Sonia Davis and his ''New York Exile;'' of course, equally vital is Mrs Davis' memoir itself, ''The Private Life of Howard Phillips Lovecraft,'' though it has never been published in its entirety (the manuscript is in the John Hay Library). Valuable also are Frank Belknap Long's ''H.P.L. in Red Hook,'' R. Alain Everts' ''Mrs Howard Phillips Lovecraft,'' and the Galpin memoir. Lovecraft's so-called ''racism,'' which flared up particularly during this time of stress, has been judiciously dealt with by Prof. Dirk W. Mosig in ''H. P. Lovecraft: Rabid Racist—or Compassionate Gentleman?'', which urges us to look at Lovecraft's views of foreigners in historical perspective.

The final ten years of Lovecraft's life have been heftily documented by Lovecraft's colleagues; important are R. H. Barlow's ''The Wind That Is in the Grass: A Memoir of H. P. Lovecraft in Florida,'' Derleth's ''Lovecraft as Mentor,'' Fritz Leiber's ''My Correspondence with Lovecraft,'' E. Hoffmann Price's ''The Man Who Was Lovecraft,'' J. Vernon Shea's ''H. P. Lovecraft: The House and the Shadows,'' Kenneth Sterling's ''Caverns Measureless to Man,'' Wilfred B. Talman's ''The Normal Lovecraft,'' and Donald Wandrei's ''The Dweller in Darkness: Lovecraft, 1927.'' R. Alain Everts' and Phillips Gamwell III's ''The Death of a Gentleman: The Last Days of Howard Phillips Lovecraft'' provides graphic data on Lovecraft's final days in the hospital.

Of articles concentrating on general aspects of Lovecraft's life, some vital ones are these: Robert Bloch's ''Inside the Outsider,'' which states that the contradictions in Lovecraft's character simply indicate that he was a human being like any of us; Derleth's *Some Notes on H. P. Lovecraft* (reprinted as ''Final Notes'' in *The Dark Brotherhood and Other Pieces*), which deals not incompetently on Lovecraft's ''racism,'' sheds light on the ''posthumous collaborations'' of Derleth, and prints Barlow's fragmentary journal of Lovecraft's visits with him in Florida; R. Alain Everts' ''Howard Phillips Lovecraft and Sex,'' noting that Lovecraft, though having a low sex drive, was neither impotent nor homosexual (on this matter see J. Vernon Shea's lively but unpublished ''The Homosexual Element in H. P. Lovecraft''); David H. Keller's ''Shadows over Lovecraft,'' which provides the celebrated but incorrect view that Lovecraft had syphilis (the noted rebuttal to this theory is by Kenneth Sterling); and Sterling's ''Lovecraft and Science,'' which explains Lovecraft's wealth of knowledge ''countless academic fields'' and his ''perennial love of science.'' The volume, *Rhode Island on Lovecraft,* ed. Donald M. Grant and Thomas P. Hadley, has, aside from the significant biographical-critical ''Lovecraft and Benefit Street'' by Dorothy Walter, relatively inessential but interesting memoirs by Mrs Eddy, Mary V. Dana, and M. F. Bonner.

Of cognate interest are Kenneth Faig's two articles, ''Lovecraft's Providence,'' describing Lovecraft's favourite sites in his native city (Henry L. P. Beckwith's forthcoming tour guide of Lovecraft's Providence should be yet more extensive), and ''The Lovecraft Circle: A Glossary.'' Some use may be made of various articles or books on Lovecraft's associates or on amateur journalism, pulp magazines, etc., but most are fairly poor or inaccurate (e.g. Spencer's *History of*

Amateur Journalism, Reginald Smith's *Weird Tales in the Thirties,* Weinberg's *The Weird Tales Story,* the chapter on C. A. Smith in de Camp's *Literary Swordsmen and Sorcerers,* de Camp's *The Miscast Barbarian: A Biography of Robert E. Howard,* etc.), and had best be avoided. Weinberg's *WT50: A Tribute to Weird Tales* is somewhat better, as is Harry Warner's *All Our Yesterdays.* Highly relevant is George T. Wetzel's "Lovecraft's Literary Executor," an article on R. H. Barlow. Barlow's life and work have been brilliantly covered in Kenneth Faig's unpublished monograph, "R. H. Barlow."

B. Critical

Lovecraft's myth-cycle has received a vast amount of attention from critics; the lengthiest is Lin Carter's *Lovecraft: A Look Behind the "Cthulhu Mythos,"* which though full of hideous factual errors and misinterpretations does manage a coherent picture of the developement of the myth-cycle, particularly after Lovecraft's death. Carter, however, accepts Derleth's concept of the mythos. Carter's "H.P.L.: The History" is recommended insofar as it maps out an history of the solar system as told by Lovecraft in his later tales. Richard L. Tierney's "The Derleth Mythos" was the first direct exposé of the many perversions of the myth-cycle perpetrated by August Derleth, and must be consulted in spite of its brevity. High hopes may be had for William Fulwiler's long forthcoming study on many aspects of the myth-cycle, which in certain areas diverges from the theories of George T. Wetzel.

Much recent work has been done in philosophical-literary interpretations of Lovecraft, though Matthew H. Onderdonk's "The Lord of R'lyeh" and "Charon—in Reverse, or, H. P. Lovecraft Versus the 'Realists' of Fantasy" were early breakthroughs in the field. Prof. Barton L. St Armand's master's thesis, "H. P. Lovecraft: The Outsider in Legend and Myth" is still valuable for its analyses of "The Rats in the Walls" and "The Horror at Red Hook," although its biographical portion is weaker; St Armand's "H. P. Lovecraft: New England Decadent" is erudite and laced with brilliance, but perhaps tries too hard to fit Lovecraft into, first, the Decadent/Symbolist mode, which he rejected in his later years, and secondly, the Puritan moral ethic, which he never in truth espoused. Prof. St Armand's book, *The Roots of Horror in the Fiction of H. P. Lovecraft,* examines "The Rats in the Walls" in some detail, and though at times making self-evident conclusions, contains much powerful philosophical and psychological analysis. Prof. Mosig's "The Prophet from Providence" champions Lovecraft's incisive thought and explains how Lovecraft predicted "future shock" in his letters and tales.

Work on Lovecraft's literary influences and sources has been extensive but still remains somewhat uncoordinated. Prof. Mabbott's "Lovecraft as a Student of Poe" is a happy addition to the field, and J. Vernon Shea's "H. P. Lovecraft and Robert Aickman: Contrast and Comparison" is brilliant but difficult to locate; asserting that Aickman is a "master of ambiguity" while Lovecraft is somewhat too explicit, and that both authors paid much attention to atmosphere. Robert Marten has done some astounding research into the source materials—occult, local colour, and historical—for Lovecraft's tales, but his work regrettably remains unpublished.

Prof. Mosig still remains almost alone in the psychoanalytical approach to Lovecraft, and his "The Four Faces of 'The Outsider' " is eminently readable and worthwhile. Much can be expected also from his forthcoming book on Lovecraft for Twayne's United States Authors Series.

Prof. John Taylor Gatto's Monarch Note, *The Major Works of H. P. Lovecraft,* is intermittently brilliant and weak, predominantly the latter. Gatto's idiosyncratic opinions on Lovecraft's work and egregious factual errors are by no means redeemed by his few penetrating insights and rhetorical flourishes. Its worth is perhaps solely derived from its sheer existence, being a concrete indication of the increasing academic interest in Lovecraft.

Peter Cannon's master's thesis, "Lovecraft's New England," studies Lovecraft's use of actual New England sites, customs, and history to achieve greater realism in his fiction. Remarking on the "significant thematic ambiguity" that "his beloved New England is the site of both beauty and horror," Cannon examines many of Lovecraft's tales, calling *The Case of Charles Dexter Ward* a "masterpiece of the supernatural historical romance."

"Out of the Ivory Tower" by Robert Bloch proclaims Lovecraft as a regional writer (on this cf. also Wetzel's "Some Thoughts on the Lovecraft Pattern") and tries also to indicate the difference between the Lovecraft of legend and the real Lovecraft.

John Vetter's "Lovecraft's Illustrators" is an extensive article summarising the work of many of the illustrators of Lovecraft's tales, from Clark Ashton Smith to the *Weird Tales* artists to Frank Utpatel to Virgil Finlay (whose illustration for "The Shunned House" is "the finest Lovecraft illustration ever done") to Hannes Bok to Lee Brown Coye and many others.

Still worthy is *H. P. Lovecraft: A Symposium,* where the five panelists (Fritz Leiber, Robert Bloch, Sam Russell, Arthur Jean Cox, and Leland Sapiro) discuss such aspects of Lovecraft's work as the themes of "psychic displacement" and hereditary degeneration, his use of overstatement, and of whether Lovecraft's tales are actually frightening. It is annotated by August Derleth.

Meade and Penny Frierson's *HPL* contains many valuable articles on Lovecraft, including Wetzel's "The Cthulhu Mythos: A Study" (revised), Tierney's "The Derleth Mythos," Shea's "HPL and Films," etc. Some spectacular illustrations also grace the book-magazine.

Of greater historical than intrinsic interest are such articles as the Lovecraft portions in Vincent Starrett's *Books and Bipeds* (reprints of his column in *The Chicago Sunday Tribune*) and certain articles by W. T. Scott, e.g. "The Haunter of the Dark: Some Notes on Howard Phillips Lovecraft" and "The Case of Howard Phillips Lovecraft of Providence, R.I.", which represent some early recognition of Lovecraft. There are many such items: cf. those by William Rose Benét, T. O. Mabbott, Fred Lewis Pattee, *et al.,* listed in my bibliography (see below).

C. Bibliographical

The most complete bibliography is *H. P. Lovecraft and Lovecraft Criticism: An Annotated Bibliography,* ed. S. T. Joshi, listing periodical publications, complete descriptions of books by Lovecraft, anthological appearances, much foreign data, Lovecraft criticism including books, articles, chapters of books, academic theses, and book reviews, and other miscellany. The bibliography was founded on George T. Wetzel's epochal seventh volume of *The Lovecraft Collectors Library,* the first Lovecraft bibliography that even approached completeness, and the basis for all future work in the field. Wetzel's "The Research of a Biblio" is still worthwhile for an outline of the difficulties he encountered in compiling his work.

August Derleth's *Thirty Years of Arkham House* is valuable for complete bibliographical information on the publishing firm and its subsidiaries. Derleth also gives an illuminating history of its founding.

The most complete bibliography of the works of the myth-cycle by writers other than Lovecraft is Robert Weinberg's and E. P. Berglund's *The Reader's Guide to the Cthulhu Mythos,* 2nd rev. ed. A 3rd rev. ed. has been announced by Berglund, to be in three volumes.

William Crawford's "Lovecraft's First Book" sheds light on the publication of Lovecraft's *The Shadow over Innsmouth* (1936) under the imprint of Crawford's Visionary Publishing Co.

Willametta Keffer's "Howard P(seudonym) Lovecraft: The Many Names of HPL" is a strong article on Lovecraft's pseudonymous authorship of work in the amateur press. Mrs Keffer was the first to hint that "El Imparcial" might be a Lovecraft pseudonym. Also to be consulted is George T. Wetzel's "The Pseudonymous Lovecraft."

For indices and glossaries, Donald Cochran's *Lovecraft: The Fiction* and *Lovecraft: The Revisions* are useful. Philip A. Shreffler's recent *The H. P. Lovecraft Companion* (admittedly intended for general readers) is somewhat shaky, filled with minor factual errors, and providing a glossary only of the characters and not the place-names in Lovecraft's fiction (excluding revisions). His synopses of the fiction are for the most part good, though giving short shrift to several important tales; and Shreffler tries a bit too hard to make Lovecraft an occultist, wasting many pages in the process. The photographs, however (taken by Shreffler), are excellent.

Attention may be drawn to T. G. L. Cockcroft's *Index to the Weird Fiction Magazines* (recently reprinted by Arno Press), which gives complete indices to *Weird Tales* and other important pulp magazines. Donald Tuck's *An Encyclopedia of Science Fiction and Fantasy Through 1968* may also be useful for bibliographic information on writers other than Lovecraft. For specific authors, see: *100 Books by August Derleth;* Glenn Lord's *The Last Celt: A Bio-Bibliography of Robert E. Howard;* and Donald Sydney-Fryer's bibliography of Clark Ashton Smith.

INDEX

Portions of this book not indexed are the Preface, the "Chronology of Selected Works by H. P. Lovecraft," and the Appendices. Thanks to Marc A. Michaud for assistance in the compilation of this index.